THE
CASE
FOR
ISRAEL

Alan Dershowitz

WILEY

John Wiley & Sons, Inc.

Published by John Wiley & Sons, Inc., Hoboken, New Jersey
Published simultaneously in Canada

Design and production by Navta Associates, Inc.

Maps used by permission: *Atlas Arab-Israeli Conflict, 7th Edition*, Sir Martin Gilbert. Published by Routledge, © 2002 ISBN: 0415281172 (PB) and ISBN: 0415281164 (HB). Please visit our web site for further details on the new edition: www.taylorandfrancis.com.

For general information about our other products and services, please contact our Customer Care Department within the United States at (800) 762-2974, outside the United States at (317) 572-3993 or fax (317) 572-4002.

Wiley also publishes its books in a variety of electronic formats. Some content that appears in print may not be available in electronic books. For more information about Wiley products, visit our web site at www.wiley.com.

Library of Congress Cataloging-in-Publication Data:

Dershowitz, Alan M.
    The case for Israel / Alan Dershowitz.
        p. cm.
Includes bibliographical references and index.
    ISBN 0-471-46502-X (cloth : alk. paper)
    1. Jews—Palestine—History. 2. Jews—Colonization—Palestine. 3. Refugees, Jewish—Palestine—History. 4. Zionists—Palestine—History. 5. Israel—History. 6. Arab-Israeli conflict. 7. Zionism. I. Title.
    DS125.D47   2003
    956.94   2003009481

Printed in the United States of America

10 9 8 7 6 5 4 3 2

This book is respectfully dedicated to my dear friend of nearly forty years, Professor Aharon Barak, the president of Israel's Supreme Court, whose judicial decisions make a better case for Israel and for the rule of law than any book could possibly do.

CONTENTS

ACKNOWLEDGMENTS

I have been working on this book since 1967, when I first began to make the case for Israel on university campuses, in the media, and in my writings. Over the years I have had the assistance—often the critical assistance—of too many colleagues to list and thank. Among those who deserve special mention are Professor Irwin Cotler, now a member of the Canadian Parliament, with whom I have worked on so many causes and projects; Justices Aharon Barak and Yitzak Zamir, who have taught me so much; Professor George Fletcher, who educates me by arguing and challenging; Professor Amnon Rubinstein, with whose writings I nearly always agree; Israel Ringel, who gently corrects my misperceptions about Israel; and generations of students who educate me about current matters.

In writing this book, I have benefited greatly from the research assistance of Owen Alterman, Mara Zusman, Eric Citron, Holly Beth Billington, Natalie Hershlag, and Ayelet Weiss. My assistant, Jane Wagner; my agent, Helen Rees; my editor, Hana Lane; and my temporary assistant, Robin Yeo, have provided invaluable assistance.

For perceptive comments on the manuscript, I thank my friends Bernard Beck, Jeffrey Epstein, Steve Kosslyn, Alan Rothfeld, and Michael and Jackie Halbreich.

My wife, Carolyn, and my daughter, Ella, inspired me, debated with me, and encouraged me. My sons, Elon and Jamin, my nephew Adam, my nieces Rana and Hannah, my brother Nathan, and my sister-in-law Marilyn all made useful suggestions, which I much appreciate.

I acknowledge the people of Israel who have sacrificed so much in their historic efforts to achieve peace, prosperity, and democracy in the face of such enduring enmity and violence. Finally, I acknowledge the peacemakers and peace seekers on both sides of this conflict, especially those who gave their lives so that others might live in peace and security.

Introduction

The Jewish nation of Israel stands accused in the dock of international justice. The charges include being a criminal state, the prime violator of human rights, the mirror image of Nazism, and the most intransigent barrier to peace in the Middle East. Throughout the world, from the chambers of the United Nations to the campuses of universities, Israel is singled out for condemnation, divestment, boycott, and demonization. Its leaders are threatened with prosecution as war criminals. Its supporters are charged with dual loyalty and parochialism.

The time has come for a proactive defense of Israel to be offered in the court of public opinion. In this book, I offer such a defense—not of every Israeli policy or action but of Israel's basic right to exist, to protect its citizens from terrorism, and to defend its borders from hostile enemies. I show that Israel has long been willing to accept the kind of two-state solution that is now on the proposed "road map" to peace, and that it was the Arab leadership that persistently refused to accept any Jewish state—no matter how small—in those areas of Palestine with a Jewish majority. I also try to present a realistic picture of Israel, warts and all, as a flourishing multiethnic democracy, similar in many ways to the United States, that affords all of its citizens—Jews, Muslims, and Christians—far better lives and opportunities than those afforded by any Arab or Muslim nation. Most important, I argue that those who single out Israel for unique criticism not directed against countries with far worse human rights records are themselves guilty of international bigotry. This is a serious accusation and I back it up. Let me be clear that I am not charging all critics of Israel with anti-Semitism. I myself have been quite critical of specific Israeli policies and actions over the years, as have most Israel supporters, virtually every Israeli citizen, and many American Jews. But I am also critical of other countries, including my own, as well as European, Asian, and Middle Eastern countries. So long as criticism is comparative, contextual, and fair, it should be encouraged, not disparaged. But when the Jewish nation is the only one criticized for faults that are far worse among other nations, such criticism crosses the line from fair to foul, from acceptable to anti-Semitic.

Thomas Friedman of the *New York Times* got it right when he said,

"Criticizing Israel is not anti-Semitic, and saying so is vile. But singling out Israel for opprobrium and international sanction—out of all proportion to any other party in the Middle East—is anti-Semitic, and not saying so is dishonest."[1] A good working definition of anti-Semitism is taking a trait or an action that is widespread, if not universal, and blaming *only* the Jews for it. That is what Hitler and Stalin did, and that is what former Harvard University president A. Lawrence Lowell did in the 1920s when he tried to limit the number of Jews admitted to Harvard because "Jews cheat." When a distinguished alumnus objected on the grounds that non-Jews also cheat, Lowell replied, "You're changing the subject. I'm talking about Jews." So, too, when those who single out only the Jewish nation for criticism are asked why they don't criticize Israel's enemies, they respond, "You're changing the subject. We're talking about Israel."

This book will prove not only that Israel is innocent of the charges being leveled against it but that no other nation in history faced with comparable challenges has ever adhered to a higher standard of human rights, been more sensitive to the safety of innocent civilians, tried harder to operate under the rule of law, or been willing to take more risks for peace. This is a bold claim, and I support it with facts and figures, some of which will surprise those who get their information from biased sources. For example, Israel is the only nation in the world whose judiciary actively enforces the rule of law against its military even during wartime.[2] It is the only country in modern history to have returned disputed territory captured in a defensive war and crucial to its own self-defense in exchange for peace. And Israel has killed fewer innocent civilians in proportion to the number of its own civilians killed than any country engaged in a comparable war. I challenge Israel's accusers to produce data supporting their claim that, as one accuser put it, Israel "is the prime example of human rights violators in the world."[3] They will be unable to do so.

When the best is accused of being the worst, the focus must shift to the accusers, who I contend may be guilty of bigotry, hypocrisy, or abysmal ignorance at the very least. It is they who must stand in the dock of history, along with others who have also singled out the Jewish people, the Jewish religion, the Jewish culture, or the Jewish nation for unique and undeserved condemnation.

The premise of this book is that a two-state solution to the Israeli and Palestinian claims is both inevitable and desirable. What precise form this solution will and should ultimately take is, of course, subject to considerable dispute—as evidenced by the failure of the Camp David and Taba negotiations in 2000–2001 to reach a mutually acceptable resolution and by the disputes surrounding the "road map" of 2003. There are really only four possible alternatives to a Jewish and a Palestinian state living side by side in peace.

The first is the preferred Palestinian solution demanded by Hamas and others who reject Israel's very right to exist (commonly referred to as rejectionists): namely, the destruction of Israel and the total elimination of a Jewish state anywhere in the Middle East. The second is preferred by a small number of Jewish fundamentalists and expansionists: the permanent annexation of the West Bank and the Gaza Strip and the expulsion or occupation of the millions of Arabs who now live in these areas. The third alternative was once preferred by the Palestinians, but they no longer accept it: some kind of federation between the West Bank and another Arab state (i.e., Syria or Jordan). The fourth, which has always been a pretext to turn Israel into a de facto Palestinian state, is the creation of a single binational state. None of these alternatives is currently acceptable. A resolution that recognizes the right of self-determination by Israelis as well as Palestinians is the only reasonable path to peace, although it is not without its own risks.

A two-state solution to the Arab–Palestinian–Israeli conflict also seems to be a rare point of consensus in what is otherwise an intractable dilemma. Any reasonable consideration of how to resolve this longstanding dispute peacefully must begin with this consensus. Most of the world currently advocates a two-state solution, including the vast majority of Americans. A substantial majority of Israelis have long accepted this compromise. It is now the official position of the Palestinian Authority as well as the Egyptian, Jordanian, Saudi Arabian, and Moroccan governments. Only the extremists among the Israelis and the Palestinians, as well as the rejectionist states of Syria, Iran, and Libya, claim that the entire landmass of what is now Israel, the West Bank, and the Gaza Strip should permanently be controlled either by the Israelis alone or by the Palestinians alone.

Some academic opponents of Israel, such as Noam Chomsky and Edward Said, also reject the two-state solution. Chomsky has said, "I don't think it's a good idea," although he has acknowledged that it may be "the best of various rotten ideas around." Chomsky has long preferred, and apparently still prefers, a single binational federal state based on the models of Lebanon and Yugoslavia.[4] The fact that both of these models failed miserably and ended in bloody fratricide is ignored by Chomsky, for whom theory is more important than experience. Said is adamantly opposed to any solution that leaves Israel in existence as a Jewish state: "I don't myself believe in a two-state solution. I believe in a one-state solution."[5] He, along with Chomsky, favors a binational secular state—an elitist and impractical solution that would have to be imposed on both sides, since virtually no Israelis or Palestinians would accept it (except as a ploy to destroy the other side's state).

To be sure, the poll numbers in favor of a two-state solution vary over time, especially according to circumstance. In times of violent conflict, more Israelis and more Palestinians reject compromise, but most reasonable people realize that whatever particular individuals would hope for in theory or even claim as a matter of God-given right, the reality is that neither the Israelis nor the Palestinians will go away or accept a one-state solution. Accordingly, the inevitability—and correctness—of some sort of two-state compromise is a useful beginning to any discussion that seeks a constructive resolution of this dangerous and painful conflict.

An agreed-upon starting point is essential, because each party to this long dispute begins the narrative of its claim to the land at a different point in history. This should not be surprising, since nations and peoples who are in conflict generally select as the beginning of their national narrative a point that best serves to support their claims and grievances. When the American colonists sought separation from England, their Declaration of Independence began the narrative with a history of "repeated injuries and usurpations" committed by "the present king," such as "imposing taxes on us without our consent" and "quartering large bodies of armed troops among us." Those who opposed separation began their narrative with the wrongs perpetrated by the colonists, such as their refusal to pay certain taxes and the provocations directed against British soldiers. Similarly, the Israeli Declaration of Independence begins its narrative with the land of Israel being "the birthplace of the Jewish People," where they "first attained statehood . . . and gave the world the Eternal Book of Books." The original Palestine National Charter begins with the "Zionist occupation" and rejects any "claim of historical or spiritual links between the Jews and Palestine," the United Nation's partition of Palestine, and the "establishment of the state of Israel."

Any attempt to unravel the complexly disputed and ultimately unverifiable historical contentions of extremist Israelis and Arabs only produces unrealistic arguments on both sides. It is, of course, necessary to have some description of the history—ancient and modern—of this land and its ever-changing demographics, for no reason other than to begin to understand how reasonable people can draw such diametrically opposed conclusions from the same basic facts on the ground. The reality, of course, is that only some of the facts are agreed upon. Much is disputed and believed to be absolute truth by some, while others believe that its opposite is equally true.

This dramatic disparity in perception results from a number of factors. Sometimes it is a matter of the interpretation of an agreed-upon event. For example, as we will see in chapter 12, everyone agrees that hundreds of thousands of Arabs who once lived in what is now Israel no longer live there. Although the precise number is in dispute, the major disagreement is whether all, most, some, or none of these refugees were chased out of Israel, left because Arab leaders urged them to, or some combination of these and other factors. There is also disagreement over how long many of these refugees had actually lived in the places they left, since the United Nations defined a Palestinian refugee—unlike any other refugee in history—as anyone who had lived in what became Israel for only two years prior to leaving.

Because it is impossible to reconstruct the precise dynamics and atmospherics that accompanied the 1948 war waged by the Arab states against Israel, the one conclusion about which we can be absolutely certain is that no one will ever know—or convince his or her opponents—whether most of the Arabs who left Israel were chased, left on their own, or experienced some combination of factors that led them to move from one place to another. Israel has recently opened many of its historical archives to scholars, and newly available information has produced more insights and interpretations but has not—and will never—end all disagreements.[6]

Similarly, the 850,000 Sephardic Jews who had lived in Arab countries before 1948, most of whom ended up in Israel, were either forced to leave, left on their own, or experienced some combination of fear, opportunity, and religious destiny. Again, the precise dynamics will never be known, especially since the Arab countries they left do not maintain, or refuse to share, historical records and archives.

Each side is entitled to its self-serving narrative so long as it recognizes that others may interpret the facts somewhat differently. Sometimes the dispute is about definition of terms rather than interpretation of facts. For example, it is often claimed by Arabs that Israel was allocated 54 percent of the land of Palestine, despite the fact that only 35 percent of the residents of that land were Jews.[7] Israelis, on the other hand, contend that Jews were a clear majority in the *parts* of the land allocated to Israel when the United Nations partitioned the disputed land. As you will see, precise definitions can sometimes narrow disparities.

Another starting point must include some kind of statute of limitations for ancient grievances. Just as the case for Israel can no longer rely exclusively on the expulsion of the Jews from the land of Israel in the first century, so too the Arab case must move beyond a reliance on events that allegedly occurred more than a century ago. One reason for statutes of limitations is the recognition that as time passes it becomes increasingly difficult to reconstruct the past with any degree of precision, and political memories harden and replace the facts. As it has been said, "There are facts and there are true facts."

With regard to the events preceding the First Aliyah in 1882 (the initial immigration of European Jewish refugees to Palestine), there are more political and religious memories than true facts. We know that there has always been a Jewish presence in Israel, particularly in the holy cities of Jerusalem, Hebron, and Safad, and that there has been a Jewish plurality or majority in Jerusalem for centuries. We know that European Jews began to move to what is now Israel in significant numbers during the 1880s—only shortly after the time when Australians of British descent began to displace Aboriginal Australians and Americans of European descent began to move into some Western lands originally populated by Native Americans.

The Jews of the First Aliyah did not displace local residents by conquest or fear as the Americans and Australians did. They lawfully and openly bought land—much of it thought to be nonarable—from absentee land-lords. No one who accepts the legitimacy of Australia being an English-speaking Christian nation, or of Western America being part of the United States, can question the legitimacy of the Jewish presence in what is now Israel from the 1880s to the present. Even before the U.N. Partition of 1947, international treaties and law recognized that the Jewish community in Palestine was there, as a matter "of right," and any rational discussion of the conflict must be premised on the assumption that the "fundamental conflict" is "of right with right." Such conflicts are often the most difficult to resolve, since each side must be persuaded to compromise what it believes is an absolute claim of right. The task becomes even more daunting when some on each side see their claim as based on God's mandate.

I begin the case for Israel by briefly reviewing the history of the Arab–Muslim–Jewish and then the Arab–Palestinian–Muslim–Israeli conflict, emphasizing the refusal of Palestinian leaders to accept a two-state (or two-homeland) solution in 1917, 1937, 1948, and 2000. I focus on Israel's pragmatic efforts to live in peace within secure boundaries despite the repeated efforts of Arab leaders to destroy the Jewish state. I point out Israel's mistakes but argue that they were generally made in a good-faith (although sometimes misguided) effort to defend its civilian population. Finally, I argue that Israel has sought to comply with the rule of law in virtually all of its activities.

Despite my own strong belief that there must be a statute of limitations for grievances, making the case for Israel requires a brief journey into the relatively recent past. This is so because the case against Israel currently being made on university campuses, in the media, and throughout the world relies on willful distortions of the historical record, beginning with the first arrival of Europeans in Palestine near the end of the nineteenth century and continuing throughout the U.N. partition, the establishment of the Jewish state, and the wars between the Arab states and Israel, and culminating in the ongoing terrorism and responses to it. The historical record must be set straight so as to heed the philosopher Santayana's warning that those who cannot remember the past are condemned to repeat it.

Each chapter of the book starts with the accusation leveled against Israel, quoting specific sources. I respond to the accusation with hard facts backed up by credible evidence. In presenting the facts, I do not generally rely on pro-Israel sources but primarily on objective, and sometimes to emphasize the point, overtly anti-Israel sources.

I prove beyond any shadow of a doubt that a pernicious double standard has been applied to judging Israel's actions: that even when Israel has been the best or among the best in the world, it has often been accused of being the worst or among the worst in the world. I also prove that this double standard has not only been unfair to the Jewish state but that it has damaged the rule of law, wounded the credibility of international organizations such as the United Nations, and encouraged Palestinian terrorists to commit acts of violence in order to provoke overreaction by Israel and secure one-sided condemnation of Israel by the international community.

In the conclusion to the book I argue that it is impossible to understand the conflict in the Middle East without accepting the reality that from the very beginning the strategy of the Arab leadership has been to eliminate the existence of any Jewish state, and indeed any substantial Jewish population, in what is now Israel. Even Professor Edward Said, the Palestinians' most prominent academic champion, has acknowledged that "the whole of Palestinian nationalism was based on driving all Israelis [by which he means Jews] out."[8] This is a simple fact not subject to reasonable dispute. The evidence from the mouths and pens of Arab and Palestinian leaders is overwhelming. Various tactics have been employed toward this end, including the mendacious rewriting of the history of the immigration of Jewish refugees into Palestine, as well as the demographic history of the Arabs of Palestine. Other tactics have included the targeting of vulnerable Jewish civilians beginning in the 1920s, the Palestinian support for Hitler and Nazi genocide in the 1930s and 1940s, and the violent opposition to the two-state solution proposed by the Peel Commission in 1937, then by the United Nations in 1948. Yet another tactic was creating, then deliberately exacerbating and exploiting, the refugee crisis.

For some, the very idea of Palestinian statehood alongside a Jewish state has itself been a tactic—a first step—toward the elimination of Israel. Between 1880 and 1967, virtually no Arab or Palestinian spokesperson called for a Palestinian state. Instead they wanted the area that the Romans had designated as Palestine to be merged into Syria or Jordan. As Auni Bey Abdul-Hati, a prominent Palestinian leader, told the Peel Commission in 1937, "There is no such country. . . . Palestine is a term the Zionists invented. . . . Our country was for centuries part of Syria." Accordingly, the Palestinians rejected the independent homeland proposed by the Peel Commission because it would also have entailed a tiny Jewish homeland alongside it. The goal has always remained the same: eliminating the Jewish state and transferring most of the Jews out of the area.

Arab realists now recognize that this goal is unattainable—at least in the foreseeable future. The hope is that pragmatism will prevail over fundamentalism and that the Palestinian people and their leaders will finally come to understand that the case for a Palestinian state is strengthened by the acceptance of a Jewish state. When the Palestinians want their own state more than they want to destroy the Jewish state, most Israelis will welcome a peaceful Palestinian state as a good neighbor. The agreement to follow the "road map," and the handshakes and promises exchanged in Aqaba on June 4, 2003, represent some hope that the two-state solution—long accepted by Israel—will finally become a reality.

I welcome vigorous discussion about the case for Israel I make in this book. Indeed I hope to generate honest, contextual debate about an issue that has become polarized by extremist arguments. There will surely be disagreement about the conclusions I reach and the inferences I draw from the historical facts. But there can be no reasonable disagreement about the basic facts: the European Jews who joined their Sephardic Jewish cousins in what is now Israel at the end of the nineteenth century had an absolute right to seek refuge in the land of their ancestors; they established by the sweat of their brows a Jewish homeland in parts of Palestine that they fairly purchased from absentee landlords; they displaced very few local fellahin (Arabs who worked the land); they accepted proposals based on international law for a partitioned Jewish homeland in areas with a Jewish majority; and, at least until recently, virtually all Palestinian and Arab leaders categorically rejected any solution that included a Jewish state, a Jewish homeland, or Jewish self-determination. These indisputable facts laid the foundation for the conflict that accompanied the establishment of Israel and that continues to this day. It is important to present these historical facts as part of the current case for Israel, because distortion or omission of the painful history is a staple of the case often made against the Jewish state.

I decided to write this book after closely following the Camp David–Taba peace negotiations of 2000–2001, then watching as so many people throughout the world turned viciously against Israel when the negotiations failed and the Palestinians turned once again to terrorism. I was lecturing at Haifa University in Israel during the summer of 2000, so I observed firsthand the enthusiasm and anticipation with which so many Israelis awaited the outcome of the peace process that had begun with the Oslo Accords in 1993 and appeared on track toward the acceptance of a two-state resolution, with Israel and Palestine finally living in peace after so many years of violent conflict.

As the process moved toward resolution, Prime Minister Ehud Barak shocked the world by offering the Palestinians virtually everything they had been demanding, including a state with its capital in Jerusalem, control over the Temple Mount, a return of approximately 95 percent of the West Bank and all of the Gaza Strip, and a $30 billion compensation package for the 1948 refugees. How could Yasser Arafat possibly reject that historic offer? Prince Bandar of Saudi Arabia, who was serving as an intermediary among the parties, urged Arafat to "take this deal." Could you ever get "a better deal"? he asked. Would you rather negotiate with Sharon? As Arafat vacillated, Bandar issued a stern warning: "I hope you remember, sir, what I told you. If we lose this opportunity, it is going to be a crime."[9]

I watched in horror as Arafat committed that crime by rejecting Barak's offer, walking away from the peace negotiations without even making a counterproposal. Prince Bandar was later to characterize Arafat's decision as "a crime against the Palestinians—in fact, against the entire region." He held Arafat personally responsible for all the ensuing deaths of Israelis and Palestinians.[10] President Clinton also placed the entire blame for the termination of the process on Arafat, as did most of those who had participated in the negotiations. Even many Europeans were furious at Arafat for walking away from this generous offer. Finally, it looked as if world public opinion was shifting away from the Palestinians, who had rejected the two-state solution once again, and toward the Israelis, who had proposed a way out of the violent impasse.

But within a few short months, international public opinion had once again shifted away from Israel and back toward the Palestinians, this time with a vengeance. Suddenly Israel was the pariah, the villain, the aggressor, and the destroyer of peace. On university campuses across the world, it was Israel—the country that had just offered so much—that was the sole object of divestment and boycott petitions. How could so many intelligent people have forgotten so quickly who was to blame for the termination of the peace process? How could the world so quickly turn Arafat, the villain of Camp David, into a hero, while turning Israel, which had heroically offered so much, into the villain? What happened in this brief period to produce such a dramatic shift in public perceptions?

I learned that what happened was precisely what Prince Bandar had predicted to Arafat would happen if he turned down Barak's peace offer: "You have only two choices. Either you take this deal or we go to war." Arafat chose to go to war. According to his own communications minister, "The P.A. [Palestinian Authority] began to prepare for the outbreak of the current intifada since its return from the Camp David negotiations, by request of President Yasser Arafat."[11]

The excuse for the escalation of suicide bombings was Ariel Sharon's visit to the Temple Mount. But as the communications minister boasted, "Arafat . . . predicted the outbreak of the intifada as a complementary stage to the Palestinian steadfastness in the negotiations, and not as a specific protest against Sharon's visit to Al-Haram Al-Sharif [the Temple

Mount]." Indeed, the escalation in terrorism had actually begun several days *before* Sharon's visit, as part of "the PA's instruct[ion]" to "the political forces and factions to run all materials of the intifada." In other words, instead of showing "steadfastness in the negotiations" by making a counterproposal to Barak's generous offer, Arafat decided to make his counteroffer in the form of suicide bombings and escalating violence. Prince Bandar has charged Arafat with responsibility for the resulting bloodbath: "I have still not recovered . . . from the magnitude of the missed opportunity," he told a reporter. "Sixteen hundred Palestinians dead so far. And seven hundred Israelis dead. In my judgment, not one life of these Israelis and Palestinians dead is justified."[12]

How then could the man who was responsible for these avoidable deaths, who chose to reject the Barak peace proposal, and who instructed his subordinates to restart the violent intifada as "a complementary stage" to the negotiations manage to turn world public opinion so quickly in favor of the Palestinians and against the Israelis? It was this daunting question that cried out for an answer, and it was the frightening answer that impelled me to write this book.

The answer comes in two parts. The first is rather obvious: Arafat played the tried-and-true terrorism card that had worked for him so many times over his long and tortuous career as a terrorist diplomat. By targeting Israel's civilians—children on school buses, pregnant women in shopping malls, teenagers at a discotheque, families at a Passover seder, university students in a cafeteria—Arafat knew he could get Israel to overreact, first by electing a more hawkish prime minister to replace the dovish Ehud Barak, then by provoking the military to take actions that would inevitably result in the deaths of Palestinian civilians. It worked perfectly, as it had in the past. Suddenly the world was seeing disturbing images of Israeli soldiers shooting into crowds, stopping women at checkpoints, and killing civilians. Arafat had "mastered" the "harsh arithmetic of pain," as one diplomat put it: "Palestinian casualties play in their favor, and Israeli casualties play in their favor. Non-violence doesn't pay."[13]

For many, the bare arithmetic was enough: more Palestinians than Israelis were dead, and that fact alone proved that Israel was the villain. Ignored was the fact that although "only" 810 Israelis were killed (as of June 2003), Palestinian terrorists had *attempted* to kill thousands more and had failed only because Israeli authorities had thwarted "about 80 percent of the attempted" terrorist attacks.[14] Ignored also was the fact that among the 2,000 or so Palestinians killed were hundreds of suicide bombers, bomb makers, bomb throwers, terrorism commanders, and even alleged collaborators who were killed by other Palestinians. When only innocent civilians are counted, significantly more Israelis than Palestinians have been killed.[15] Indeed, Israel has killed fewer innocent Palestinian civilians during the decades it has been fighting terrorism than any other nation in history facing comparable violence, and these tragic deaths have been the unintended consequences of fighting terrorism, rather than the object of the violence.

Why then have so many people in the international community—diplomats, media pundits, students, politicians, religious leaders—fallen for Arafat's transparent and immoral ploy? Why were they not blaming Arafat for the escalation of bloodshed, as Prince Bandar and others were doing? Why were they so quick to place the blame on Israel? Why were moral and religious leaders who ordinarily drew a sharp distinction between those who *purposefully* target innocent civilians and those who *inadvertently* kill civilians in an effort to protect their own civilians failing to draw that important distinction when it came to Israel? Why did they not understand how the Palestinian leadership was manipulating and exploiting the arithmetic of death? Why could they not see beyond the gross body count and focus on the correct moral calculus: how many *innocent* people were deliberately being targeted and killed by each side?

In seeking to answer these disturbing questions, it became clear to me that darker forces were at play. The dramatic and almost total shift in public perceptions over so brief a period of time could not be explained by reference exclusively to principles of logic, morality, justice—even politics. The answers lay, at least in part, in the fact that Israel is the Jewish state and the "Jew" among the states of the world. A full understanding of so much of the world's bizarre reactions to Israel's generous peace offer and the Palestinians' violent response to it requires a recognition of the world's long and disturbing history of judging the Jewish people by different, and far more demanding, standards.

So too with the Jewish nation. Since shortly after its establishment as the world's first modern Jewish state, Israel has been subjected to a unique double standard of judgment and criticism for its actions in defending itself against threats to its very existence and to its civilian population. This book is about that double standard—both its unfairness toward Israel and, even more important, its pernicious effect on encouraging terrorism by Palestinians and others.

If the tone of this book sometimes sounds contentious, it is because the accusations currently being made against Israel are so often shrill, uncompromising, one-sided, and exaggerated: "Nazi-like," "genocidal," "the prime example of human rights violators in the world," and so on. These false charges must be answered directly and truthfully before a tone of compromise and mutual acknowledgment of wrongdoing can be restored and the issues debated on their often complex merits and demerits. But all too often, today's debate, especially on university campuses, is characterized by contentious and one-sided accusations made by those seeking to demonize Israel. They are often answered by far more candid acknowledgments of wrongdoing by defenders of Israel and a tone of apology that often panders to the accusers.

Progress toward peace will come only when both sides are willing to acknowledge their own wrongdoing and blameworthiness and move beyond the finger-pointing past to a future of mutual compromise. An atmosphere conducive to such compromise will not be achieved unless the air is cleared of the false, exaggerated, and one-sided accusations that now pollute the discussion in so many settings. The purpose of this book is to help clear the air by providing direct and truthful defenses to false accusations. The tone of these defenses sometimes necessarily mirrors the tone of the accusations. The hallmark of my writing, speaking, and teaching over the years has always been to be direct and not to pander to, or worry about, offending those who, on the basis of their own bigoted actions and false accusations, deserve to be offended. I try to follow that path in this book.

Once the air is cleared of the pollutants of bigotry and falsehood, a more nuanced debate can begin over specific Israeli policies—as well as specific Palestinian policies. This book is not part of *that* debate, although I have my own views on many of these issues. So long as Israel stands singularly and falsely accused of being the worst offender, the first obligation of those committed to truth and fairness is to disprove those accusations—firmly and unequivocally.

I am frequently asked how I, as a civil libertarian and liberal, can support Israel. The implication behind the question is that I must be compromising my principles in supporting so "repressive" a regime. The truth is that I support Israel precisely *because* I am a civil libertarian and a liberal. I also criticize Israel whenever its policies violate the rule of law. Nor do I try to defend egregious actions by Israelis or their allies, such as the 1948 killings by irregular troops of civilians at Deir Yassin, the 1982 Phalangist massacre of Palestinians in the Sabra and Shatilla refugee camps, or the 1994 mass murder of Muslims at prayer by Baruch Goldstein. Like any other democracy, Israel and its leaders should be criticized whenever their actions fail to meet acceptable standards, but the criticism should be proportional, comparative, and contextual, as it should be with regard to other nations as well.

I make the case for Israel based on liberal and civil libertarian considerations, although I believe that conservatives should also support the Jewish state based on conservative values. I am not asking anybody to compromise their principles. Rather, my request is that all people of goodwill should simply apply the same principles of morality and justice to the Jewish state of Israel that they do to other states and peoples. If they would only apply a single standard, the case for Israel would largely make itself. But since so many people insist on applying a more demanding standard to Israel, I now make the case that, judged by any rational standard, Israel deserves the support—although certainly not the uncritical support—of all people of goodwill who value peace, justice, fairness, and self-determination.

1 Is Israel a Colonial, Imperialist State?

THE ACCUSATION

Israel is a colonial, imperialist, settler state, comparable to apartheid South Africa.

THE ACCUSERS

"[A Jewish state in Palestine] could only emerge as the bastard child of imperialist powers, and it could only come into existence by displacing the greater part of the Palestinian population, by incorporating them into an apartheid state, or through some combination of the two. In addition, once created, Israel could only survive as a militarist, expansionist, and hegemonic state, constantly at war with its neighbours." (M. Shahid Alam, professor of economics at Northeastern University[1])

"Occupied Palestine [which includes all of Israel] must be decolonized, deracialized and restored to the Palestinian people as a single sovereign state. In plain English, the Zionist State must be dismantled." (Imam Achmed Cassiem, national chairperson, Islamic Unity Conviction, South Africa[2])

THE REALITY

Israel is a state comprising primarily refugees and their descendants exercising their right of self-determination. Beginning in the 1880s, the Jews who moved to what is now Israel were refugees escaping the oppressive anti-Semitism of colonial Europe and the Muslim states of the Middle East and North Africa. Unlike colonial settlers serving the expansionist commercial and military goals of imperial nations such as Great Britain, France, the Netherlands, and Spain, the Jewish refugees were escaping from the countries that had oppressed them for centuries. These Jewish refugees were far more comparable to the American colonists who had left England because of religious oppression (or the Europeans who later immigrated to America) than they were to eighteenth- and nineteenth-century English imperialists who colonized India, the French settlers who colonized North Africa, and the Dutch expansionists who colonized Indonesia.

THE PROOF

Those who absurdly claim that the Jewish refugees who immigrated to Palestine in the last decades of the nineteenth century were the "tools" of European imperialism must answer the following question: *For whom* were these socialists and idealists working? Were they planting the flag of the hated czar of Russia or the anti-Semitic regimes of Poland or Lithuania? These refugees wanted nothing to do with the countries from which they fled to avoid pogroms and religious discrimination. They came to Palestine without any of the weapons of imperialism. They brought with them few guns or other means of conquest. Their tools were rakes and hoes. The land they cultivated was not taken away from its rightful owners by force or confiscated by colonial law. It was purchased, primarily from absentee landlords and real estate speculators, at fair or often exorbitant prices.

As Martin Buber, a strong supporter of Palestinian rights, observed in 1939: "Our settlers do not come here as do the colonists from the Occident, to have natives do their work for them; they themselves set their shoulders to the plow and they spend their strength and their blood to make the land fruitful."[3] Nor was the land they sought to cultivate rich in natural resources such as oil or gold, or strategically positioned as a trade route. It was a materially worthless piece of real estate in a backwater of the world whose significance to Jews was religious, historical, and familial.

Clearly these Jewish workers were not your typical imperialists. They were refugees from oppressive regimes who were seeking to begin new lives in a place their ancestors had long ago settled and from which most but not all of them had eventually been driven. Moreover, as the British historian Paul Johnson has documented, the colonial powers did everything possible to thwart the establishment of a Jewish homeland: "Everywhere in the West, the foreign offices, defense ministries and big business were against the Zionists."[4] The Jewish refugees who came to live in Palestine had to overcome Turkish, British, and Pan-Arab imperialism in order to achieve self-determination.

To prove beyond any reasonable doubt that Israel is not and has never been an imperialist or colonialist state, it is necessary to briefly recount the early history of the Jewish refugees from Europe who joined the mostly Sephardic Jews who had lived in Palestine for generations. The first wave of immigration (or Aliyah as it was called), beginning in 1882 and ending in 1903, was not very different in many respects from the first large-scale immigration of Eastern European Jews to America at about the same time. This was a time of massive emigration and immigration throughout the world, especially from the crowded cities and towns of Europe. Enormous population shifts took place, with people settling in places far away from their birthplaces. Irish, Italian, Greek, German, Polish, and Jewish families, as well as Chinese, Japanese, and Caribbean families, sought better lives in the United States, Canada, South America, Australia, and other places where they could work with their hands and develop their minds.

Approximately 10,000 Eastern European Jews immigrated to Palestine, as compared to nearly a million Jews who immigrated to the United States.[5] Most of the Jews of the First Aliyah had no realistic hope of establishing a Jewish nation in Palestine. Although some Jewish intellectuals, such as Leo Pinsker, had advocated "autoemancipation" as early as 1882, there was no political movement advocating a Jewish state until near the end of the First Aliyah in 1897, when Theodore Herzl organized the first Zionist Congress in Basel, Switzerland.

The Jews of the First Aliyah produced a manifesto in 1882, in which they explicitly referred to the recent wave of pogroms as well as the more distant autos-da-fe that had threatened to destroy European Jewry. They did not necessarily want a state but "a home in our country," perhaps a "state within a larger state," where they could have their "civil and political rights" and could also "help our brother Ishmael in the time of his need."

Like the Jews who sought refuge in America, most of the Jews who first returned to Zion were simply looking for a place to live in peace, without discrimination and without physical threats to their survival. They certainly had that right. Palestine, the land of their forebears, seemed to be an appropriate place for several important reasons, including that there has always been a significant Jewish presence in Palestine.

Historians believe that the Hebrews arrived in present-day Israel sometime in the second millennium B.C.E. Under Joshua, and later King David and his successors, independent Hebrew kingdoms existed. "For more than one thousand six hundred years the Jews formed the main settled population of [what the Romans later called] Palestine," according to historian Martin Gilbert.[6] After conquest by the Babylonians, Persians, and Greeks, an independent Jewish kingdom was revived in 168 B.C.E., but Rome took effective control in the next century. The Romans suppressed Jewish revolts in 70 C.E. and 135 C.E., and Judea was renamed Palestine, in order

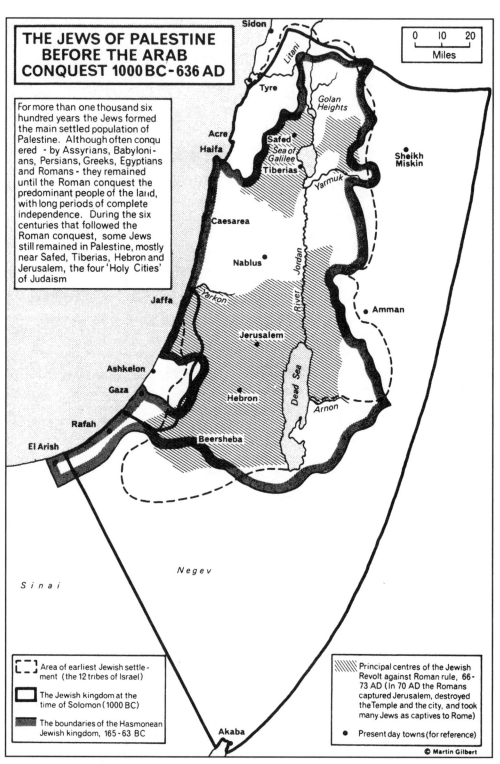

THE JEWS OF PALESTINE BEFORE THE ARAB CONQUEST 1000 BC – 636 AD

For more than one thousand six hundred years the Jews formed the main settled population of Palestine. Although often conquered - by Assyrians, Babylonians, Persians, Greeks, Egyptians and Romans - they remained until the Roman conquest the predominant people of the land, with long periods of complete independence. During the six centuries that followed the Roman conquest, some Jews still remained in Palestine, mostly near Safed, Tiberias, Hebron and Jerusalem, the four 'Holy Cities' of Judaism

0   10   20
Miles

Sidon
Tyre
Golan Heights
Acre
Haifa
Safed
Sea of Galilee
Tiberias
Sheikh Miskin
Litani
Yarmuk
Caesarea
Nablus
River Jordan
Amman
Jaffa
Yarkon
Jerusalem
Ashkelon
Gaza
Dead Sea
Hebron
Arnon
Rafah
Beersheba
El Arish
Negev
Sinai
Akaba

Area of earliest Jewish settlement (the 12 tribes of Israel)

The Jewish kingdom at the time of Solomon (1000 BC)

The boundaries of the Hasmonean Jewish kingdom, 165 - 63 BC

Principal centres of the Jewish Revolt against Roman rule, 66 - 73 AD (In 70 AD the Romans captured Jerusalem, destroyed the Temple and the city, and took many Jews as captives to Rome)

• Present day towns (for reference)

© Martin Gilbert

16

to de-Judaize it; the Romans renamed it after the earlier coastal inhabitants, the Philistines.[7] From then on, despite repeated efforts by the Romans, the Crusaders, and some Muslims to make Palestine empty of Jews, thousands of Jews managed to remain in its holy cities, especially Jerusalem, Safad, Tiberias, and Hebron. There were also Jewish communities in Gaza, Rafah, Ashkelon, Caesarea, Jaffa, Acre, and Jericho.

Among the Jews who lived in Jericho during the seventh century were refugees from Muhammad's bloody massacre of two Arabian Jewish tribes. The Jews of Khaibar had lived peacefully among their Arab neighbors until the prophet Muhammad "visited upon his beaten enemy inhuman atrocities," massacring Jewish men, women, and children. The Jews of Khaibar "had prided themselves on the purity of their family life; now their women and daughters [the ones who were spared execution] were distributed among and carried away by the conquerors."[8] Those Jews who managed to escape the sword of the prophet were forbidden to remain on the Arab Peninsula, pursuant to the prophet's command: "Never do two religions exist in Arabia."[9] Many settled in Palestine, joining Jewish refugees from post-Roman Christian oppression.

The Crusaders massacred thousands of Jews along with Muslims in the eleventh century, but soon thereafter Jews from France, England, and later Spain, Lithuania, Portugal, Sicily, Sardinia, Rhodes, and Naples established centers of Jewish learning and commerce. From this time on, Palestine was never without a significant and well-documented Jewish presence. By the time the Ottoman Turks occupied Palestine in 1516, approximately 10,000 Jews lived in the Safad region alone. In the sixteenth century, according to British reports, "as many as 15,000 Jews" lived in Safad, which was "a center of rabbinical learning."[10] Many more Jews lived in Jerusalem, Hebron, Acre, and other locations. Jerusalem, in fact, has had a Jewish majority since the first population figures were gathered in the nineteenth century, and, according to the British consul in Jerusalem, the Muslims of Jerusalem "scarcely exceed[ed] one quarter of the whole population."[11] Jerusalem was a predominantly Jewish city well before the First Aliyah. By the middle of the nineteenth century—thirty years before the First Aliyah of European Jews—Jews also constituted a significant presence, often a plurality or majority, in Safad, Tiberias, and several other cities and towns.[12] Tel Aviv has been a predominantly Jewish city since European Jews founded it on sand dunes in 1909.

Palestine remained a center of Jewish learning, piety, and mysticism throughout the ages. European Jews contributed to the Jewish religious institutions in Palestine and prayed daily for a return to Zion (which was originally a religious, rather than a political, term; hence its recurring mention in Christian sources). Although most of the Jews of the First Aliyah were secular to the core, the longing for Zion transcended theology and was an important aspect of Jewish history. Jews who lived outside of Palestine were referred to as the diaspora or the exiles. The Jewish people never abandoned their claim to return to the land from which so many of their ancestors had been forcibly driven.

Well before the first European Zionists arrived in Palestine, religiously inspired pogroms and other forms of violence victimized local Jews whose ancestors had called Palestine home for centuries. During the Egyptian occupation of Palestine in the 1830s, the indigenous Jews were persecuted mercilessly by Muslim zealots for no reason other than religious bigotry. In 1834, Jewish homes in Jerusalem "were sacked and their women violated."[13] Later that year, Jews in Hebron were massacred. The British consul, William Young, in a report to the British Foreign Office—40 years before the First Aliyah—painted a vivid and chilling picture of the life of the Jews of Jerusalem in 1839:

> I think it my duty to inform you that there has been a Proclamation issued this week by the Governor in the Jewish quarter—that no Jew is to be permitted to pray in his own house under pain of being severely punished—such as want to pray are to go into the Synagogue. . . .
>
> There has also been a punishment inflicted on a Jew and Jewess—most revolting to human nature, which I think it is my duty to relate.
>
> In the early part of this week, a House was entered in the Jewish Quarter, and a robbery was committed—the House was in quarantine—and the guardian was a Jew—he was taken before the Governor—he denied having any knowledge of the thief or the circumstances. In order to compel him to confess, he was laid down and beaten, and afterwards imprisoned. The following day he was again brought before the Governor, when he still declared his innocence. He was then burned with a hot iron over his face, and various parts of the body—and beaten on the lower parts of his body to the extent that the flesh hung in pieces from him. The following day the poor creature died. He was a young Jew of Salonica about 28 years of age—who had been here but a very short time, he had only the week before been applying to enter my service.
>
> A young man—a Jew—having a French passport was also suspected—he fled—his character was known to be an indifferent one—his mother, an aged woman, was taken under suspicion of concealing her son—She was tied up and beaten in the most brutal way. . . .
>
> I must say I am sorry and am surprised that the Governor could have acted so savage a part—for certainly what I have seen of him, I should have thought him superior to such wanton inhumanity—but it was a Jew—without friends or protection—it serves well to show, that it is not without reason that the poor Jew, even in the nineteenth century, lives from day to day in terror of his life.[14]

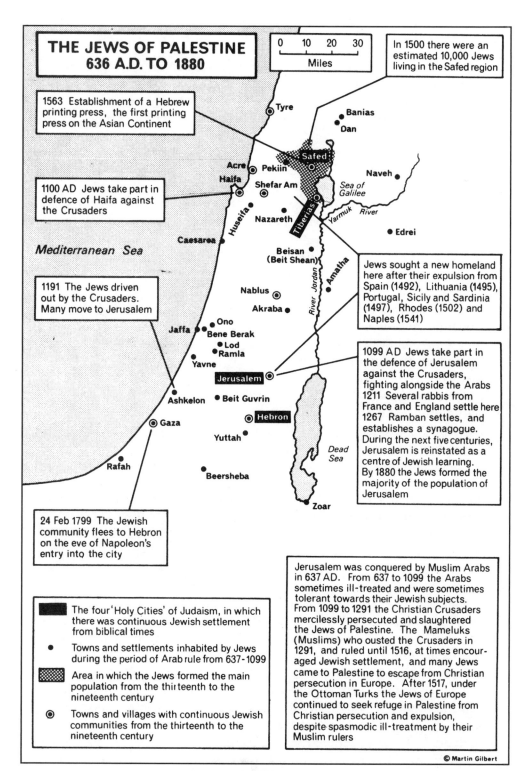

THE JEWS OF PALESTINE 636 A.D. TO 1880

0   10   20   30
Miles

In 1500 there were an estimated 10,000 Jews living in the Safed region

1563 Establishment of a Hebrew printing press, the first printing press on the Asian Continent

1100 AD Jews take part in defence of Haifa against the Crusaders

Mediterranean Sea

1191 The Jews driven out by the Crusaders. Many move to Jerusalem

Tyre

Banias
Dan

Acre   Pekiin
Haifa
Shefar Am

Safed

Naveh

Sea of Galilee

Tiberias

Yarmuk River

Nazareth

Edrei

Caesarea   Huseifa

Beisan (Beit Shean)

Amatha

Jews sought a new homeland here after their expulsion from Spain (1492), Lithuania (1495), Portugal, Sicily and Sardinia (1497), Rhodes (1502) and Naples (1541)

Nablus
Akraba

River Jordan

Jaffa   Ono
Bene Berak
Lod
Ramla
Yavne

Jerusalem

Ashkelon   Beit Guvrin

Gaza

Hebron

Yuttah

Dead Sea

Rafah

Beersheba

Zoar

1099 AD Jews take part in the defence of Jerusalem against the Crusaders, fighting alongside the Arabs 1211 Several rabbis from France and England settle here 1267 Ramban settles, and establishes a synagogue. During the next five centuries, Jerusalem is reinstated as a centre of Jewish learning. By 1880 the Jews formed the majority of the population of Jerusalem

24 Feb 1799 The Jewish community flees to Hebron on the eve of Napoleon's entry into the city

The four 'Holy Cities' of Judaism, in which there was continuous Jewish settlement from biblical times

Towns and settlements inhabited by Jews during the period of Arab rule from 637-1099

Area in which the Jews formed the main population from the thirteenth to the nineteenth century

Towns and villages with continuous Jewish communities from the thirteenth to the nineteenth century

Jerusalem was conquered by Muslim Arabs in 637 AD. From 637 to 1099 the Arabs sometimes ill-treated and were sometimes tolerant towards their Jewish subjects. From 1099 to 1291 the Christian Crusaders mercilessly persecuted and slaughtered the Jews of Palestine. The Mameluks (Muslims) who ousted the Crusaders in 1291, and ruled until 1516, at times encouraged Jewish settlement, and many Jews came to Palestine to escape from Christian persecution in Europe. After 1517, under the Ottoman Turks the Jews of Europe continued to seek refuge in Palestine from Christian persecution and expulsion, despite spasmodic ill-treatment by their Muslim rulers

© Martin Gilbert

19

Nor could the Jew seek redress, as the report observed:

> Like the miserable dog without an owner he is kicked by one because he crosses his path, and cuffed by another because he cries out—to seek redress he is afraid, lest it bring worse upon him; he thinks it better to endure than to live in the expectation of his complaint being revenged upon him.[15]

Several years later, the same consul attributed the plight of the Jew in Jerusalem to "the blind hatred and ignorant prejudice of a fanatical populace," coupled with an inability of the poverty-stricken Jewish community to defend itself either politically or physically.[16] This was half a century before the advent of modern Zionism and the arrival of European Jews. It was pure religious bigotry directed against a native population that had lived in Palestine for centuries and had just as much right to be there, and to be treated fairly, as any Arabs or Muslims.

As we shall see, it was only after European Jews began to join their Sephardic cousins in Palestine that these Jewish refugees were able to mount any kind of defense against the religiously inspired violence that made life in Palestine so difficult. Certainly the indigenous Jews of Palestine, who had at least as much right to be there as any Muslim or Christian, were entitled to be protected against religious discrimination and victimization, and their European coreligionists had the right to offer them such protection by introducing institutions of self-defense.

Although the Jews who immigrated from Eastern Europe to Palestine were similar in many ways to the Jews who came to America in that both groups were refugees from European anti-Semitism and were seeking new lives in a place free from old bigotries, they were different in that some of those who moved to Israel had ideological reasons for their choice of a new home, whereas those who came to America picked "the Goldena Medina" (the golden nation) largely on the basis of practical considerations (such as economic opportunity, political freedom, religious equality, and family unification).

American Jews moved into Jewish neighborhoods, established Jewish communal institutions, and continued to speak Yiddish as their children mastered English. Although they experienced discrimination and exploitation, as did other immigrant groups, they eventually assimilated into the mainstream economically, politically, and even socially.

The Jews of the First Aliyah found a very different reality in late nineteenth-century Palestine. They too established their own neighborhoods, built their own communal institutions, and revived the ancient language of Hebrew. But assimilation, even for those Jews or Arabs who wanted it, was not feasible. Organized gangs of Arabs attacked unprotected and unarmed Jewish settlements, and efforts were made to prevent additional European Jews from seeking asylum in Palestine. Although some Arab leaders welcomed the Jewish refugees and saw them as a potential source of employment for local Arabs, many wanted to discourage any immigration by non-Muslims or non-Arabs. Unlike in America, where Jewish immigrants could eventually live and work alongside non-Jewish Americans, in Palestine the Jewish refugees had to live in separate communities and cultivate their own land. As the Peel Commission was later to conclude, assimilation was not feasible because of anti-Jewish prejudice stimulated by Muslim leaders.

The initial phase of the *yishuv* ("return" or "community") was thus more of an immigration of refugees than a determined political or nationalistic movement, although the seeds of political Zionism were certainly planted during the First Aliyah (and perhaps even earlier) by those whose decision was motivated, at least in part, by a desire to return to Zion. At about the time the first wave of European Jewish refugees were immigrating to Palestine, other waves of Jewish refugees from Muslim countries such as Yemen, Iraq, Turkey, and North Africa were also beginning to arrive in Palestine. These Arab Jews had no knowledge of political Zionism. They were simply returning home to escape persecution, having learned that the Ottoman Empire was permitting (or closing its eyes to) some Jewish immigration into Palestine.

Based on the actual history of the Jewish refugees who immigrated to Palestine, the claim that Israel is a colonial or imperialist state is so far-fetched that it simply serves to illustrate how language is willfully distorted in the service of a partisan agenda.

2 Did European Jews Displace Palestinians?

THE ACCUSATION

The European Jews who came to Palestine displaced Palestinians who had lived there for centuries.

THE ACCUSERS

"The Jews stole our land. What else do you want us to do, just go away?" (Mohammad Abu Laila, professor of comparative religion at Al-Azhar University in Cairo, in the context of defending suicide bombers as "martyrs"[1])

"The Jews hate the Arabs. They hate the Palestinians because the Jews stole the land of the Arabs and Palestine. A thief hates the owner of the right." ("Iraqi President Says Tel Aviv Bombing 'Just Great'; Cabinet Endorses Oil Export Halt," released June 4, 2001)

"Zionists . . . conceived their plan for a colonial-settler state in Palestine, as they went about executing this plan on the backs of imperialist powers—with wars, massacres and ethnic cleansing—and, later, as they have persisted in their plans to dispossess the Palestinians of the last fragments of their rights and legacy whose Canaanite roots were more ancient than Isaiah, Ezekiel, David and Moses." (M. Shahid Alam[2])

"Now in this respect I want to say that the Palestinians are the indigenous people of Palestine. They are descendants of the Semitic tribes that came and inhabited Palestinian territory since thousands and thousands of years, certainly long before Abraham set foot on the Palestinian territory. . . . And I say that we Palestinians, we are the descendants and indigenous people of Palestine. . . . Now we concede that the Jews, the Israelis have historical relations to Palestine, although not as long and not as fundamental as our relations being the indigenous people." (Haider Abdel Shafi, then head of the Palestinian peace talks delegation, now an independent activist[3])

"So there are two national groups which claim national self-determination. One group is the indigenous population, or what's left of it—a lot of it's been expelled or driven out or fled. The other group is the Jewish settlers who came in, originally from Europe, later from other parts of the Middle East and some other places. So there are two groups, the indigenous population and the immigrants and their descendants." (Noam Chomsky[4])

THE REALITY

The Palestine to which the European Jews of the First Aliyah immigrated was vastly underpopulated, and the land onto which the Jews moved was, in fact, bought primarily from absentee landlords and real estate speculators.

In addition to Palestine being an appropriate place for Jewish refugees because of its close connection to their history and ideology, it was also seen as appropriate because of the demographics of the land to which they were moving, or, in their word, *returning*.

Mark Twain, who visited Palestine in 1867, offered this description:

Stirring scenes . . . occur in the valley [Jezreel] no more. There is not a solitary village throughout its whole extent—not for thirty miles in either direction. There are two or three small clusters of Bedouin tents, but not a single permanent habitation. One may ride ten miles hereabouts and not see ten human beings. . . . Come to Galilee for that . . . these unpeopled deserts, these rusty mounds of barrenness, that never, never, never do shake the glare from their harsh outlines, and fade and faint into vague perspective; that melancholy ruin of Capernaum: this stupid village of Tiberias, slumbering under its six funereal palms. . . . We reached Tabor safely. . . . We never saw a human being on the whole route.

Nazareth is forlorn. . . . Jericho the accursed lies in a moldering ruin today, even as Joshua's miracle left it more than three thousand years ago; Bethlehem and Bethany, in their poverty and their humiliation, have nothing about them now to remind one that they once knew the high honor of the Savior's presence, the hallowed spot where the shepherds watched their flocks by night, and where the angels sang, "Peace on earth, good will to men," is untenanted by any living creature. . . . Bethsaida and Chorzin have vanished from the earth, and the "desert places" round about them, where thousands of men once listened to the Savior's voice and ate the miraculous bread, sleep in the hush of a solitude that is inhabited only by birds of prey and skulking foxes.[5]

Other travelers recorded similar accounts of Palestine prior to the arrival of the Jews of the First Aliyah, who began the process of revitalizing the land and increasing its population by creating jobs and an infrastructure.

THE PROOF

There have been two competing mythologies about Palestine circa 1880. The extremist Jewish mythology, long since abandoned, was that Palestine was "a land without people, for a people without a land." (This phrase was actually coined by the British lord Shaftesbury in his 1884 memoir.) The extremist Palestinian mythology, which has become more embedded with time, is that in 1880 there was a Palestinian people; some even say a Palestinian nation that was displaced by the Zionist invasion.

The reality, as usual, lies somewhere in between. Palestine was certainly not a land empty of all people. It is impossible to reconstruct the demographics of the area with any degree of precision, since census data for that time period are not reliable, and most attempts at reconstruction—by both Palestinian and Israeli sources—seem to have a political agenda. But rough estimates are possible. The entire population of Palestine (defined for these purposes as current Israel, the West Bank, and the Gaza Strip) was probably in the neighborhood of half a million at the time of the First Aliyah in the early 1880s. That same area today supports a population of more than 10 million, and is capable of sustaining a far larger population. The area that was eventually partitioned into a Jewish state by the United Nations in 1947 contained only a fraction of that number, with estimates varying between 100,000 and 150,000. As a geographic entity, Palestine had uncertain and ever-shifting boundaries. Palestine was not a political entity in any meaningful sense. Under Ottoman rule, which prevailed between 1516 and 1918, Palestine was divided into several districts, called *sanjaks*. These *sanjaks* were part of administrative units called *vilayets*. The largest portion of Palestine was part of the *vilayet* of Syria and was governed from Damascus by a pasha, thus explaining why Palestine was commonly referred to as southern Syria. Following a ten-year occupation by Egypt in the 1830s, Palestine was divided into the *vilayet* of Beirut, which covered Lebanon and the northern part of Palestine (down to what is now Tel Aviv); and the independent *sanjak* of Jerusalem, which covered roughly from Jaffa to Jerusalem and south to Gaza and Be'er Sheva. It is thus unclear what it would mean to say that the Palestinians were the people who originally populated the "nation" of Palestine.

Furthermore, absentee landowners owned much of the land that was eventually partitioned into Israel. According to land purchase records, many lived in Beirut or Damascus, and some were tax collectors and merchants living elsewhere. These landlords were real estate speculators from foreign countries who had no connection to the land and who often exploited the local workers or fellahin. Like refugees in other countries, the Jewish refugees in Palestine bought land, much of it nonarable. Palestinian propagandists have wildly exaggerated the number of Arab families actually displaced by Jewish land purchases. Benny Morris is an Israeli historian whose writings have been criticized by some for their "one-sidedness . . . against Israel,"[6] and he is frequently cited by Noam Chomsky, Edward Said, and other critics of Israel as among the "new historians" who do not present the "Zionist line." Said has characterized Morris, and other "revisionist historians," as having "a genuine will to understand the past;" and what they say about it is "without a desire to lie or conceal the past"—high praise indeed from one so harshly critical of Zionism. Morris has been praised by the *New York Times Book Review* for having written "the most sophisticated and nuanced account of the Zionist–Arab conflict."[7] He summarizes the historical record as follows: "Historians have concluded that only 'several thousand' families were displaced following land sales to Jews between the 1880s and the late 1930s."[8] This is a fraction of the number of people displaced by the Egyptian construction of the Aswân Dam, the Iraqi displacement of the Marsh Arabs, and other forced movements by Arab governments of fellow Arabs.

Even years later, when Jewish land purchases were increasing, it was found that "the quantity of Arab land offered for sale was far in excess of the Jewish ability to purchase."[9] A professional analysis of land purchases between 1880 and 1948 established that three-quarters of the plots purchased by Jews were from mega-landowners rather than those who worked the soil.[10] Even as pro-Palestinian a writer as Professor Rached Khalidi acknowledges that there were considerable land sales by "absentee landlords (both Palestinian and non-Palestinian)."[11] David Ben-Gurion, former prime minister of Israel, instructed the Jewish refugees never to buy land belonging to local "fellahs or worked by them."[12] I challenge anyone making the case against Israel to produce any objective data—from census reports, land transfer records, or demographic reports—that contradict this historical reality. No one will be able to do so. Yet the false claim continues to be made that the Jews stole the land from local Arab fellahin. A related claim, and one that is equally false, is that the few fellahin who were displaced were all local Arabs who had lived and worked the land "uninterruptedly for 1300 years"[13]—that they were descendants of indigenous Arabs "whose Canaanite roots were more ancient than Isaiah, Ezekiel, David, and Moses."[14]

There is considerable dispute about the ethnicity of the people who worked the land in what eventually became Israel. Many Greeks who fled Muslim rule in their home country had moved to Palestine. By the middle of the eighteenth century, the biblical port city of Jaffa, from where Jonah began his fateful journey, had become a town populated by Turks, Arabs, Greeks, Armenians, and others. A Christian historian has reported that several villages throughout Palestine "are populated wholly by settlers from other portions of the Turkish Empire within the nineteenth century. There are villages of Bosnians, Druzes, Circassians and Egyptians."[15] The 1911 edition of *Encyclopaedia Britannica* described the population of Palestine as comprising widely differing "ethnological" groups speaking "no less than fifty languages." It was daunting therefore to "write concisely" about "the ethnology of Palestine," especially following the influx of population from Egypt "which still persists in the villages." In addition to Arabs and Jews, the other ethnic groups in Palestine at the end of the nineteenth and the beginning of the twentieth century included Kurds, German Templars, Persians, Sudanese, Algerians, Samaritans, Tatars, Georgians, and many people of mixed ethnicities. As one scholar, writing in 1984, summarized the situation: "The few Arabs who lived in Palestine a hundred years ago, when Jewish settlement began, were a tiny remnant of a volatile population, which had been in constant flux, as a result of unending conflicts between local tribes and local despots. Malaria and disease had taken a heavy toll of the inhabitants."[16]

Prior to the arrival of the European Jews at the beginning of the 1880s, the number of Arabs, particularly in the part of Palestine that was to be partitioned into a Jewish state, was small and shrinking. An 1857 communiqué from the British consul in Jerusalem reported that "the country is in a considerable degree empty of inhabitants and therefore its greatest need is that of a body of population."[17] It also noted that although the Arabs tended to leave and not return, the Jewish population was more stable: "[W]e have Jews who have traveled to the United States and Australia," and "instead of remaining there, do return hither."[18] Four years later, it was reported that "depopulation is even now advancing."[19] And four years after that, it was noted that in certain parts of the country "land is going out of cultivation and whole villages are rapidly disappearing . . . and the stationary population extirpated."[20]

Other historians, demographers, and travelers described the Arab population as "decreasing,"[21] and the land as "thinly populated,"[22] "unoccupied,"[23] "uninhabited,"[24] and "almost abandoned now." The Plain of Sharon, which the Jews of the First Aliyah later cultivated, was described by Reverend Samuel Manning in 1874 as "a land without inhabitants" that "might support an immense population."[25]

Moreover, the conditions of local life before the arrival of the European Jewish refugees were hardly enviable. Only a tiny proportion of the population could read or write.[26] Health care was abominable,[27] infant mortality high, life expectancy short, and water scarce.[28] All this would improve dramatically after the European Jews arrived.

Not surprisingly, the small and decreasing Arab–Muslim population of the area was also a transient and migratory population, as contrasted with the more stable, if smaller, Jewish population. The myth of a stable and settled Palestinian–Arab–Muslim population that had lived in villages and worked the land for centuries, only to be displaced by the Zionist invaders, is simply inconsistent with the recorded demographic data gathered not by the Jews or Zionists but rather by the local authorities themselves. J. L. Burkhardt reported that as early as in the second decade of the nineteenth century, "Few individuals . . . die in the same village in which they were born. Families are continually moving from one place to another . . . in a few years . . . they fly to some other place, where they have heard that their brethren are better treated."[29]

By the mid-1890s—only a dozen years after the beginning of the First Aliyah—Jews were becoming an important part of the ethnic and religious mix of Palestine, especially in the area eventually partitioned by the United Nations for a Jewish state in 1947. At the time of the partition, there was a clear Jewish majority in that area[30] (538,000 Jews and 397,000 Arabs). According to some disputed accounts—which I do not rely on for my argument—even as early as the mid-1890s, there may have been a plurality of Jews in parts of Palestine that became the heartland of the Jewish area under the U.N. partition.[31] Without any doubt, there was already a significant Jewish presence in that area before the beginning of the twentieth century.

Some Muslims—the numbers are uncertain—had been attracted to the new areas of Jewish settlement by the jobs made available by Jewish immigration and cultivation of land. A study of the Jewish settlement of Rishon L'Tzion, first established in 1882, showed that the 40 Jewish families that settled there had attracted "more than 400 Arab families," many of which were Bedouin and Egyptian. These families moved into areas around the Jewish settlement and formed a new Arab village on the site of "a forsaken ruin."[32] The report observed a similar pattern with regard to other settlements and villages.

Although it is impossible to reconstruct with any confidence the precise number of Arabs–Muslims–Palestinians who had lived for generations in what eventually became the Jewish area under the partition, the number is far below that claimed by Palestinian polemicists. According to one historian, "at least 25% of [the Muslims who lived in all of Palestine in 1882] were newcomers or descendants of those who arrived after [the Egyptian conquest of 1831]."[33] In addition to the Egyptian influx, there was a considerable immigration of Turks, Greeks, and Algerians. Moreover, many of the Palestinian Muslims who were attracted to western Palestine between 1882 and 1893 came from eastern Palestine (the West and East Banks of the Jordan). Combining these figures leads to the inescapable conclusion that the number of Palestinians with deep roots in the areas of Jewish settlement—although impossible to estimate with confidence—constitutes a tiny fraction of the more than a million Palestinian Arabs who now live in Israel.

The number of Muslims who lived in the Jewish areas grew dramatically after the Jewish settlements blossomed not only because many Arabs were attracted to the newly settled areas and newly cultivated land but also because the Jewish presence improved health care, cut infant mortality, and expanded adult life expectancy. A British official reported in 1937 that "the growth in [the numbers of Arab fellahin] had been largely due to the health services combating malaria, reducing infant death rates, improving water supply and sanitation."[34] These improvements began with modern hospitals and water and sanitary systems introduced into Palestine by the Jewish refugees from Europe.

Because of the absence of precise census or land records, no one will ever be able to reconstruct, with any degree of certainty, the precise demographics of the area eventually assigned to the Jewish state by the U.N. partition of 1947 at the time the Jewish refugees from Europe began to arrive there. But it is beyond reasonable dispute—based on census figures, authoritative reports, eyewitness accounts, and simple arithmetic—that the myth of displacement by the European Jewish refugees of a large, stable, long-term Muslim population that had lived in that part of Palestine for centuries is demonstrably false. Even many Arab intellectuals acknowledge the mythical nature of this claim. As the Palestinian leader Musa Alami said in 1948, "The people are in great need of a 'myth' to fill their consciousness and imagination."[35] King Abdullah of Jordan also recognized that the story of Jewish displacement of local Palestinians was a fictional one, acknowledging that "the Arabs are as prodigal in selling their land as they are in . . . weeping [about it]."[36]

3 Was the Zionist Movement a Plot to Colonize All of Palestine?

THE ACCUSATION

Even if the First Aliyah can be characterized as an immigration of refugees merely seeking a home in Palestine, the Second Aliyah was the beginning of a Zionist imperialist plot to colonize all of Palestine.

THE ACCUSERS

"My premise is that Israel developed as a social polity out of the Zionist thesis that Palestine's colonization was to be accomplished for and by Jews and by the displacement of the Palestinians; that in its conscious and declared idea about Palestine, Zionism attempted first to minimize, then to eliminate, then, all else failing, finally to subjugate the natives as a way of guaranteeing that Israel would not be simply the state of its citizens (which included Arabs, of course) but the state of the whole Jewish people, having a kind of sovereignty over land and peoples that no other state possessed or possesses." (Edward Said[1])

"[The 60,000 Jews who lived in Palestine by the end of the Second Aliyah] "were overwhelmingly anti-Zionist and their descendants still are unanimously [of that view]." (Noam Chomsky[2])

THE REALITY

The Second Aliyah, although largely inspired by Zionist ideology, was also an immigration from persecution, and it contemplated cooperation with local Muslims to create better lives for all residents of Palestine.

THE PROOF

The Second Aliyah (1904–1914) was, if anything, even more an immigration of refugees seeking asylum from persecution. The historian Benny Morris writes, "The [Russian] pogroms of 1903–1906 were a major precipitant of the Second Aliya."[3] These governmentally inspired waves of violence were even "more vicious than those of the 1880's."[4] The first of the twentieth-century pogroms, on Passover of 1903 in Kishinev, resulted in the murder of 49 Jews, the injury of hundreds more, and the destruction of 1,500 Jewish houses, shops, and institutions. Hundreds of pogroms followed throughout the Pale of Settlement, killing and injuring thousands of Jewish men, women, and children. Jews could not defend themselves without inviting even more retribution. The only option was to become refugees. Hundreds of thousands left for America and western Europe. Tens of thousands sought refuge in Palestine. Many were ardent Zionists, following Herzl's dream of a Jewish homeland. Others were simply refugees willing to bear the hardships of a land they hoped to turn into a socialist paradise.

The Second Aliyah, not unlike the wave of refugees who came to America during the same period, included many working-class people who formed labor unions and labor parties. They also established a Hebrew press and a small self-defense organization to protect the Jews from the Arab violence that had victimized the earlier refugees.

In 1905, an Arab writer, Najib Azouri, published an anti-Jewish screed that reverberated throughout Palestine. It warned of a secret Jewish plot to establish a Zionist state "stretching from Mount Herman to the Arabian Desert and the Suez Canal."[5] The young David Ben-Gurion worried that "Azouri's pupils" were "sowing the seed of hatred for the Jews at all levels of Arab society."[6]

Many, although not all, of the Jewish refugees sought to establish good relations with their Arab neighbors. One of the earliest publications by a Zionist living in Israel was a small book by Yitzhak Epstein entitled *The Hidden Question,* which proposed giving local Arabs access to Jewish hospitals, schools, and libraries.[7] Others urged the Jewish refugees to learn Arabic and to refrain from purchasing any land containing Arab villages or holy sites.[8] But conflicts persisted as the number of Jewish refugees increased. In 1913, a leading Arab personality published a poem that included the following lines:

> Jews, sons of clinking gold, stop your deceit:
> We shall not be cheated into bartering away our country!
> . . . The Jews, the weakest of all peoples and the least of them,
> Are haggling with us for our land;
> How can we slumber on?

Despite these provocations and continuing religiously inspired violence against the Jewish refugees, efforts persisted at reaching some rapprochement. In early 1914, a leading Zionist, Nachum Sokolov, gave an interview to a Cairo newspaper urging the Arabs to view the Jewish refugees as fellow Semites "returning home" who could help them prosper together. Jewish–Arab dialogues were planned for the summer of 1914, but the outbreak of World War I, which was to have momentous consequences for the Jews and Arabs of Palestine, put all such cooperative efforts on hold.

4 Was the Balfour Declaration Binding International Law?

THE ACCUSATION

The Balfour Declaration, which called for the establishment of a "Jewish home in Palestine," has no legal effect, since it was merely the opinion of the government of England.

THE ACCUSERS

"[The Balfour] [D]eclaration was made (a) by a European power, (b) about a non-European territory, (c) in a flat disregard of both the presence and the wishes of the native majority resident in that territory, and (d) it took the form of a promise about this same territory to another foreign group so that this foreign group might quite literally *make* this territory a national home for the Jewish people. . . . Balfour's statements in the declaration take for granted the higher right of a colonial power to dispose of a territory as it saw fit." (Edward Said[1])

"[I]n 1917, the Balfour Declaration promised a national home for the Jewish people. Under international law the declaration was null and void since Palestine did not belong to Britain—under the pact of the League of Nations it belonged to Turkey." (Faisal Bodi, British journalist[2])

THE REALITY

A de facto Jewish homeland already existed in parts of Palestine, and its recognition by the Balfour Declaration became a matter of binding international law when the League of Nations made it part of its mandate.

THE PROOF

By the beginning of the First World War, the number of Jews living in the area of Palestine that was to become Israel was somewhere between 80,000 and 90,000. Even before the Balfour Declaration of 1917, there was a de facto Jewish national home in Palestine consisting of several dozens of Jewish moshavim and kibbutzim in western and northeastern Palestine, as well as in Jewish cities such as Tel Aviv, Jerusalem, and Safad. The Jewish refugees in Palestine had established this homeland on the ground without the assistance of any colonial or imperialist powers. They had relied on their own hard work in building an infrastructure and cultivating land they had legally purchased.

World War I pitted the British (among others) against the Germans and the Ottoman Empire (among others). The United States entered the war on the British side in 1917, and President Woodrow Wilson declared that the principle of self-determination should govern any postwar reorganization of territories that were formerly controlled by the Ottoman Empire. Support for Jewish self-determination in those areas of Palestine in which Jews constituted a majority was seen by many as part of Wilsonian self-determination.[3]

After all, there had never been a Palestinian state in this area. A Jewish homeland would not be carved out of a preexisting Palestinian state. Instead, a decision would have to be made about how to allocate a 45,000-square-mile area of land that had been captured from the Ottoman Empire and was populated by Arabs, Jews, and others. There were four basic alternatives: (1) give all the land, even that in which the Jews were a majority, to some new Arab state; (2) give all the land, even the part in which Arabs were the majority, to the Jews; (3) turn all the land over to Syria, to be ruled from Damascus; or (4) divide the land fairly between the Arabs and the Jews so that each could create a homeland based on self-determination. The last of these options was selected and the decision was made to allocate a portion of the land to the group that lived there, worked the land, and built the infrastructure. What could be fairer and more in the spirit of self-determination?

Winston Churchill, "a lifelong Zionist," had long favored Jewish self-determination in Palestine. As far back as 1908, he saw the establishment of "a strong, free Jewish state" as "a notable step toward a harmonizing

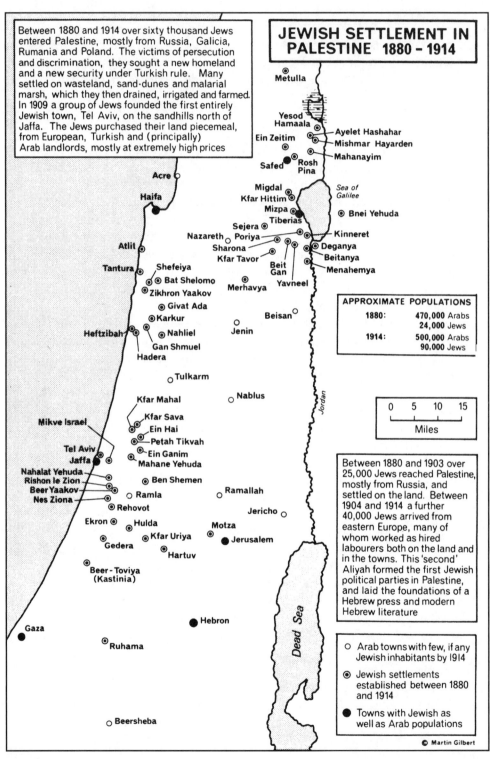

Between 1880 and 1914 over sixty thousand Jews entered Palestine, mostly from Russia, Galicia, Rumania and Poland. The victims of persecution and discrimination, they sought a new homeland and a new security under Turkish rule. Many settled on wasteland, sand-dunes and malarial marsh, which they then drained, irrigated and farmed. In 1909 a group of Jews founded the first entirely Jewish town, Tel Aviv, on the sandhills north of Jaffa. The Jews purchased their land piecemeal, from European, Turkish and (principally) Arab landlords, mostly at extremely high prices

JEWISH SETTLEMENT IN PALESTINE 1880 – 1914

Metulla

Yesod Hamaala
Ein Zeitim
Ayelet Hashahar
Mishmar Hayarden
Mahanayim
Safed   Rosh Pina

Acre

Haifa

Migdal
Kfar Hittim
Mizpa
Sejera   Tiberias
Nazareth Poriya
Sharona
Kfar Tavor
Beit Gan
Yavneel

Sea of Galilee

Bnei Yehuda

Kinneret
Deganya
Beitanya
Menahemya

Atlit

Tantura

Shefeiya
Bat Shelomo
Zikhron Yaakov
Givat Ada
Karkur
Nahliel
Gan Shmuel
Hadera

Heftzibah

Merhavya

Beisan

Jenin

Tulkarm

Nablus

Kfar Mahal
Kfar Sava
Ein Hai
Petah Tikvah
Ein Ganim
Mahane Yehuda

Mikve Israel

Tel Aviv
Jaffa
Nahalat Yehuda
Rishon le Zion
Beer Yaakov
Nes Ziona

Ben Shemen

Ramla

Ramallah

Rehovot

Jericho

Ekron   Hulda
Gedera
Kfar Uriya
Hartuv

Motza
Jerusalem

Beer-Toviya
(Kastinia)

Gaza

Ruhama

Hebron

Beersheba

Jordan

Dead Sea

APPROXIMATE POPULATIONS

1880:	470,000	Arabs
	24,000	Jews
1914:	500,000	Arabs
	90,000	Jews

0   5   10   15

Miles

Between 1880 and 1903 over 25,000 Jews reached Palestine, mostly from Russia, and settled on the land. Between 1904 and 1914 a further 40,000 Jews arrived from eastern Europe, many of whom worked as hired labourers both on the land and in the towns. This 'second' Aliyah formed the first Jewish political parties in Palestine, and laid the foundations of a Hebrew press and modern Hebrew literature

○   Arab towns with few, if any Jewish inhabitants by 1914

◉   Jewish settlements established between 1880 and 1914

●   Towns with Jewish as well as Arab populations

© Martin Gilbert

disposition of the world among its people."[4] When Britain was finally in a position to help bring about such a "harmonizing disposition," Churchill was even more explicit:

> It is manifestly right that the scattered Jews should have a national center and a national home and be reunited and where else but in Palestine with which for 3,000 years they have been intimately and profoundly associated? We think it will be good for the world, good for the Jews, good for the British Empire, but also good for the Arabs who dwell in Palestine. . . . They shall share in the benefits and progress of Zionism."[5]

It should not be surprising, therefore, that as the British government planned for victory over the Ottoman Empire, it announced through a letter from British Foreign Minister Lord Arthur Balfour that "His Majesty's Government view with favor the establishment in Palestine of a national home for the Jewish people." It also announced that such a home must not "prejudice the civil and religious rights of existing non-Jewish communities in Palestine."[6] Ironically, one of the biggest objections many Arabs had to the Balfour Declaration was that it seemed to regard Palestine as a separate entity rather than as part of Syria. As the Peel Commission was later to observe, "The Arabs had always regarded Palestine as included in Syria." The last thing they wanted was a separate Palestine, because they realized that a separate Palestine meant a Palestine that, under the Balfour Declaration, might include a small home for its substantial Jewish population.

The French foreign minister had issued a statement similar to the Balfour Declaration several months earlier, describing as "a deed of justice and of reparation" the "renaissance of the Jewish nationality in the land from which the people of Israel were expelled so many centuries ago."[7] The text of the Balfour Declaration had been submitted to President Wilson and approved by him in advance. The French and Italian governments also subsequently approved it. In 1919, President Wilson stated, "I am persuaded that the Allied nations, with the fullest concurrence of our own government and people, are agreed that in Palestine shall be laid the foundations of a Jewish commonwealth."[8] In 1922, the U.S. Congress adopted a resolution declaring that a "national home for the Jewish people" be established in Palestine. Winston Churchill also confirmed that the British government "contemplated the eventual establishment of a Jewish state,"[9] and he noted that the substance of the Balfour Declaration had been reaffirmed in several binding multinational treaties, as well as the League of Nations mandate itself, and "is not susceptible of change." It then became a matter of binding international law.

Churchill also recognized that a Jewish home in Palestine already existed on the ground without any help from the British:

During the last two or three generations the Jews have recreated in Palestine a community, now numbering 80,000 of whom about one-fourth are farmers or workers upon the land. This community has its own political organs: an elected assembly for the direction of its domestic concerns; elected councils in the towns; and an organization for the control of its schools. It has its elected Chief Rabbinate and Rabbinical Council for the direction of religious affairs. Its business is conducted in Hebrew as a vernacular language, and a Hebrew Press serves its need. It has its distinctive intellectual life and displays considerable economic activity. This community, then, with its town and country population, its political, religious and social organizations, its own language, its own customs, its own life, has in fact "national" characteristics. When it is asked what is meant by the development of the Jewish National Home in Palestine, it may be answered that it is not the imposition of a Jewish nationality upon the inhabitants of Palestine as a whole, but the further development of the existing Jewish community, with the assistance of Jews in other parts of the world, in order that it may become a center in which the Jewish people as a whole may take, on grounds of religion and race, an interest and pride. But in order that this community should have the best prospect of free development and provide a full opportunity for the Jewish people to display its capacities, it is essential that it should know it is in Palestine as of right and not on sufferance. That is the reason why it is necessary that the existence of a Jewish National Home in Palestine should be internationally guaranteed, and that it should be formally recognized to rest upon ancient historic connection.

This, then, is the interpretation which His Majesty's Government place upon the Declaration of 1917, and so understood, the Secretary of State is of the opinion that it does not contain or imply anything which need cause either alarm to the Arab population of Palestine or disappointment to the Jews.[10]

International law recognized that the Jewish community was "in Palestine by right" and that effort to "facilitate the establishment of the Jewish National Home [by increasing Jewish immigration] was a binding international obligation on the Mandatory."[11] The political and legal seeds were thus sown for a two- (or three-) state solution to the "Palestinian problem." This was a perfect example of self-determination at work.

The Jews of Palestine had certainly earned the Balfour Declaration through their sweat and blood. They had drained the malaria-filled swamps of Hulah and planted orange groves in their place, employing thousands of Arabs and Jews. The Jewish Legion fought alongside the British Army to defeat the Ottoman Army and welcomed General Edward Allenby's capture of Jerusalem. By contrast, most of the Palestinian Arabs, as well as most Arabs in general, fought on the side of the losing Ottoman Empire. As Lloyd George, the British prime minister, noted, "Most of the Arab races fought throughout the war for the Turkish oppressors . . . the Palestinian Arabs [in particular] fought for Turkish rule."[12] It was the Palestinians who had sided with the imperialist, colonialist Turkish Empire against those who favored self-determination. Despite picking the wrong side—which they did again in World War II—the Arabs emerged from the Turkish defeat with significant gains. Most important, they got 80 percent of Palestine set aside as an exclusively Arab state, with no Jewish settlement permitted. This large area of eastern Palestine was renamed Transjordan.

The first state established in Palestine was thus an emirate with a large Palestinian majority. Abdullah, the brother of neighboring Iraq's new ruler, would rule it. Many of the Jews who lived in what became Trans-jordan—some of whom had lived there for generations—had been forced to leave because of episodic outbreaks of violence and, by law, the few remaining Jews were forbidden from living in Transjordan.[13] The newly formed kingdom of Transjordan consisted of a large territorial expanse with a minuscule total population of 320,000 people, many of whom were transient Bedouins.[14] The population of Transjordan was far smaller than that of Palestine, yet no Jews were permitted to live there.

The remaining one-fifth of Palestine could now be shared or divided between its Jewish and Arab residents. At least that was the theory. But Arab opposition to *any* Jewish home in *any* part of Palestine—to any Jewish self-determination in areas in which Jews were a majority, coupled with Arab self-determination in areas in which Arabs were a majority—turned increasingly violent after the First World War and the Balfour Declaration. The last thing most Arab leaders wanted was mutual self-determination. They were satisfied with the imperialistic decision to create a Hashemite emirate in Transjordan, and they would have been equally satisfied with an imperialistic decision to hand all of Palestine over to the rule of a distant Syrian pasha—anything to prevent the creation of a Jewish homeland, even in a small portion of what was left of Palestine!

The opposition was not only to a Jewish homeland. Increasingly, Arab leaders began to demand elimination of a Jewish *presence* in Palestine. The goal was to make Palestine as empty of Jews as Transjordan had become. As Aref Pasha Dajana, a Jerusalem notable, candidly put it, "It is impossible for us to make an understanding with [the Jews] or even to live with them. . . . In all the countries where they are at present they are not wanted . . . because they always . . . suck the blood of everybody. If the League of Nations will not listen to the appeal of the Arabs, this country will become a river of blood."[15] His prediction became self-fulfilling as the Arabs turned increasingly to bloodshed.

Some moderate Arab leaders recognized the benefits of Jewish self-determination in Palestine. Emir Feisal, the son of Hussein, sherif of Mecca, who represented the Arab Kingdom of Hedjaz, signed an agreement in 1919 with Chaim Weizmann, who represented the Zionist organization. This agreement called for the taking of all necessary measures to "encourage and stimulate immigration of Jews into Palestine on a large scale [in order to achieve] closer settlement and intensive cultivation of the land," so long as "Arab peasant and tenant farmers shall be protected in their rights, and shall be assisted in forwarding their economic development."[16] In a follow-up letter to Professor Felix Frankfurter, Feisel made the following statements:

> We feel that the Arabs and Jews are cousins in race, having suffered similar oppressions at the hands of powers stronger than themselves, and by a happy coincidence have been able to take the first step towards the attainment of their national ideals together. . . .
>
> We Arabs, especially the educated among us, look with the deepest sympathy on the Zionist movement. Our deputation here in Paris is fully acquainted with the proposals submitted yesterday by the Zionist Organization to the Peace Conference, and we regard them as moderate and proper. We will do our best, in so far as we are concerned, to help them through: we will wish the Jews a most hearty welcome home. . . . We are working together for a reformed and revised Near East, and our two movements complete one another. The Jewish movement is national and not imperialist. Our movement is national and not imperialist, and there is room in Syria for us both. Indeed I think that neither can be a real success without the other.[17]

Unfortunately, this farsighted view was blocked by the virulent anti-Jewish bigotry of the man selected to become the leader of Palestine's Muslim community.

5 Were the Jews Unwilling to Share Palestine?

THE ACCUSATION

While the Arabs were willing to share Palestine with the Jews, the Jews wanted the entire country for themselves.

THE ACCUSERS

"From the beginning of serious Zionist planning for Palestine . . . we can note the increasing prevalence of the idea that Israel was to be built on the ruins of the Arab Palestine." (Edward Said[1])

"[A] territory once full of Arabs emerged from a war (a) essentially emptied of its original residents and (b) made impossible for Palestinians to return to. Both the ideological and organizational preparations for the Zionist effort to win Palestine, as well as the military strategy adopted, envisioned taking over territory, and filling it with new inhabitants." (Edward Said[2])

THE REALITY

The goal of the Arab leadership was not only to prevent the establishment of a Jewish state in any part of Palestine but to transfer the Jews of Palestine out of their historic home and to make all of Palestine empty of

Jews. Jewish leaders, on the other hand, were willing to make painful compromises as long as they could have a Jewish homeland in those areas of Palestine in which they were a majority.

THE PROOF

Shortly after the Balfour Declaration became binding international law, several organized pogroms were directed against the Jewish refugees. A Christian Arab educator described what he observed in western Jerusalem and the Jewish quarter of the old city that had been Jewish for generations:

> [A] riot broke out, the people began to run about and stones were thrown at the Jews. The shops were closed and there were screams. . . . I saw a Zionist [that is, Jewish British] soldier covered in dust and blood. . . . Afterwards, I saw one Hebronite approach a Jewish shoeshine boy, who hid behind a sack in one of the [Old City] wall's corners next to Jaffa Gate, and take his box and beat him [the shoeshine boy] over the head. He screamed and began to run, his head bleeding and the Hebronite left him and returned to the procession. . . . The riot reached its zenith. All shouted, "Muhammad's religion was born with the sword." . . . I immediately walked to the municipal garden . . . my soul is nauseated and depressed by the madness of humankind."[3]

Shortly thereafter, Jewish women were raped and synagogues destroyed in a pogrom organized by a nationalist group called Al-Nadi Al-Arabi.[4] A British investigation concluded, "All the evidence goes to show that these attacks were of a cowardly and treacherous description, mostly against old men, women and children—frequently in the back."[5]

Other attacks against Jewish refugees took place in Jaffa, where thirteen Jews were murdered. A few days later, six more Jews were murdered in an orange grove. Soon thereafter, hundreds of Palestinian Arabs from Tulkarm attacked the Jewish moshav at Hadera. Attacks against vulnerable civilians by Palestinian terrorists were becoming the norm.

In an effort to control this violence, the British appointed Haj Amin al-Husseini the grand mufti of Jerusalem, the spiritual and effectively political leader of the Muslims in Palestine.[6] The hope was that by centralizing the religious and political power in one man, whom the British thought they could control, they could limit the passions of the mob. But they picked the wrong man. Husseini was a virulent anti-Semite[7] whose hatred of Jews was both religious and racial. He was eventually to become a close ally and adviser to Adolf Hitler, and an active supporter of the "final solution"—the mass murder of European Jewry. In 1940, he asked the Axis powers to settle the Jewish problem in Palestine in accordance with the "racial interests of the Arabs and along lines similar to those used to solve the Jewish question in Germany."[8] He urged Hitler to extend the final solution to the Jewish refugees who had reached Palestine, and he advised Hitler, in 1943—when it was well known what was happening in Poland's death camps—to send the Jews to "Poland, in order thereby to protect oneself from their menace."[9]

Husseini's racist hatred of Jews was manifested early in his long career as grand mufti. He instigated anti-Jewish riots and preached anti-Jewish incitements. "Itbah al-Yahud" (kill the Jews) was the message, along with "Nashrab dam al-Yahud" (we will drink the blood of the Jews). The result was an increase in anti-Jewish violence. Although there had been earlier attacks, especially throughout 1920, now these attacks had the formal blessing of the official leader of Palestine's Muslims.

The grand mufti also lent his imprimatur to the unwillingness of his people to compromise. Before his ascendancy to the leadership of Palestinian Muslims, there had been Arab voices of compromise with regard to division of authority over the land and its people. For example, one Arab newspaper had written that the known "energies" and "labors" of the Jewish people "would improve and develop the country to the benefit of its Arab inhabitants."[10] Even some who were critical of the Balfour Declaration, such as a group of 100 Arab dignitaries who petitioned Britain in 1918, wrote that they had "always sympathized profoundly with the persecuted Jews and their misfortunes in other countries," but they refused to be ruled by these Jews, thus suggesting that some form of mutual self-determination in an equitably partitioned Palestine might be feasible.[11]

All this talk would quickly end with the appointment of Husseini as grand mufti. What would otherwise have been a political dispute, subject to a political compromise resolution, now became an absolute religious prohibition that was not amenable to any compromise: according to the grand mufti of Jerusalem, it would violate Islamic law for even one inch of Palestine to be controlled by Jews. Jewish self-determination in areas with a Jewish majority—Jewish cities and settlements and Jewish historical roots—was prohibited by Islamic law, as Husseini expounded it, and every Muslim must be prepared to fight a holy war to prevent this from happening. As quickly as the two- (or three-) state solution based on self-determination and the international acceptance of the principles of the Balfour Declaration seemed to hold some promise, it was taken off the table by Husseini. According to the grand mufti, the only solution was either for the Jews to be driven from the land by violence or for a small number of Jews to remain in a Muslim land as Dimmi—second-class noncitizens subject to the absolute control of the Muslims.[12] He made it eminently clear that if Muslims ever controlled all of Palestine, most of the Jews would be transferred out.[13]

There were, of course, Jews who wanted to control all of Palestine—or at least the 20 percent that was left after Transjordan was partitioned from what was originally Palestine into an exclusively Arab state. But compromise was always seen as a pragmatic necessity by the mainstream Zionists and their leadership. The reality of a Jewish homeland with a Jewish majority population was far more important than the size of that homeland. Indeed, self-determination was realistic only in those parts of Palestine that were already Jewish by demographics and by the presence of Jewish institutions on the ground. The Jewish refugees from Europe, together with the Sephardic Jews and their descendants, were creating a Jewish home only in certain areas of Palestine, making territorial compromise inevitable and leaving room for another Palestinian state on the west bank of the Jordan.

The developing clash between the Jews of Palestine, led by the pragmatic socialist David Ben-Gurion, and the Muslims of Palestine, led by the uncompromising Jew-hater Haj Amin al-Husseini, was *not* over whether the Jews or the Muslims would control all of Palestine that was left after Transjordan was made into an exclusively Arab emirate. Instead, it was—realistically viewed—whether the remainder of Palestine was to be given exclusively to the Muslims of Palestine or whether it would be fairly divided between the Jews and the Muslims of Palestine, each of whom effectively controlled certain areas. Put another way, the question was whether the Wilson principle of self-determination would allow each group to control its own people and its own destiny. To this question, the grand mufti had a simple answer: no for the Jews; yes for the Muslims.

The grand mufti's approach to the Jews of Palestine—destroy them by force, frighten them into leaving by directing violence against their most vulnerable civilians, or transfer them by law—culminated in the Hebron massacre of 1929. The Jews of Hebron were neither all Zionists nor European refugees. Many were religiously observant Sephardic, Jews who lived in Hebron because of its biblical significance as the birthplace of Judaism and the several Jewish seminaries and ancient synagogues that were in that holy city.

The Hebron massacre was the culmination of a series of religiously inspired massacres deliberately incited by the grand mufti. In October 1928, the grand mufti organized a series of provocations against the Jews who prayed at the Western Wall, Judaism's holiest site because it is believed to be the only remnant of the Second Temple. The mufti ordered new construction "next to and on top of the wall" with bricks often falling on Jewish worshipers, the driving of mules "through their praying area, often dropping excrement," and the turning up of the volume of muezzins (Islamic callers) during Jewish prayer.[14] The Jews protested and tensions remained high for months. In August 1929, leaflets prepared by the mufti instructed Muslims to attack the Jews. One such leaflet said that Jews had "violated the honor of Islam"[15] and had "raped the women and murdered widows and babies." It was a blood libel demanding a holy war against the Jews. A well-organized mob burned Jewish prayer books at the Western Wall and destroyed notes of supplication left in its crevices. This was followed by attacks on Jews and the burning of Jewish stores, with Arab policemen joining in the attacks.

On August 23, Hebron was attacked. Unarmed yeshiva students were murdered, Jewish homes were attacked, and their occupants were slaughtered. Sixty Jews were killed and the remainder were chased out of town. The synagogues were desecrated. For the first time in centuries, Hebron was made empty of Jews. The grand mufti's policy of ethnic cleansing of Jewish inhabitants was being implemented with a vengeance. The British police chief of Hebron later gave the following testimony:

> On hearing screams in a room, I went up a sort of tunnel passage and saw an Arab in the act of cutting off a child's head with a sword. He had already hit him and was having another cut, but on seeing me, he tried to aim the stroke at me but missed: he was practically in the muzzle of my rifle. I shot him low in the groin. Behind him was a Jewish woman smothered in blood with a man I recognized as a[n Arab] police constable named Issa Sheril from Jaffa. . . . He was standing over the woman with a dagger in his hand. He saw me and bolted into a room close by and tried to shut me out—shouting in Arabic, "Your Honor, I am a policeman." I got into the room and shot him.[16]

The rioting soon reached Safad, where 45 Jews were murdered or seriously injured.[17] Additional murders took place throughout the Jewish areas of Palestine. Before the orchestrated bloodshed was over, 133 Jews had been murdered and 339 injured.[18]

The British condemned "the atrocious acts committed by bodies of ruthless and bloodthirsty evildoers." They railed against the "murders perpetrated upon defenseless members of the Jewish population . . . accompanied, as in Hebron, by acts of unspeakable savagery."[19] They blamed the murders on "racial animosity on the part of the Arabs."[20]

In trying to defend himself against charges that he incited the pogroms, the grand mufti blamed the victims. Citing *The Protocols of the Elders of Zion* (a notorious czarist forgery long used by anti-Semites), Husseini claimed that it was the Jews who attacked the Muslims.

The British knew that the premeditated violence was inspired by the mufti to send a clear message that even more violence would ensue unless the British agreed to curtail immigration. But instead of responding to Muslim violence by cracking down on its perpetrators, the British punished its victims by giving the mufti exactly what he was seeking: a reduction in

Jewish immigration and a statement by the British high commissioner that the Balfour Declaration was a "colossal blunder."[21] It would not be the last time that the British would reward the calculated terrorist violence directed against unarmed Jewish civilians. Indeed, it was the beginning of a pattern: nearly every time the Jewish community made any progress, the mufti would play the terrorism card and murder innocent Jews. This would persuade the British that the Arabs were "irrational" and that their demands must be met. (As we will see later, Husseini's relative, Yasser Arafat, was to repeat this pattern with regard to terrorism, and the world would repeat its response by rewarding, and thus encouraging, it.) Less was expected of the "irrational" Arabs than of the "civilized" Jews. (This form of double-standard racism—racism against but ultimately favorable to the Arabs—has recurred in current times.)

The grand mufti characterized the murder of Jewish women, children, and students in Hebron as the beginning of a revolt, which continued through the 1930s, with even greater rewards from the British. The curtailment of Jewish immigration into Palestine could not have come at a worse time for the Jews, since Adolf Hitler was soon to become the führer of Germany with a program to rid Europe of its Jews, either by emigration or by genocide.

6 Have the Jews Always Rejected the Two-State Solution?

THE ACCUSATION

The Jews have always rejected the two-state solution, whereas the Arabs have accepted it.

THE ACCUSERS

"Most importantly of all, the Palestinians did not believe, and were right not to believe, that Ben-Gurion and the other leading Zionists would be satisfied with, or abide by, a compromise. They feared, in other words, that the Zionist "acceptance" of the UN plan was disingenuous, that the Zionist leaders were adamantly bent on expanding a Jewish state to include all of biblical Palestine, and that they would simply use a partition compromise as the base from which to expand later." (Jerome Slater, research scholar in political science at SUNY–Buffalo[1])

"We must only recall the real world, in which the PLO had been calling for negotiations and a peaceful settlement with Israel for many years while the U.S. and Israel never countered with any 'reasonable people ready to make peace,' just as they do not today." (Noam Chomsky[2])

"If you use the term [rejectionist] in a non-racist sense, we instantly conclude that the United States leads the rejection front and has for many years, and that both political groupings in Israel . . . are strict rejectionists, and this is completely non-controversial up until the mid-90s. . . . I think it holds right up to the present." (Noam Chomsky[3])

THE REALITY

As soon as partition into two states or homelands was proposed, the Jews accepted it and the Arabs rejected it.

THE PROOF

In 1937—in the midst of the terrorist revolt inspired by the grand mufti— the British published the *Peel Commission Report,* based on its investigation of the "causes of the disturbances." It left no doubt about who was at fault: "one side put itself, not for the first time, in the wrong by resorting to force, whereas the other side patiently kept the law."[4] The commission realized that the murderous violence against civilians that had begun in the 1920s had been deliberately ordered by the mufti and the Arab High Committee.[5] It also confirmed that the Jews who had come to Palestine were refugees, calling Zionism "a creed of escape" from the persecution suffered by the Jews of the Diaspora. In the broadest sense, it saw the problem as "fundamentally a conflict of right with right" that was rooted deeply in the past. After reviewing the historic claims of the Jews and the Arabs, the commission found them both compelling.

Turning to the present, the Peel Commission found that "the sympathy of the Palestinian Arabs with their kinsmen in Syria had been plainly shown. . . . Both peoples clung to the principle that Palestine was part of Syria and should never have been cut off from it."[6] It also found that it would be "wholly unreasonable to expect" the Jews to accept minority status in a Muslim state,[7] especially since they had essentially created a Jewish home, with Hebrew newspapers, Hebrew schools and universities, a Jewish hospital system, an active political and labor union system, and all the other attributes of statehood. The Jewish areas of Palestine were more like an ongoing state than were the Arab areas. Tel Aviv was a Jewish metropolis with a population exceeding 150,000. West Jerusalem had a Jewish population of 76,000, far exceeding the Muslim population. Haifa, with its population of 100,000, was half Jewish, and much of the business at its port "is Jewish business." Local democratic governments, as well as a national agency, featured nearly twenty political parties. Democracy had come to Palestine, at least to its Jewish areas. So had art and culture:

With every year that passes, the contrast between the intensely democratic and highly organized modern community and the old-fashioned Arab world around it grows sharper, and in nothing perhaps more markedly than on its cultural side. The literary output of the National Home is out of all proportion to its size. Hebrew translations have been published of the works of Aristotle, Descartes, Leibnitz, Fichte, Kant, Bergson, Einstein and other philosophers, and of Shakespeare, Goethe, Heine, Byron, Dickens, the great Russian novelists, and many modern writers. In creative literature the works of Bialik, who died in 1935, have been the outstanding achievement in Hebrew poetry and that of Nahum Sokolov, who died in 1936, in Hebrew prose. A number of Hebrew novels have been written reflecting the influence on the Jewish mind of life in the National Home. The Hebrew Press has expanded to four daily and ten weekly papers. Of the former, the *Ha'aretz* and the *Davar* are the most influential and maintain a high literary standard. Two periodicals are exclusively concerned with literature and one with dramatic art. But perhaps the most striking aspect of the culture of the National Home is its love of music. It was while we were in Palestine, as it happened, that Signor Toscanini conducted the Palestine Symphony Orchestra, composed of some 70 Palestinian Jews, in six concerts mainly devoted to the works of Brahms and Beethoven. On each occasion every seat was occupied, and it is noteworthy that one concert was reserved for some 3,000 workpeople at very low rates and that another 3,000 attended the Orchestra's final rehearsal. All in all, the cultural achievement of this little community of 400,000 people is one of the most remarkable features of the National Home."[8]

In 1937, the Peel Commission recommended a partition plan by which to resolve what it characterized as an "irrepressible conflict . . . between two national communities within the narrow bounds of one small country."[9] Because of the general hostility and hatred of the Jews by the Muslims, "national assimilation between Arabs and Jews is . . . ruled out."[10] Nor could the Jews be expected to accept Muslim rule over them, especially since the grand mufti made it clear that most of the Jews would be transferred out of Palestine if the Muslims gained complete control.[11] The Peel Commission concluded that partition was the only just solution:

Manifestly the problem cannot be solved by giving either the Arabs or the Jews what they want. The answer to the question "Which of them in the end will govern Palestine?" must surely be "Neither." We do not think that any fair-minded statesman would suppose, now that the hope of harmony between the races has proved untenable, that Britain ought either to hand over to Arab rule 400,000 Jews . . . or that if the Jews should become a majority, a million or so of Arabs should be handed over to their rule. But, while neither race can justly rule all Palestine, we see no reason why, if it were practicable, each race should not rule part of it.

No doubt the idea of Partition as a solution of the problem has often occurred to students of it, only to be discarded. There are many who would have felt an instinctive dislike to cutting up the Holy Land. The severance of Transjordan, they would have thought, from historic Palestine was bad enough. On that point we would suggest that there is little moral value in maintaining the political unity of Palestine at the cost of perpetual hatred, strife and bloodshed, and that there is little moral injury in drawing a political line through Palestine if peace and goodwill between the peoples on either side of it can thereby in the long run be attained. . . . Partition seems to offer at least a chance of ultimate peace. We can see none in any other plan.[12]

The Peel Commission plan proposed a Jewish home in areas in which there was a clear Jewish majority, divided into two noncontiguous sections. The northern portion extended from Tel Aviv to the current border with Lebanon. It consisted largely of a 10-mile-wide strip of land from the Mediterranean east to the end of the coastal plain, then a somewhat wider area from Haifa to the Sea of Galilee. A southern portion, disconnected from the northern one by a British-controlled area that included Jerusalem, with its majority Jewish population, extended from south of Jaffa to north of Gaza.

The proposed Arab area was, on the other hand, entirely contiguous and encompassed the entire Negev, the West Bank, and the Gaza Strip. It was many times larger than the proposed Jewish home. The population of the proposed Jewish area would have included 300,000 Jews and 190,000 Arabs. More than 75,000 additional Jews lived in Jerusalem, which would have remained under British control.

The commission suggested that over time there could be exchanges of land and population:

[T]he Jews may wish to dispose of some or all of the lands now owned by them which lie within the boundaries of the Arab state, and their occupants may wish to move into the Jewish state. . . . The Arabs . . . may likewise be willing to sell the land they own within the boundaries of the Jewish state [and move to the Arab state].[13]

The commission summarized the advantages of partition for both sides:

The advantages to the Arabs of Partition on the lines we have proposed may be summarized as follows:

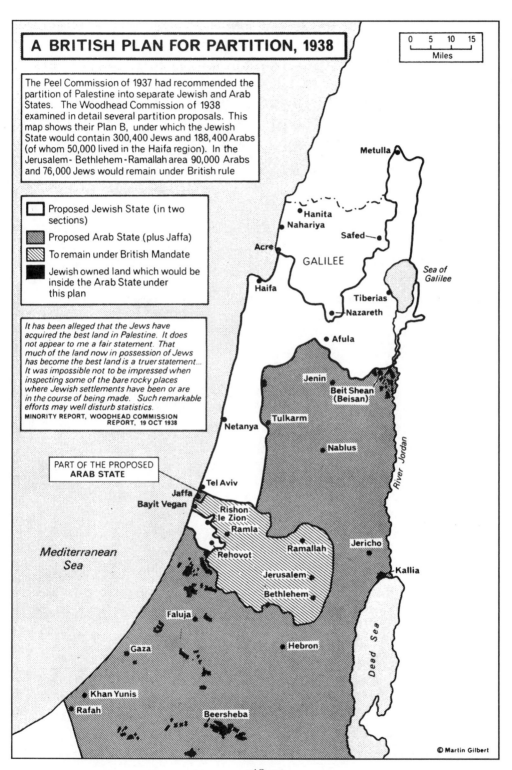

A BRITISH PLAN FOR PARTITION, 1938

The Peel Commission of 1937 had recommended the
partition of Palestine into separate Jewish and Arab
States. The Woodhead Commission of 1938
examined in detail several partition proposals. This
map shows their Plan B, under which the Jewish
State would contain 300,400 Jews and 188,400 Arabs
(of whom 50,000 lived in the Haifa region). In the
Jerusalem-Bethlehem-Ramallah area 90,000 Arabs
and 76,000 Jews would remain under British rule

0 5 10 15
Miles

☐ Proposed Jewish State (in two
   sections)

▨ Proposed Arab State (plus Jaffa)

▨ To remain under British Mandate

■ Jewish owned land which would be
   inside the Arab State under
   this plan

*It has been alleged that the Jews have
acquired the best land in Palestine. It does
not appear to me a fair statement. That
much of the land now in possession of Jews
has become the best land is a truer statement...
It was impossible not to be impressed when
inspecting some of the bare rocky places
where Jewish settlements have been or are
in the course of being made. Such remarkable
efforts may well disturb statistics.*
**MINORITY REPORT, WOODHEAD COMMISSION
REPORT, 19 OCT 1938**

PART OF THE PROPOSED
ARAB STATE

Metulla

Hanita
Nahariya
Safed
Acre
GALILEE
Sea of
Galilee
Haifa
Tiberias
Nazareth

Afula

Jenin
Beit Shean
(Beisan)

Netanya
Tulkarm
Nablus

River Jordan

Tel Aviv
Jaffa
Bayit Vegan
Rishon
le Zion
Ramla
Rehovot
Ramallah
Jericho
Jerusalem
Kallia
Bethlehem

Mediterranean
Sea

Faluja

Gaza
Hebron

Dead Sea

Khan Yunis
Rafah
Beersheba

© Martin Gilbert

49

I. They obtain their national independence and can cooperate on an equal footing with the Arabs of the neighboring countries in the cause of Arab unity and progress.

II. They are finally delivered from the fear of being "swamped" by the Jews and from the possibility of ultimate subjection to Jewish rule.

III. In particular, the final limitation of the Jewish National Home within a fixed frontier and the enactment of a new Mandate for the protection of the Holy Places, solemnly guaranteed by the League of Nations, removes all anxiety lest the Holy Places should ever come under Jewish control.

IV. As a set-off to the loss of territory the Arabs regard as theirs, the Arab State will receive a subvention from the Jewish State. It will also, in view of the backwardness of Trans-Jordan, obtain a grant of £2,000,000 from the British Treasury; and if an arrangement can be made for the exchange of land and population, a further grant will be made for the conversion, as far as may prove possible, of uncultivable land in the Arab State into productive land from which the cultivators and the state alike will profit.

The advantages of Partition to the Jews may be summarized as follows:

I. Partition secures the establishment of the Jewish National Home and relieves it from the possibility of its being subjected in the future to Arab rule.

II. Partition enables the Jews in the fullest sense to call their National Home their own: for it converts it into a Jewish State. Its citizens will be able to admit as many Jews into it as they themselves believe can be absorbed. They will attain the primary objective of Zionism—a Jewish nation planted in Palestine, giving its nationals the same status in the world as other nations give theirs. They will cease at last to live a "minority life."[14]

Finally, the commission alluded to how partition would help the rescue of Europe's Jews from Nazism:

To both Arabs and Jews Partition offers a prospect—and we see no such prospect in any other policy—of obtaining the inestimable boon of peace. It is surely worth some sacrifice on both sides if the quarrel, which the Mandate started, could be ended with its termination. It is not a natural or old-standing feud. An able Arab exponent of the Arab case told us that the Arabs throughout their history have not only been free from anti-Jewish sentiment but have also shown that the spirit of compromise is deeply rooted in their life. And he went on to express his sympathy with the fate of the Jews in Europe. "There is no decent-minded person," he said, "who would not want to do everything humanly possible to relieve the distress of those persons," provided that it was "not at the cost of inflicting a corresponding distress on another people." Considering what the possibility of finding a refuge in Palestine means to many thousand suffering Jews, we cannot believe that the "distress" occasioned by Partition, great as it would be, is more than Arab generosity can bear. And in this, as in so much else connected with Palestine, it is not only the peoples of that country that have to be considered. The Jewish Problem is not the least of the many problems, which are disturbing international relations at this critical time and obstructing the path to peace and prosperity. If the Arabs at some sacrifice could help to solve that problem, they would earn the gratitude not of the Jews alone but of all the Western World.[15]

The Jews reluctantly accepted the Peel partition plan, while the Arabs categorically rejected it, demanding that all of Palestine be placed under Arab control and that most of the Jewish population of Palestine be "transferred" out of the country, because "this country [cannot] assimilate the Jews now in the country."[16] The Peel Commission implicitly recognized that it was not so much that the Arabs wanted self-determination as that they did not want the Jews to have self-determination or sovereignty over the land the Jews themselves had cultivated and in which they were a majority. After all, the Palestinians wanted to be part of Syria and be ruled over by a distant monarch. They simply could not abide the reality that the Jews of Palestine had created for themselves a democratic homeland pursuant to the League of Nations mandate and binding international law. Even if turning down the Peel proposal resulted in no state for the Palestinians, that was preferable to allowing even a tiny, noncontiguous state for the Jews. When the British convened a meeting between the parties, "the Arabs would not sit in the same room as the Jews."[17] Further, they responded to the Peel plan with massive violence directed at Jewish civilians, as well as at British police and civil servants.

This impasse, resulting from Arab rejection of "all attempts to give any part of Palestine over to Jewish sovereignty,"[18] coupled with Arab violence, led directly to the British decision to curtail the flow of Jewish refugees into Palestine, despite acknowledgment in the *Peel Commission Report* that "Jews enter Palestine as of right and not on sufferance," and that "Jewish Immigration is not merely sanctioned but required by solemn international agreements."[19] The British White Paper of 1939 limited Jewish immigration to 75,000 over the next five years. Britain had become the barrier to independence and statehood for the Jewish community in Palestine. British imperialistic goals now favored the Arabs over the Jews.

As Michael Oren put it, "Though the British had steadily abandoned their support for a Jewish National Home, the home was already a fact: an inchoate, burgeoning state."[20] But it was a state that was being prevented by Britain, at the demand of the Arabs, from opening its gates to those refugees most in need. This coincided with the beginning of the Holocaust, in which six million Jews were murdered. Had the Arabs accepted the two-state solution recommended by the Peel Commission, instead of responding with violence, hundreds of thousands—perhaps even a million or more—European Jews could have been saved, since the Nazi program, up until 1941, called for Jews to be expelled from Europe but not necessarily murdered. The "final solution" became the solution of choice for the Nazis only when it became clear that there was nowhere for the Jews of Europe to go, except to the gas chambers and killing fields.

7 Have the Jews Exploited the Holocaust?

THE ACCUSATION

The Jews have exploited the Holocaust to gain sympathy for a Jewish state at the expense of the Palestinians, who bear no responsibility for Hitler's genocide against the Jews.

THE ACCUSERS

"The Holocaust has proved to be an indispensible ideological weapon. Through its deployment, one of the world's most formidable military powers, with an horrendous human rights record, has cast itself as a 'victim' state, and the most successful ethnic group in the US has likewise acquired victim status. Considerable dividends accrue from this specious victimhood—in particular, immunity to criticism, however justified." (Norman Finkelstein[1])

"What makes many Palestinians and Arabs EXTREMELY ANGRY is that the memories of the Holocaust are being exploited to paint Palestinians as Nazis. Such dangerous comparison and propaganda tactics are continuously fed to many Israeli and Jewish school children from inception, especially upon visiting the Holocaust museum at Yad Vashem. It should be emphasized that many life size pictures of al-Hajj Amin standing alongside Hitler are on display at Yad Vashem, just West of Jerusalem not far from Deir Yassin. It is hypocritical to hold Palestinians responsible for the 'ill fated' choice of al-Hajj Amin, while Israelis and Jews still blind themselves to the choices some of their leaders made during WW II." (www.PalestineRemembered.com responding to "Israeli Zionists propaganda" that Hajj Amin al-Husseini collaborated with Nazis during WWII)

THE REALITY

The Palestinian leadership with the acquiescence of most of the Palestinian Arabs actively supported and assisted the Holocaust and Nazi Germany and bears considerable moral, political, and even legal culpability for the murder of many Jews.

THE PROOF

Shortly after Hitler came to power, the grand mufti decided to emulate him. He informed the German consul in Jerusalem that "the Muslims inside and outside Palestine welcome the new regime of Germany and hope for the extension of the fascist anti-democratic, governmental system to other countries."[2] In an effort to bring it to his own country, Husseini organized the "Nazi Scouts," based on the "Hitler Youth."[3] The swastika became a welcome symbol among many Palestinians.

The mid- to late 1930s were marked by Arab efforts to curtail immigration and Jewish efforts to rescue as many Jews as possible from Hitler's Europe. These years were also marked by escalating Muslim violence orchestrated by Husseini and other Muslim leaders. In 1936, Arab terrorism took on a new dimension. In the beginning, the targets were defenseless Jewish civilians in hospitals, movie theaters, homes, and stores. This was followed by strikes and shop closures, then by the bombing of British offices. The Nazi regime in Germany and the Italian fascists supported the violence, sending millions of dollars to the mufti.[4]

The SS, under the leadership of Heinrich Himmler, provided both financial and logistical support for anti-Semitic pogroms in Palestine. Adolf Eichmann visited Husseini in Palestine and subsequently maintained regular contact with him. The support was mutual, as one Arab commentator put it: "Feeling the whip of Jewish pressure and influence, the Arabs sympathize[d] with the Nazis and Fascists in their agony and trials at the hands of Jewish intrigues and international financial pressure."[5] The initial British response was appeasement in the form of a reduction in the Jewish immigration quota. Eventually, they responded with force, blowing up houses as punishment and deterrence. In Jaffa, they systematically destroyed parts of the old city, blowing up 220 homes.[6]

The Palestinians and their Arab allies were anything but neutral about the fate of European Jewry. The official leader of the Palestinians, Haj Amin al-Husseini, the grand mufti of Jerusalem who formed an alliance with the Nazis and eventually spent the war years in Berlin with Hitler, serving as a consultant on the Jewish question, was taken on a tour of Auschwitz by Himmler and expressed support for the mass murder of European Jews. He also sought to "solve the problems of the Jewish element in Palestine and other Arab countries" by employing "the same method" being used "in the Axis countries." He would not be satisfied with the Jewish residents of Palestine—many of whom were descendants of Sephardic Jews who had lived there for hundreds, even thousands, of years—remaining as a minority in a Muslim state. Like Hitler, he wanted to be rid of "every last Jew." As Husseini wrote in his memoirs,

> Our fundamental condition for cooperating with Germany was a free hand to eradicate every last Jew from Palestine and the Arab world. I asked Hitler for an explicit undertaking to allow us to solve the Jewish problem in a manner befitting our national and racial aspirations and according to the scientific methods innovated by Germany in the handling of its Jews. The answer I got was: "The Jews are yours."[7]

The mufti was apparently planning to return to Palestine in the event of a German victory and to construct a death camp modeled after Auschwitz, near Nablus. Husseini incited his pro-Nazi followers with the words "Arise, o sons of Arabia. Fight for your sacred rights. Slaughter Jews wherever you find them. Their spilled blood pleases Allah, our history and religion. That will save our honor." In 1944, a German–Arab commando unit under Husseini's command parachuted into Palestine in an effort to poison Tel Aviv's wells.

Husseini also helped to inspire a pro-Nazi coup in Iraq and to organize thousands of Muslims in the Balkans into military units known as Handselar divisions, which carried out atrocities against Yugoslav Jews, Serbs, and Gypsies. After a meeting with Hitler, he recorded the following in his diary:

> The Mufti: "The Arabs were Germany's natural friends. . . . They were therefore prepared to cooperate with Germany with all their hearts and stood ready to participate in a war, not only negatively by the commission of acts of sabotage and the instigation of revolutions, but also positively by the formation of an Arab Legion. In this struggle, the Arabs were striving for the independence and the unity of Palestine, Syria and Iraq.
>
> Hitler: "Germany was resolved, step by step, to ask one European nation after the other to solve its Jewish problem, and at the proper time

direct a similar appeal to non-European nations as well. Germany's objective would then be solely the destruction of the Jewish element residing in the Arab sphere under the protection of British power. The moment that Germany's tank divisions and air squadrons had made their appearance south of the Caucasus, the public appeal requested by the Grand Mufti could go out to the Arab world."[8]

It is fair to conclude that the official leader of the Muslims in Palestine, Haj Amin al-Husseini, was a full-fledged Nazi war criminal, and he was so declared at Nuremberg. He was sought by Yugoslavia and Great Britain as a war criminal after the war, escaping to Egypt, where he was given asylum and helped to organize many former Nazis and Nazi sympathizers against Israel.

It is also fair to say that Husseini's pro-Nazi sympathies and support were widespread among his Palestinian followers, who regarded him as a hero even after the war and the disclosure of his role in Nazi atrocities. According to his biographer, "Haj Amin's popularity among the Palestinian Arabs and within the Arab states actually increased more than ever during his period with the Nazis," because "large parts of the Arab world shared this sympathy with Nazi Germany during the Second World War." Nor was it merely a hatred of Zionism that animated this support for Nazi ideology. The grand mufti's "hatred of Jews . . . was fathomless, and he gave full vent to it during his period of activity alongside the Nazis (October 1941–May 1945)." His speeches on Berlin Radio were anti-Semitic to the core: "Kill the Jews wherever you find them—this pleases God, history and religion." In 1948, the National Palestinian Council elected Husseini as its president, even though he was a wanted war criminal living in exile in Egypt.[9] Indeed, Husseini is still revered today among some Palestinians as a national hero, while others try hard to erase him from Palestinian history. Yasser Arafat fits plainly into the former category. In an interview conducted in 2002 and reprinted in the Palestinian daily *Al-Quds* on August 2, 2002, the chairman of the Palestinian Authority calls Haj Amin al-Husseini "our hero," referring to the Palestinian people. Arafat also boasted of being "one of his troops," even though he knew he was "considered an ally of Nazis."[10] (If a German today were to call Hitler "our hero," he would appropriately be labeled a neo-Nazi!) Even Professor Edward Said believes that "Hajj Amin al-Hussaini represented the Palestinian Arab national consensus, had the backing of the Palestinian political parties that functioned in Palestine, and was recognized in some form by Arab governments as the voice of the Palestinian people."[11] He was "Palestine's national leader"[12] when he made his alliance with Hitler and played an active role in the Holocaust.

Although it would be unfair to hold the Palestinian people responsible

THE CASE FOR ISRAEL 57

for the murder of European Jewry, its official leadership was certainly far from blameless in the Holocaust. It actively supported Hitler's final solution as well as Nazi victory over the Americans and their Allies. The grand mufti of Jerusalem was personally responsible for the concentration camp slaughter of thousands of Jews. In one instance, when he learned that the Hungarian government was planning to allow thousands of children to escape from the Nazis, he intervened with Eichmann and demanded they reverse the plan. They did and the children were sent to the death camps.[13] The mufti also supported the Nazis militarily, offering his Arab Legion to fight against the Allies, so as to counteract the Jewish Brigade, which was fighting on the side of the Allies.[14]

In light of the close association between the Palestinian leadership and Nazism throughout the 1930s and 1940s, it is ironic that many pro-Palestinian groups have chosen the swastika as the symbol with which to attack Israel. Just as the Nazis called the Jews *communists* and Stalin called the Jews *fascists,* many Palestinians and their supporters—both on the extreme right and the extreme left—now use the word "Nazi" to characterize Israel, the Jews, and Zionism. The Jews have always been caught between the black and the red, as one scholar put it. They are back in the uncomfortable position once again, as the extreme left and the extreme right both seek to demonize the Jewish state by falsely comparing it to an ideology that practiced genocide against the Jewish people—a genocide widely supported and assisted by Palestinian leaders.

The Palestinian police chief, Ghazi Jabali, has compared Israel's first prime minister, the Socialist David Ben-Gurion, to the evil monster against whom he fought: "There is no difference between Hitler and Ben Gurion."[15] On today's college campuses, you can often hear Israel's prime minister compared to Hitler with the following chant: "Sharon and Hitler—just the same—the only difference is the name." No one ever compares Sharon to, say, Pinochet, or even Stalin. It is always Hitler and Nazism. Signs juxtaposing the Star of David and the swastika are commonplace. These sign-carriers are, of course, deliberately using George Orwell's "turnspeak" by trying to associate the Star of David with the swastika, knowing how deeply offensive the swastika is to Jews.

Some Jewish groups have called me over the years and asked me to try to ban the use of the swastika in attacks on Israel. Since I am opposed to censorship, I have always urged them to use the Palestinian attempt to equate Israel with Nazism as an educational opportunity to remind the world of the widespread Palestinian support for Nazism and of the fact that Nazi war criminals were given asylum in Egypt and helped the Egyptian government in its attacks against Israeli civilian targets. If Palestinian supporters insist on using the swastika, they certainly cannot complain when this symbol is turned against them to remind the world of indisputable historical facts regarding the role of their revered leader in actively supporting Hitler's genocide against the Jews and Hitler's failed attempt to bring the Holocaust to Palestine. Hitler's partner in genocide is now the "hero" of the chairman of the Palestinian Authority, while its prime minister once tried to "prove" that Hitler's Holocaust against the Jews never occurred. That is the reality, and no attempt to turn the victims into perpetrators or the villains into heroes will change history.

Generally, those who support the losing side in a war—especially a side so egregiously evil as the Nazis—do not benefit from the postwar reconstruction that inevitably follows from the surrender of the losing side. Most Palestinian Muslims were on the losing side of World War I, while the Jews of Palestine were on the winning side. The Jewish support for the British in World War I, which included fighting alongside British forces, helped earn them the Balfour Declaration of 1917. The Jewish support—including the military support of thousands of Palestinian Jews—for the Allies during World War II helped to earn the U.N. Partition of 1947. Churchill believed that the Arabs were "owed . . . nothing in a postwar settlement" because of their widespread support for Nazism. Winston Churchill had characterized the leader of the Palestinians as "the deadliest enemy."[16]

In the view of many decent people, the Palestinian (and widespread Arab) support for the Nazis should have disqualified them from having much of a say in the postwar rearrangements, much as it disqualified the Sudeten Germans from having a voice in their transfer from the Sudetenland in the borderlands of Czechoslovakia, where they had lived for centuries, to the new, smaller borders of Germany. As Winston Churchill said, "Of course there must be a transfer," despite the objections of those being transferred and his own concerns over its humanitarian implications.[17]

Instead, in 1947, the Palestinians were offered nearly the same deal they had rejected in 1937 (with the exception of the barren Negev), despite the greater need for a place for the hundreds of thousands of Jewish refugees from the death camps of Europe. At the time of the U.N. partition plan, a quarter-million Jewish refugees were living in deplorable prison camps in the very country that had murdered their parents, children, and siblings. They could not return to Poland because the Poles continued to murder Jews even after the Nazis had been defeated, and the last thing the Communist leaders of Poland wanted was an influx of Jewish refugees. Nor could they be expected to remain in Germany, where the refugee camps were temporarily located.

Immigration into a Jewish homeland in partitioned Palestine was the only feasible solution to the refugee problem. There was also a growing problem with regard to Arab countries containing significant Jewish populations. Jews in Muslim countries were always treated as second-class noncitizens (at best) and as appropriate targets of mass violence (at worst).

Although the Jews of Islam were never subjected to anything like the Holocaust, they had long been victims of pogroms and religious discrimination.

Some Islamic governments had an apartheid-like system under which Dhimmis—a religious category that includes Jews and Christians—were, by law and theology, deemed inferior and subjected to separate but unequal rules. Dhimmis were, and in some places still are, barred from public office, forced to wear distinctive dress, and subject to restrictions on the building and maintenance of synagogues and churches. It is true that Dhimmis are permitted to practice their religion and preserve their culture, but only if they pay a special *jizya*, or poll tax, not required of Muslims. The Dhimmis pay the tax in exchange for protection by the state. As such, they are outside the political community. So it is not that the Dhimmis are second-class citizens—essentially, Dhimmis are not citizens at all. Even if certain Muslim regimes treat them tolerably, they still live largely at the government's whim, as designated outsiders.

Following the Holocaust and especially the widespread Muslim and Arab support for it, it became clear that Jews could no longer be expected to live as an inferior Dhimmi minority subject to the whimsical protection of a discriminatory majority. The Jews of Islam were refugees in waiting. They were waiting for a place to move—a place in which they could live as legal equals, without regard to their religion or ethnicity. Israel was that place, and shortly after its establishment, approximately 850,000 Sephardic and Mizrahi Jews were forced to leave, or "chose" to leave, places in the Arab world that they and their ancestors had inhabited for thousands of years. As we will see in chapter 12, the situation of those Sephardic Jews who left their ancient homelands out of fear, coercion, or an unwillingness to live as a persecuted minority was, in many ways, comparable to the situation of the Arab refugees who left Israel following the massive Arab attacks on the newly declared Jewish state.

It is sometimes argued that although the Jewish survivors of the Holocaust, who became refugees at the end of the war, were entitled to a homeland *somewhere,* such a homeland should not have come at the expense of the Arabs in general and the Palestinians in particular. The Holocaust, it is argued, was the fault of the Germans and of countries including the United States that refused to accept Jewish refugees from Germany, Poland, and Austria. As Iranian president Khatami put it in 2001, "If Nazis and Fascists in the West committed crimes against the Jews, why should the Palestinians pay the price now? Those who have committed the crimes [Westerners] should pay the price."[18]

This argument fails for at least two reasons. First, the state of Israel did not come into existence at the expense of either the Arabs or the Palestinians. The area partitioned for a Jewish state had a Jewish majority that had a right to self-determination vis-à-vis the British (and the Ottomans before them). The land in question was neither Arab nor Palestinian. It had passed from one empire to another, and the time had come for self-determination by the two groups that lived in different parts of it. It was historically, demographically, economically, and legally *both* a Jewish and an Arab land. (The last independent state to have existed in Palestine was the Jewish state that had been destroyed by the Romans in 70 C.E.)

Second, the argument closes its eyes to the reality that some Arab and Palestinian leaders bore significant responsibility for the Holocaust. They supported it, aided it, used it to their advantage, and expected to benefit from it. Moreover, it was as the direct result of Arab and Palestinian pressure that the gates of immigration to Palestine were closed to Jews during the crucial years when hundreds of thousands of Jews, perhaps even more, could have been saved if they had been permitted to enter Palestine—even the tiny portion of Palestine proposed for a Jewish home by the Peel Commission in 1937.

The Arabs and Palestinians bore sufficient guilt for the Holocaust and for supporting the wrong side during World War II to justify their contribution, as part of the losing side, in the rearrangement of territory and demography that inevitably follows a cataclysmic world conflict. Just as the Sudeten Germans bore some of the burden of being on the wrong side, so too the Arabs and the Palestinians were justly required by the United Nations to contribute to a resolution of the postwar refugee problem. Moreover, all the United Nations did by partitioning Palestine was to grant the Jewish *majority,* in the land area allocated to the Jewish state, the right of self-determination—a right that has long been valued by supporters of human rights and civil liberties, and a right claimed today by Palestinians on the West Bank and in the Gaza Strip.

The Arab and Muslim nations were *completely* responsible for the second-class (or worse) status that their religions and political leaders had imposed on their Jewish minorities over the centuries. The myth of benign treatment by the Arab and Muslim world of their Jewish minority has been shattered by modern scholarship. The Jews were victims of an apartheid-like system comparable in many respects to that inflicted on black South Africans by the apartheid government of pre-Mandela South Africa. In addition to the legal and theological discrimination—the requirement to wear distinctive clothing, not to own self-defense weapons, and to pay a special tax—they were subject to periodic pogroms and blood libels, such as in Damascus in 1840. According to Morris, there were also

massacres in Tetuan in Morocco in 1790; in Mashhad and Barfurush in Persia in 1839 and 1867, respectively; and, in Baghdad in 1828. The Jewish quarter of Fez was almost destroyed in 1912 by a Muslim mob;

and *pro-Nazi mobs* slaughtered dozens of Jews in Baghdad in 1941. Repeatedly, in various parts of the Islamic world, Jewish communities—contrary to the provisions of the *dhimma*—were given the choice of conversion or death. Usually, though not always, the incidents of mass violence occurred in the vulnerable extremities of the Muslim empire rather than at its more self-confident core. But the underlying attitude, that Jews were infidels and opponents of Islam, and necessarily inferior in the eyes of God, prevailed throughout Muslim lands down the ages.[19]

Less lethal but quite degrading was another widespread practice:

One measure and symbol of Jewish degradation was the common phenomenon—amounting in certain places, such as Yemen and Morocco, to a local custom—of stone throwing at Jews by Muslim children. A nineteenth century Western traveler wrote: "I have seen a little fellow of six years old, with a troop of fat toddlers of only three and four, teaching (them) to throw stones at a Jew, and one little urchin would, with the greatest coolness, waddle up to the man and literally spit upon his Jewish gabardine. To all this the Jew is obliged to submit: it would be more than his life was worth to offer to strike a Mohammedan."[20]

One historian summarized the historic treatment of Jews by Muslims as "contemptuous tolerance."[21] They were treated as an "inferior race."[22] The fact that there were no Inquisitions or Holocausts only shows that matters were even worse in Christian Europe. Both the Christians of Europe and the Muslims of the Arab nations treated their Jewish minorities so horribly that the need for Jewish self-government, in a Jewish state with a Jewish majority, where Jews could be treated as equals and defend themselves from persecution, became evident to most of the world at the close of the Second World War.

If rights come from wrongs, as I have argued at length elsewhere,[23] then the *wrongs* imposed on Jewish minority residents of Muslim and Christian states demonstrated to the world that the Jewish people had the right to self-determination in a place in which Jews were a majority. As Winston Churchill had correctly observed a quarter of a century earlier, such a state already existed, in fact and in law, in those areas of Palestine with a Jewish majority, Jewish political, economic, and cultural institutions, and a Jewish army that had fought alongside the victors in World War I—and subsequently in World War II. All the United Nations did was recognize the reality of Jewish self-determination in areas in which they had every right—recognized by international law, treaties, the League of Nations, and a majority of the United Nations—to live and cultivate land they had lawfully purchased from absentee landlords. As the *London Times* editorialized at the time, "It is hard to see how the Arab world, still less the Arabs of Palestine, will suffer from what is mere recognition of accomplished fact—the presence in Palestine of a compact, well organized, and virtually autonomous Jewish community."[24]

Even for those who reject any blameworthiness on the part of Palestinians and Arabs for the plight of the Jewish refugees from Nazism and Islamic apartheid—an untenable position in light of the history of widespread Palestinian support for Nazism—the case for some affirmative action for a people who suffered so grievously at the hands of others is powerful. Those of us who support affirmative action with regard to African Americans do so, at least in part, on a theory of reparation for past wrongs. Although our own forebearers may bear none of the responsibility for slavery, since they were not even in the country, we must all be willing to share some of the burdens of reparation. Our children and grandchildren may be denied places in the colleges or jobs of their first choice, because these places are allocated to the descendants of slaves and other minorities. Certainly those who directly benefited from slavery bear a special responsibility for making reparations, just as those who benefited from the Holocaust bear special responsibility to those who were its victims.

But in a larger sense, the entire world owes the victims of slavery, the Holocaust, and other humanly imposed genocides a special form of affirmative action. Even the Peel Commission seemed to recognize an affirmative action component in its decision to recognize the existence of a Jewish national home:

> It is impossible, we believe, for any unprejudiced observer to see the National Home and not wish it well. It has meant so much for the relief of unmerited suffering. It displays so much energy and enterprise and devotion to a common cause. In so far as Britain has helped towards its creation, we would claim, with Lord Balfour, that to that extent, at any rate, Christendom has shown itself "not oblivious of all the wrong it has done."[25]

The Muslim world too should recognize all the wrong it has done to the Jews it historically treated as second-class noncitizens (Dhimmi).

Even for those who did not believe in 1947 that partition of Palestine was just to the Palestinians, when the partition is viewed as a form of international affirmative action it seems more than fair. For those who support affirmative action based on the need for diversity, a Jewish state certainly adds considerable diversity to a world with more than forty Muslim states and numerous Christian, Hindu and Buddhist states. Although there already exists a state with a majority of Palestinians in Jordan, a new Palestinian state in the West Bank and Gaza, governed by Palestinians, would also add an element of diversity.

8 Was the U.N. Partition Plan Unfair to Palestinians?

The U.N. Partition Plan of 1947 was unfair to the Palestinians.

Shavit: "Would you have accepted the 1947 Partition Plan?"

Said: "My instinct is to say no. It was an unfair plan based on the minority getting equal rights to those of the majority. Perhaps we shouldn't have left it there. Perhaps we should have come up with a plan of our own. But I can understand that the Partition Plan was unacceptable to the Palestinians of the time." (Edward Said[1])

"[I]n 1947, the UN proposed a solution which was accepted only by one side, the Jewish one. And, in the history of the United Nations, usually, if you don't have an agreement of both sides, you don't implement that solution. There, the story began to turn bad. The fact is that you force the solution on a majority of the people living in Palestine who oppose that solution, then you shouldn't be surprised that they opposed it even by force.

". . . But we don't even have the right to say they were wrong to refuse the partition. They viewed Zionism as a colonialist movement. And there are very little reasons not to understand that point of view. Just imagine the Algerian national movement agreeing in the fifties to divide Algeria

63

into two states, between them and the white settlers ('les pieds-noirs')! Who would have said to the Algerian leadership 'Don't miss the historic chance?'!" (Ilan Pappe, political science lecturer at Haifa University[2])

THE REALITY

The U.N. plan was fair to both sides and was a reflection of mutual self-determination both for Arabs and for Jews and is now the consensus of world opinion.

THE PROOF

As the United Nations concluded when it partitioned Palestine in 1947, it is impossible to base any solution to the problems on the claimed "historical origins of the conflict" or "the rights and wrongs" alleged by each side. The "basic premise underlying" partition was that "the claims to Palestine of the Arabs and Jews, both possessing validity, are irreconcilable." It is useful to quote from the U.N. findings, since they form the basis for the current international consensus regarding the two-state solution to the Palestinian–Israeli conflict:

> 1.) The basic premise underlying the partition proposal is that the claims to Palestine of the Arabs and Jews, both possessing validity, are irreconcilable, and that among all the solutions advanced, partition will provide the most realistic and practicable settlement, and is the most likely to afford a workable basis for meeting in part the claims and national aspirations of both parties.
>
> 2.) It is a fact that both of these peoples have their historic roots in Palestine, and that both make vital contributions to the economic and cultural life of the country. The partition solution takes these considerations fully into account.
>
> 3.) The basic conflict in Palestine is a clash of two intense nationalisms. Regardless of the historical origins of the conflict, the rights and wrongs of the promises and counter-promises, and the international intervention incident to the Mandate, there are now in Palestine some 650,000 Jews and 1,200,000 Arabs who are dissimilar in their ways of living and, for the time being, separated by political interests which render difficult full and effective political cooperation.
>
> 4.) Only by means of partition can these conflicting national aspirations find substantial expression and qualify both peoples to take their places as independent nations in the international community and in the United Nations.

As stated earlier, the two-state solution is the premise of this book as well. I reject—as the Peel Commission did in 1937, as the United Nations did in 1947, as Ehud Barak did in 2000, and as most of the world does now—the extremist claims on both sides: I reject the extremist Jewish claim that "all of Greater Israel" should be a Jewish state, and I reject the extremist Arab claim that the Jewish state, even if it were "the size of a postage stamp, . . . has no right to exist."[3]

The current worldwide consensus supports this premise: that there should be two states, one Jewish and one Palestinian, existing side by side. There is no consensus as to the relative size and precise borders of the two states. But the principle of a two-state solution is even more accepted today than it was in 1947, since most Arab states and the Palestinian Authority seem to accept it, at least when talking to outsiders. Those who currently reject it include a small minority of Israelis and American Jews at the fringe of Israeli and Jewish society; Palestinian terrorist groups such as Hamas, Hezbullah, Islamic Jihad, and the Popular Front for the Liberation of Palestine; as well as the rejectionist states of Syria, Iran, and Libya. (In February 2003, Tariq Aziz, the former Iraqi deputy prime minister, refused even to accept a question from an Israeli journalist at an open press conference in Rome.) Because the two-state solution is the best hope for peace, its acceptance by Israel first in 1937 and then in 1948, coupled with its categorical and violent rejection by the Arab states, the Palestinians, and virtually every Muslim leader—first in 1937 and again in 1948— is a central component in making the case for Israel. It must be answered by anyone seeking to make the case against Israel.

The decision to partition Palestine—at least that portion not already allocated to an exclusively Arab emirate, renamed Transjordan and then Jordan—into Jewish and Arab states was not a reflection of the discredited colonialism or imperialism of the past. Rather, it was among the first examples of the new self-determination that President Woodrow Wilson and many other progressives had championed. Since the U.N. partition of Palestine into Jewish and Arab political units, many new states have emerged as a result of self-determination, including several Islamic states. Some, like Pakistan, have resulted from partitions. Yet the self-determination of the Jewish majority in those areas of Palestine portioned for the Jewish state is, alone among newly declared states, characterized by some enemies of Israel as colonialism and imperialism.[4] This is no more than argument by name-calling or sloganizing, even though neither the name nor the slogan fits the facts or the history.

The establishment of Jordan and the selection of its Hashemite ruler by the British government in 1923 *was* an act of imperialism and colonialism. Its formal exclusion of all Jews was an act of blatant racism. Yet these characterizations are rarely heard with regard to the illegitimate birth certificate of that nation. The Jewish claim to govern the Jewish area of Palestine allocated to it by the United Nations is certainly more consistent with self-determination than the Hashemite claims to rule over the majority of the Palestinian population of Jordan. Yet the selective name-callers and sloganizers aim their misguided rhetoric only at the Jewish state. The burden falls on them to explain why.

9 Were Jews a Minority in What Became Israel?

THE ACCUSATION

The Jewish state was established in Palestine, despite the fact that Jews constituted only a minority of the total population of Palestinians.

THE ACCUSERS

"Americans receive most of their information regarding the Israeli/Palestinian conflict from corporate controlled, politically manipulated mainstream media. Few have the opportunity to scrutinize the reality of the history that has resulted in the tensions that exist in the mid-east. Few know that Palestinians are, in all legitimate ways, the indigenous population of the area; that the land now occupied by the Israelis was owned by the Palestinians; that in 1870, 98% of the population was Arab and only 2% Jewish; that in 1940, Palestinians accounted for 69% of the population even as Jews thronged to the area from Europe in an attempt to escape the Nazis; that in 1946, the year that the UN created Israel without the approval of the indigenous population, the Palestinians represented 65% and the Israelis less than 35% of the 1,845,000 who lived there." (William A. Cook, English professor at the University of La Verne, in California[1])

"In 1947 there were 600,000 Jews and a million three hundred thousand Palestinian Arabs. So, when the United Nations divided Palestine, the

Jews were a minority (31% of the population). This division, promoted by the main imperialist powers—with support from Stalin—gave 54% of the fertile land to the Zionist movement." (Cecilia Toledo, Brazilian journalist[2])

"It is worth noting that even after five decades of ethnic cleansing, occupation, and dispossession the demographic ratio between Palestinians (8.2 million) and Israeli Jews (4.5–5 million) is still the same as it was in December 1947, which was (and still is) 2 to 1 in favor of the Palestinian people. However, for Israel to maintain its democratic "Jewish State," and above all its "Jewish character," it opted to ethnically cleanse 80% of the Palestinian people out of their homes, farms, businesses, boats, banks, . . . etc." (www.PalestineRemembered.com, in response to the "Israeli Zionists [sic] propaganda" that "the Arabs rejected the 1947 U.N. partition of Palestine, and consequently attacked the Jewish state, and lost the 1948 war")

THE REALITY

The Jews were a substantial majority in those areas of Palestine partitioned by the United Nations for a Jewish state.

THE PROOF

Advocates often play games with the demographics in order to support their agenda-driven conclusions. In estimating the Arab population of Palestine at the time of the U.N. partition of 1947, advocates of the Arab cause sometimes include the population of what is now Jordan, as well as what is now the West Bank and Gaza. In assessing the fairness of the U.N. Partition Plan of 1947, when the United Nations divided Palestine, the relevant Palestinian population of the area is that assigned to the Jewish state in 1947.[3] Even with regard to that population, estimates vary, but the official U.N. estimate was that the land assigned to the Jewish state contained approximately 538,000 Jews and 397,000 Arabs (a number that included Christians, Bedouins, Druze, and others).

No one doubts that had there been a referendum on the issue of self-determination and separation, the residents of the area partitioned by the United Nations for a Jewish state would have voted overwhelmingly in favor of what the United Nations decreed. In terms of the division of land, the Jewish state received somewhat more than the Arabs, but only if one counts fully the Negev Desert, which was deemed uninhabitable and uncultivatable. If the Negev is excluded or substantially discounted, the usable land allocated to the Arabs was larger than that allocated to the

Jews. Moreover, much of the land allocated to the Jewish state was originally swamp and desert land that had been irrigated and made fertile by Jewish labor and investment. The land allocated to the Arabs was also contiguous with and proximate to Transjordan, whose population has always been predominantly Palestinian, although a Hashemite monarchy was imposed on the population by Great Britain.

The land allocated to the Jews did not include western Jerusalem, which had a Jewish majority, or Hebron, two of Judaism's holiest and most historic cities. Jerusalem, with a Jewish population of 100,000, was to be internationalized but cut off from the Jewish areas. Hebron was to be part of the Arab sector, with no Jewish presence, despite the fact that Jews had lived there for thousands of years until Palestinian massacres of Jewish women, children, and old men drove out the Jewish population in 1929 and again in 1936.

Because the land in which the Jews were to live was divided into noncontiguous areas and separated by Arab land, it would be difficult to defend in the face of the threatened Arab attack. In addition to Jerusalem, Safad was isolated. Even Tel Aviv could easily be cut off by enemy forces at the narrow waistline of the Jewish area, which measured approximately 9 miles between the Arab area and the Mediterranean.

Nevertheless, Israel quickly accepted the U.N. partition and soon declared statehood. The Arabs rejected the partition and attacked the new Jewish state from the air and the ground. What remained of the proposed Palestinian state after Israel repelled these attacks was quickly gobbled up by Jordan and Egypt.

Had the Arabs accepted the U.N. partition, there would have been a large, contiguous Palestinian state alongside a Jewish state. The two-state solution that is now the international consensus would have been achieved without bloodshed. Surely anyone who now accepts the two-state solution must place the blame for it not being implemented in 1947 (or even earlier in 1937) on the Arab and Palestinian leaders who rejected a Palestinian state when it was offered to them. (As we will see in chapters 16 and 17, a Palestinian state, with its capital in Jerusalem, was again offered at Camp David and Taba in 2000 and again rejected by the Palestinians, who responded to the offer not by making any counterproposal but by increasing suicide bombings against Israeli civilians.)

10 Has Israel's Victimization of the Palestinians Been the Primary Cause of the Arab–Israeli Conflict?

THE ACCUSATION

Israel is the cause of the Arab–Israeli conflict.

THE ACCUSERS

"There is no symmetry in this conflict. One would have to say that. I deeply believe that. There is a guilty side and there are victims. The Palestinians are the victims." (Edward Said[1])

THE REALITY

Arab rejection of Israel's right to exist has long been the cause of the problem.

THE PROOF

The repeated rejection by the grand mufti, the Palestinian Liberation Organization, the Arab world, and the Palestinian people of the two-state (or homeland) solution from 1937 when it was first officially proposed until relatively recently lies at the heart of the conflict. The reason for the rejection has been that most Arab and Muslim leaders cared more about denying the Jews the right of self-determination in those areas of Palestine in which they were a majority than in exercising their own right of self-

70

determination in those areas with a Muslim majority. This sad reality is demonstrated by the words of so many Palestinian and Arab leaders over a long period of time. This reality is beyond reasonable dispute. When the Peel Commission questioned the grand mufti in 1937, he not only refused to accept any Jewish self-rule, "political power," or "privilege," he categorically refused even to "provide guarantees for the safety of the Jewish population in the event of an Arab Palestinian state." This made it certain, of course, that there would be no Palestinian state or federal division. After the grand mufti concluded his testimony, the committee "noted ironically":

> We are not questioning the sincerity or the humanity of the Mufti's intentions and those of his colleagues, but we cannot forget what recently happened, despite treaty provisions and explicit assurances, to the Assyrian minority in Iraq; nor can we forget that the hatred of the Arab politicians for the National Home has never been concealed and that it had now permeated the Arab population as a whole."[2]

Little has changed over the years. The official radio of the Palestinian Authority broadcast a sermon on April 30, 1999, in which the following was said:

> The Land of Muslim Palestine is a single unit which cannot be divided. There is no difference between Haifa and Shechem (Nablus), between Lod and Ramallah, and between Jerusalem and Nazareth . . . the land of Palestine is sacred waqf land for the benefit of all Muslims, east and west. No one has the right to divide it or give up any of it. The liberation of Palestine is obligatory for all the Islamic nations and not only for the Palestinian nation.[3]

And in 2002, the chief justice of the Muslim Trust in Jerusalem, appointed by Yasser Arafat, said the following:
"All Palestine is Islamic land. . . . The Jews usurped it. . . . There can be no compromise on Islamic land."[4] A fatwa prohibits even the sale of any Palestinian land to Jews, declaring it to be "an act of apostasy and rejection of Islam." And it is prohibited, according to some Islamic scholars, for Jews to rule over Muslims or Muslim land.[5]

In recent years, the mainstream Palestinian leadership has finally said— though not without some ambiguity and backpedaling—that they accept the existence of Israel, so long as it returns to boundaries that the Palestinians had previously rejected by violence. But many other Palestinian and Arab leaders still reject the two-state solution. These include not only the rejectionist states (such as Syria, Iran, and Libya) and the rejectionist

Palestinian organizations (such as Hamas, Hezbullah, and Islamic Jihad) but also important "mainstream" voices that purport to speak for Palestinians. These voices include Professor Edward Said of Columbia University, who has tried to put his categorical rejection of Israel's existence in terms "politically acceptable" to secularists:

> The only reasonable course . . . is to recommend that Palestinians and their supporters renew the struggle against the fundamental principle that relegates "non-Jews" to subservience on the land of historical Palestine. . . . Only if the inherent contradiction is faced between what in effect is a theocratic and ethnic exclusivism on the one hand and genuine democracy on the other, can there be any hope for reconciliation and peace in Israel/Palestine.[6]

What Said fails to mention is that every single Muslim and Arab state, including the Palestinian Authority, relegates Jews to a position that is far inferior to that of non-Jews in largely secular Israel. Said also suggests that the alternative to Israel would be a "genuine democracy," without acknowledging that no Arab or Islamic state, including the Palestinian authority, comes close to being as democratic as Israel. Although Israel is by far the least theocratic and most democratic state in the Middle East—both by law and by practice—Said singles out Israel for condemnation, as if it were the only state in the region to elevate one religion over another. The burden of explanation for this double standard falls squarely on him.

Recent public opinion polls taken by Palestinian polling organizations also show that a majority of Palestinians do not accept the two-state solution. As many as 87 percent in one poll were in favor of "liberating all of Palestine."[7] Even Yasser Arafat, who long rejected the two-state solution, then appeared to accept it, has spoken out of both sides of his mouth. After signing the Oslo Accords, which contemplated an eventual two-state solution, Arafat was caught making the following statement to Arab leaders in Stockholm's Grand Hotel:

> We of the PLO will now concentrate all our efforts on splitting Israel psychologically into two camps. . . . Within five years, we will have six to seven million Arabs living on the West Bank and in Jerusalem. All Palestinian Arabs will be welcomed by us. If the Jews can import all kinds of Ethiopians, Russians, Uzbeks and Ukrainians as Jews, we can import all kinds of Arabs to us. . . . [The PLO plans] to eliminate the State of Israel and establish a purely Palestinian State. We will make life unbearable for the Jews by psychological warfare and population explosion; Jews won't want to live among us Arabs.[8]

This was entirely consistent with views expressed earlier by Abu Iyad, one of Arafat's chief deputies: "According to the Phased Plan, we will establish a Palestinian state on any part of Palestine that the enemy will retreat from. The Palestinian state will be a stage in our prolonged struggle for the liberation of Palestine on all of its territories."[9]

Whatever the current views of Palestinians and Arabs, there can be no dispute that until relatively recently the rejection of the two-state solution was virtually unanimous among Palestinians and Arabs. Nor can there be any dispute that this rejection, over so many years and so many missed opportunities for compromise, has contributed greatly to the bloodshed.

11 Was the Israeli War of Independence Expansionist Aggression?

THE ACCUSATION

The Israeli War of Independence was an expansionist aggression started by Israel.

THE ACCUSERS

"In order to paint Israel as the victim, the Zionist narrative claims that Arab armies from Egypt, Syria and Jordan attacked Israel the day after it was created on May 14, 1949 [sic].

"Were the Arabs attacking an established state with a historical, moral and legal right to Palestine, or were they merely defending themselves—their lands, their homes, their historical rights—against a foreign occupation supported successively by two imperialist powers, Britain and the United States?

"In 1948, the Arabs had done what I have no doubt the Americans would have done: they defended themselves against an alien invasion." (M. Shahid Alam[1])

THE REALITY

Israel defended itself against a genocidal war of extermination.

74

THE PROOF

As soon as Israel declared its independence, Egypt, Jordan, Syria, Iraq, and Lebanon attacked it, with help from Saudi Arabia, Yemen, and Libya. Arab armies, with the help of Palestinian terrorists, determined to destroy the new Jewish state and exterminate its population.

The first attack on Israel came from the air. Egyptian aircraft bombed Israel's largest civilian center, the city of Tel Aviv. An Associated Press account on May 17, 1948, described the attack: "Arab Planes Hit Tel Aviv, Tiberias; Invader Hammering Jewish Outposts." As with virtually every previous Arab attack against the Jews since the first refugees arrived in Palestine—and even before—the targets were innocent civilians. "Dispatches from Arab capitals said the invasion armies of five Arab nations hammered away with air and artillery attacks at outlying Jewish settlements in Palestine."

The article went on to describe the shelling of Jewish civilian homes. "A Jewish settler who arrived in Haifa gave this account of the fighting in the Galilee area: enemy planes attacked Ashdot Yaacov, Afikim and Ein Geg as well as Tiberias. Ein Geg was pounded from the trans-Jordan hills." The Haganah, the Israeli citizen army, "claimed to have killed 200 enemy soldiers at Malikya on the Lebanese border just inside the Jewish state."[2]

The Egyptian air attacks persisted and civilians were killed, especially in an air attack that targeted the central civilian bus station in Tel Aviv. Efforts were also made to shell the city from the ground. The fledgling Israeli air force responded by targeting military installations in and around Amman and Damascus, killing no civilians.

The pattern of past and future fighting was thus established: the Arabs would target soft civilian areas—cities, towns, kibbutzim, and moshavim—trying to kill as many children, women, elderly, and other unarmed civilians as possible, while the Israelis would respond by targeting soldiers, military equipment, and other lawful targets. Military attacks that target civilians are in violation of international law and the law of war, yet these have always been and continue to be the targets of choice not only by Arab terrorists and guerrillas but also by the regular armies of Jordan, Egypt, Syria, and Iraq. This is simply historical fact, and no reasonable military historian has even tried to dispute it.

As we shall see in chapters 13 and 20, the regular Israeli army has not responded by targeting Arab population centers, such as Amman, Damascus, and Cairo, even though these cities have been well within the range of Israeli aircraft. The Israeli army, like every other army in the world, has killed civilians while attacking military targets, especially since the Arab armies and terrorist groups often hide and protect their military targets by deliberately surrounding them with civilian shields. Israel, on the other hand, has isolated its military bases as far as possible from its civilian population centers. There is, of course, an enormous difference in morality as well as law in *expressly targeting* civilians, as the Arabs have long done, and *collaterally* hitting civilians who are close to appropriate military targets that pose a continuing danger. The former is a crime against humanity absolutely prohibited by international law. The latter is permissible under the laws of war so long as the response is proportional and reasonable and efforts are made to minimize inevitable civilian casualties.

The Israeli War of Independence was started by the Arabs, whose express aim was genocidal. "Murder the Jews" and "Drive the Jews into the sea" were the battle cries of the invading armies. The Arab Liberation Army was commanded by Fawzi al-Qawuqji, who had sat out the war years in Germany, broadcasting the Nazi message to the Arab world. Other former Nazi operatives also participated in this war of extermination against the Jews, many of whom were survivors of the Holocaust. The initial means selected was the targeting of civilians by "major urban terrorist attacks, probably mounted with Husseini's personal blessing."[3] The Arab armies also massacred civilians, *even after they surrendered*. They repeatedly and deliberately dropped bombs on civilian population centers near absolutely no legitimate military targets. Husseini's "chief bomb maker, Fawzi al-Katab, had learned his craft in an SS course in Nazi Germany."[4] The goal was to finish the job Hitler had started: "This will be a war of extermination."[5] Yet Professor Edward Said insists on calling the 1947–1948 attack on Israel "the Palestinian bicommunal war!"[6]

At great cost in human life—Israel lost 1 percent of its total population—the ragtag Israeli army defeated the invading Arab armies and the Palestinian attackers. They won in large part because, as Morris argues, the stakes were much greater for them. They had the "morale-boosting stimulus" of fighting for their

> own home and fields (in many cases literally) and in defense of one's loved ones. Moreover, as during the first "civil" half of the war, the Jews felt that they faced slaughter should they be defeated. With the memory of the Holocaust still fresh in their minds, the Haganah troopers were imbued with unlimited motivation.[7]

The Arab soldiers on the other hand, were fighting an aggressive war, far away from home, and for a somewhat "abstract cause."[8]

In defeating the Arab armies, Israel captured more land than that allotted to it by the U.N. partition. Much of the newly captured land had significant Jewish populations and settlements, such as in western Galilee. This land had to be captured in order to assure the safety of its Jewish civilian residents. The Egyptians and Jordanians also captured land, but for no reason other than to increase their own territory and to control their Palestinian residents. Indeed, by the end of the war, according to Morris, the "Arab war Plan changed . . . into a multinational land grab focusing on the Arab areas of the country. The evolving Arab 'plans' failed to assign any of these whatsoever to the Palestinians or to consider their political aspirations."[9]

A key part of the Arab plan was the complete "marginalization" of the Palestinians.[10] The Jordanians wanted the West Bank and the Egyptians wanted the Gaza Strip. Neither wanted an independent Palestinian state. Nobody can blame Israel for the Egyptian and Jordanian decision to occupy the lands allocated to the Palestinians for a state and for denying the Palestinians the right of self-determination in those lands. These are incontrovertible historical facts not subject to reasonable dispute but omitted from pro-Palestinian pseudohistories of the period. The occupation of Palestine by Jordan and Egypt was never the subject of U.N. condemnation or even expression of concern from human rights groups. Indeed, it was not even widely protested by Palestinians.

12 Did Israel Create the Arab Refugee Problem?

THE ACCUSATION

Israel created the Arab refugee problem.

THE ACCUSERS

"The state of Israel was established as a settler-colonial project that was sponsored by different colonial powers for different reasons. Because it was not possible to establish a Jewish state in Palestine without expelling the indigenous people who constituted the majority of the population, the 1948 war provided a cover for their widespread and systematic expulsion." (Azmi Bishara, member of the Israeli Knesset[1])

Shavit: "And in 1948, does the moral responsibility for the Palestinian tragedy of that year lie only with the Jews? Don't the Arabs share the blame?"

Said: "The war of 1948 was a war of dispossession. What happened that year was the destruction of Palestinian society, the replacement of that society by another, and the eviction of those who were considered undesirable. Those who were in the way. It is difficult for me to say that all responsibility lies with one side. But the lion's share of responsibility for depopulating towns and destroying them definitely lies with the Jewish-Zionists. Yitzhak Rabin evicted the 50,000 inhabitants of Ramle and Lydda, so it is difficult for me to see anyone else as responsible for

78

that. The Palestinians were only responsible for being there." (Edward Said[2])

"The Israelis engaged in 'ethnic cleansing,' during the 1947–1948 War. The Zionist claim that Arab leaders told the Palestinians to leave is 'not believed by anyone. . . . No one even claims this any more.' Benny Morris has shown that the Arab population 'was driven out' by the Israelis." (Noam Chomsky[3])

THE REALITY

The problem was created by a war initiated by the Arabs.

THE PROOF

The aggressive war waged against Israel in 1947 and 1948 by the Palestinians and the Arab armies not only took land from the Palestinians but also created the first refugee problem. While the Arab armies tried to kill Jewish civilians and did in fact massacre many who tried to escape, the Israeli army allowed Arab civilians to flee to Arab-controlled areas. For example, when the Arab Legion's Sixth Battalion conquered Kfar Etzion, they left no Jewish refugees. The villagers surrendered and walked, hands in the air, into the center of the compound. Morris reports that the Arab soldiers simply "proceeded to mow them down."[4] The soldiers massacred 120 Jews; 21 of them were women. This was part of a general Arab policy: "Jews taken prisoner during convoy battles were generally put to death and often mutilated by their captors."[5] It is precisely because the Israeli army, unlike Arab armies, did not deliberately kill civilians that the refugee problem arose.[6]

Several distinct, although overlapping, refugee problems were created by the Arab attack on Israel in 1947 and 1948. The first was created between December 1947 and March 1948 during the attacks by Palestinians in the months before the invasion of the Pan-Arab armies. According to Benny Morris, the historian who is quite critical of Israel and Zionists and an expert on the refugee issue, "The Yishuv [the Jews of Palestine who would soon become the Israelis] was on the defensive and upper and middle-class Arabs—as many as seventy-five thousand—fled." Morris described how the families that had the means to move to Cairo, Amman, or Beirut did so, expecting to return as they had done after the violence of the late 1930s. Among those who left were "many of the political leaders and/or their families . . . including most members of the AHC and of the Haifa National Committee." These notables, according to Morris "may have feared a Husseini-ruled Palestine" as much as they worried about Jewish domination.

Morris pointed out that the Jewish-Arab conflict was only part of a "more general breakdown of law and order in Palestine after the UN Partition resolution." Public services collapsed following the withdrawal of the British and their replacement by "Arab irregulars, who extorted money from prosperous families and occasionally abused people in the streets."[7]

The second refugee problem began when the Haganah, the official Jewish army of self-defense, began to gain the offensive between April and June 1948. Once Haifa and Jaffa were captured by the Israelis, a domino effect began, with the flight from cities leading to flight from surrounding villages, which in turn led to flight from other villages.

Contrary to Noam Chomsky's characterization of Morris's conclusion—Chomsky says that Morris does not believe that any Arab leaders "told the Palestinians to leave"—Morris actually says that:

> In some areas Arab commanders ordered the villagers to evacuate to clear the ground for military purposes or to prevent surrender. More than half a dozen villages—just north of Jerusalem and in the Lower Galilee—were abandoned during these months as a result of such orders. Elsewhere, in East Jerusalem and in many villages around the country, the [Arab] commanders ordered women, old people, and children to be sent away to be out of harm's way. Indeed, psychological preparation for the removal of dependents from the battlefield had begun in 1946–47, when the AHC and the Arab League had periodically endorsed such a move when contemplating the future war in Palestine.[8]

Morris estimates that between two and three thousand Arabs fled their homes during this phase of the Arab-initiated fighting.

Again contrary to Chomsky's characterization of Morris's views, Morris notes that during the first phase "there was no Zionist policy to expel the Arabs or intimidate them into flight," although some Jews were certainly happy to see them leave. During the second stage as well, "there was no blanket policy of expulsion,"[9] but the military actions of the Haganah certainly contributed to the flight. Such flight from the scenes of battle occurs in most wars, if the winning side allows it, rather than seeking to kill those running away, as the Arabs did. There is little doubt that if the Arab armies had captured Jewish cities, they would not have allowed the civilian refugees to flee to other Jewish cities. They would have massacred them in order to prevent the creation of a Jewish refugee problem in the Arab state they hoped would result from an Arab victory.

The grand mufti declared "a holy war" and ordered his "Muslim brothers" to "murder the Jews. Murder them all."[10] There were to be no survivors or refugees. The position of the grand mufti had always been that an Arab Palestine could not absorb even 400,000 Jews.[11] By 1948, the Jewish population exceeded 600,000. Extermination, not the creation of a difficult refugee population, was the goal of the Arab attack on Jewish civilian populations. As the Arab League's secretary general, Abd al-Ahlman Azzah Pasha, candidly put it, "This will be a war of extermination and momentous massacre, which will be spoken of like the Mongolian massacres and the Crusades." The grand mufti's spokesman, Ahmad Shukeiry, called for "the elimination of the Jewish state" with regard to the goal of the Arab attack. There was no talk of, or planning for, a large Jewish refugee population in the event of an Arab victory. "It does not matter how many [Jews] there are. We will sweep them into the sea," the Arab League's secretary general announced.[12] The Jews fully understood that they "faced slaughter should they be defeated."[13]

Israel, on the other hand, was prepared to extend full citizenship to whatever number of Arabs remained in the Jewish state. Although many Jews surely preferred a smaller, rather than a larger, Arab minority, the official Jewish organizations took no steps to assure a reduction in the Arab population in general, although Israeli military commanders did order the evacuation of several hostile towns that had served as bases for Arab irregular units, which were preventing access to the main road to Jerusalem and which "proved a permanent threat both to all north-south and to east-west (Tel Aviv–Jerusalem) communications."[14]

Although it was not the policy of the Haganah to encourage the flight of local Arabs, that certainly seems to have been the policy of the Irgun (or Etzel), the paramilitary wing of the revisionist movement headed by Menachem Begin, and Lechi (or the Stern gang) headed by Yitzhak Shamir. On April 9, 1948, paramilitary units fought a difficult battle for control of Deir Yassin, an important Arab village on the way to Jerusalem. The battle was fierce, with Etzel and Lechi forces losing more than a quarter of their fighters. The Jewish fighters were pinned down by sniper fire and threw grenades through the windows of many of the houses from which the snipers were firing. Most of the villagers eventually fled. An Etzel armored car with a loudspeaker demanded that the remaining villagers lay down their arms and leave their houses. Morris reports that "the truck got stuck in a ditch"[15] and the message was not heard. The fighting continued, and when it was over, 100 to 110 Arabs were dead.[16]

Many of the dead were women, because Arab fighters dressed as women and shot Israelis to whom they had "surrendered"[17]—a tactic employed by some Iraqis in 2003. Some children and old people were also killed. Although there was and continues to be considerable dispute surrounding the circumstances of these deaths, the event was called a massacre, and as word spread, it clearly contributed to the flight of Arabs in surrounding villages. "Everyone had an interest" in publicizing and exaggerating the number of people killed and the brutality of the killings. The Arab side wanted to discredit the Jews by arguing—quite hypocritically, in light of their own policy over the decades of deliberately massacring civilians—that the Jews were worse than they were. The British also wanted to discredit the Jews. Etzel and Lechi wanted to "provoke terror and frighten Arabs into fleeing." And the Haganah wanted "to tarnish" Etzel and Lechi.[18]

The Haganah and the Jewish Agency—the official organs of the state-to-be—immediately condemned the massacre and those who had participated in it. A formal note of apology and explanation was sent to King Abdullah. Indeed, the Deir Yassin massacre certainly contributed to the controversial decision by David Ben-Gurion—Israel's first prime minister—to disarm, by force, these paramilitary groups in June 1948. But the effect of Deir Yassin, and the publicity surrounding it, was clearly to provoke even more flight by Arabs.

Some Palestinian leaders actually circulated false rumors that women had been raped. When confronted with the reality that no rapes had taken place, Hussein Khalidi, a Palestinian leader, said, "We have to say this, so that Arab armies will come to liberate us from the Jews."[19] Hazam Nusseibi, who was a journalist at the time, told the BBC years later that the deliberate fabrication of the rape charge "was our biggest mistake . . . as soon as they heard that women had been raped at Deir Yassin, Palestinians fled in terror."[20]

Deir Yassin stands out in the history of Arab–Jewish conflict in Palestine precisely because it was so unusual and so out of character for the Jews. No single Arab massacre of Jews has that status, because there are too many to list. Yet every Arab schoolchild and propagandist knows of and speaks of Deir Yassin, while few ever mention Hebron, Kfar Etzion, Hadassah Hospital, Safad, and the many other well-planned Arab massacres of Jews to come, except when extremists proudly take credit for them.

The Arabs retaliated for the Deir Yassin massacre not by attacking those responsible for perpetrating it—Etzel or Lechi military targets—but rather by deliberately committing a far more premeditated massacre of their own. In a well-planned attack four days after Deir Yassin, Arab forces ambushed a civilian convoy of doctors, nurses, medical school professors, and patients headed toward the Hadassah hospital to treat the sick, murdering seventy of them. To assure there were no survivors, the Arab attackers doused the buses and cars containing the medical personnel with gasoline, "setting them alight."[21]

No apologies or excuses were offered for this carefully planned massacre of medical noncombatants. Israeli forces did not retaliate for the Hadassah massacre by targeting Arab *civilians.* They went after those armed murderers who had perpetrated the massacre. Deir Yassin remained an isolated although tragic and inexcusable blemish on Israeli paramilitary actions in defense of its civilian population,[22] while the deliberate targeting of civilians remained—and still remains—the policy of Palestinian terrorist groups, as well as of many Arab governments.

Another phase of the Arab refugee problem took place when the Haganah won the battle for Haifa at the end of April 1948. According to Morris, "The Arab leaders, preferring not to surrender, announced that they and their community intended to evacuate the town, despite a plea by the Jewish mayor that they stay."[23] Similarly, in Jaffa, the fierce fighting with many Jewish casualties caused a panic among the town's Arab population and many fled. Morris writes that "the behavior of Jaffa's Arab military also contributed: they looted the empty houses and occasionally robbed and abused the remaining inhabitants." When he visited Jaffa after the fighting had died down, David Ben-Gurion wrote in his diary, "I couldn't understand. Why did the inhabitants . . . leave?"[24]

Of course, Jaffa remained an Arab city, and today its population includes thousands of Arabs. Haifa remained a mixed city, whose current population also includes thousands of Arabs. Some other towns and villages from which Arabs fled remain mixed today, while some have not seen a return of Arab populations. Morris, who is harshly critical of traditional Israeli history with regard to the refugee issue, summarizes the problem caused by the Palestinian and Pan-Arab attack: "The Palestinian Refugee problem was born of war, not by design. . . . The Arab leadership inside and outside Palestine probably helped precipitate the exodus. . . . No guiding hand or central control is evident."[25] Morris states that "[d]uring the first months, the flight of the middle and upper classes from the towns provoked little Arab interest."[26]

It looked like a repeat of the exodus that had taken place during the riots of the late 1930s, and the Husseinis "were probably happy that many of these wealthy, Opposition-linked families were leaving."[27] Morris points out that "no Arab government closed its borders or otherwise tried to stem the exodus."[28] Finally, Morris notes that these refugees would

> be utilized during the following years by the Arab states as a powerful political and propaganda pawn against Israel. The memory or vicarious memory of 1948 and the subsequent decades of humiliation and deprivation in the refugee camps would ultimately turn generations of Palestinians into potential or active terrorists and the "Palestinian problem" into one of the world's most intractable.[29]

In his public speeches, Noam Chomsky mischaracterizes Morris's conclusions by telling his audiences that Morris does not claim—indeed, Chomsky says that no one today claims—that Arab leaders contributed to the flight of Palestinians. He says (falsely) that Morris places the entire blame on Israel, that there were "never any such calls" by Arab leaders, and that this story was "Zionist propaganda" that was "abandoned almost 15 years ago" and is "not believed by anyone."[30] The truth, of course, is that Morris does indeed conclude that some "Arab commanders ordered the villagers to evacuate" and that the Arab League had "periodically endorsed such a move."

Morris, like other historians and unlike Chomsky, finds a shared responsibility for the creation of the refugee problem and concludes that neither side deliberately caused it "by design," but that "the Arab leadership inside and outside Palestine helped precipitate the exodus"—a conclusion Chomsky assures his audience is "not believed by anyone," especially not Morris. It is always important to check the sources cited by Chomsky, especially when he is discussing Israel.

In his 1972 memoirs, the former prime minister of Syria, Khalid al-Azm, placed the entire blame for the refugee problem on the Arabs:

> Since 1948 it is we who demanded the return of the refugees . . . while it is we who made them leave. . . . We brought disaster upon . . . Arab refugees, by inviting them and bringing pressure to bear upon them to leave. . . . We have rendered them dispossessed. . . . We have accustomed them to begging. . . . We have participated in lowering their moral and social level. . . . Then we exploited them in executing crimes of murder, arson, and throwing bombs upon . . . men, women and children—all this in the service of political purposes.[31]

Even Mahmoud Abbas (Abu Mazen), the prime minister of the Palestinian Authority, has accused the Arab armies of having abandoned the Palestinians after they "forced them to emigrate and to leave their homeland and threw them into prisons similar to the ghettos in which the Jews used to live."[32]

Other sources sympathetic to the Arab cause agree. In 1980, the Arab National Committee of Haifa wrote a memorandum to the Arab states that included the following: "The removal of the Arab inhabitants . . . was voluntary and was carried out at our request. The Arab delegation proudly asked for the evacuation of the Arabs and their removal to the neighboring Arab countries. . . . We are very glad to state that the Arabs guarded their honour and traditions with pride and greatness."[33] And a research report by the Arab-sponsored Institute for Palestine Studies concluded that the majority of the Arab refugees were not expelled and 68 percent of them "left without seeing an Israeli solder."[34] At the very least, the issue is too complex and multifaceted for simple finger-pointing in only one direction.

There is some dispute about the total number of Arabs who left their cities, towns, and villages as a result of the Palestinian and Arab attacks on the Jews. There is even greater disagreement about the proportion of those who left of their own accord, were chased, or were told by Arab leaders to leave. There is also considerable disagreement over how long many of these refugees had actually lived in the areas they left. And there is little agreement about how many Arabs who currently call themselves refugees of the 1947–1948 war actually belong in that category.

Most scholars have put the total number of Arab refugees from the Palestinian–Arab attacks of 1947–1948 at between 472,000 and 750,000. The U.N. mediator on Palestine counted only 472,000, of which 360,000 required aid.[35] The official Israeli count was 520,000. Morris puts it at 700,000. Palestinians put it as high as 900,000. Whatever the real figure was, it is impossible to subdivide that total figure into voluntary, forced, or some combination of factors. As Morris concludes, "The creation of the problem was almost inevitable, given the geographical intermixing of the populations, the history of Arab–Jewish hostility since 1917, the rejection by both sides of a binational [as distinguished from a two-state] solution, and the depth of Arab animosity toward the Jews and fears of coming under Jewish rule."[36] Put another way, the last thing many Arabs wanted was to remain as minority citizens of the Jewish state of Israel in the villages and homes they had left.

The claimed right of return has never contemplated their return as a *minority* group, based on any personal desire to live in a particular village or house in Jewish Israel. The right to return has always contemplated returning as a *majority* group so as to eliminate the Jewish state and live in a Muslim state. On August 4, 1948, Emile Ghoury, the secretary of the Arab Higher Command, told the *Beirut Telegraph* that "it is inconceivable that the refugees should be sent back to their homes while they are occupied by the Jews . . . it would serve as a first step toward their recognition of Israel."[37] Shortly thereafter, the foreign minister of Egypt acknowledged that "it is well known and understood that the Arabs, in demanding the return of the refugees to Palestine, mean their return as masters of their homeland, and not as slaves. More explicitly: they intend to annihilate the state of Israel."[38] In other words, the refugees were not primarily a humanitarian concern but rather a political tactic designed to produce the intended destruction of Israel. Surely no one would expect Israel to facilitate its own politicide.

As to how long these refugees had actually lived in the villages and towns they left, even Morris documents that as a result of "economic and social processes that had begun in the mid-nineteenth century [well before the First Aliyah] large parts of the rural population [had] been left landless" prior to the events of 1947–1948:[39]

In consequence there was a constant, growing shift of population from the countryside to urban shantytowns and slums; to some degree this led to both physical and psychological divorce from the land. [They also] lost their means of livelihood. For some, exile may have become an attractive option, at least until Palestine calmed down.[40]

The United Nations, recognizing that many of the refugees had not lived for long in the villages they left, made a remarkable decision to change the definition of refugee—*only* for purposes of defining who is an *Arab* refugee *from Israel*—to include any Arab who had lived in Israel for *two years* before leaving.[41] Moreover, an Arab was counted as a refugee if he moved just a few miles from one part of Palestine to another—even if he *returned* to the village in which he had previously lived and in which his family still lived, from a village to which he had moved only two years earlier. Indeed a significant number of Palestinian refugees simply moved from one part of Palestine to another. Some preferred to live in an area controlled by Arabs rather than Jews, just as the Jews who had lived in cities that came under Arab control chose to move to the Israeli side of the partition. The Jews who moved a few miles (even those who had no choice) were not called refugees, but the Arabs who moved the same distance were. It was the most unusual definition of refugee in history.

Unlike all other refugees worldwide, Palestinian refugees are treated to a separate U.N. agency, with a separate definition of refugee and a separate mission. If the standard definition of refugee (which applies to all other refugee groups) were to apply to the Palestinians, the number of Palestinian refugees would fall precipitously.

The United Nations High Commissioner for Refugees (UNHCR), the general refugee agency that serves refugee groups other than the Palestinians, includes in its definition of refugee someone who (1) leaves out of a "well-founded fear of being persecuted," (2) is "outside the country of [his] nationality," and (3) "is unable to, or . . . unwilling to avail himself of the protection of that country." But the United Nations Relief and Works Agency (UNRWA), the separate agency specifically for Palestinian refugees, applies a far broader set of guidelines. It defines Palestinians as refugees regardless of whether they left out of a "well-founded fear of persecution" and regardless of the country where they live. Specifically, UNRWA defines a Palestinian refugee as anyone (1) "whose normal place of residence was Palestine between June 1946 and May 1948," and (2) "who lost both their homes and means of livelihood as a result of the 1948 Arab–Israeli conflict" (regardless of the reason for leaving). Plus, UNRWA defines as refugees all of the descendants of those who meet these two criteria.[42]

In addition, UNHCR and UNRWA have very different missions. The UNHCR is charged with finding permanent homes for refugees. UNRWA mandate is not concerned with permanent solutions and is designed only to maintain and support Palestinians within refugee camps, where many of them remain today. With its broad refugee definition and a mission geared toward dependency, UNRWA's refugee count has risen from under a million in 1950 to over 4 million (and counting) today.[43]

This approach to the refugee issue was calculated to keep it from being resolved and to allow it to fester and even be exacerbated. The Arab refugee problem could easily have been solved between 1948 and 1967 when Jordan controlled and annexed the West Bank, which was an under-populated and undercultivated area. But instead of integrating the refugees into the religiously, linguistically, and culturally identical society, they were segregated into ghettos called refugee camps and made to live on the U.N. dole, while being fed propaganda about their glorious return to the village down the road that had been their home for as little as two years.

At about the same time that 472,000 to 750,000 Arabs became refugees from Israel, tens of millions of other refugees had been created as the result of World War II. In virtually all of those cases, the refugees were displaced from locations in which they and their ancestors had lived for decades, sometimes centuries—certainly more than the two years required for being considered a Palestinian refugee. For example, the Sudeten Germans, who were moved en masse out of the borderlands of Czechoslovakia, had lived there for hundreds of years. The Jews of Europe—what remained of them after the Holocaust—had lived in Poland, Germany, Czechoslovakia, Hungary, and the Soviet Union for hundreds of years.

As the result of having lived in what became Israel for as little as two years, thousands upon thousands of Arabs and their descendants have been kept in refugee camps for more than half a century to be used as political pawns in an effort to demonize and destroy Israel. During that same period of time, many other refugee problems in the world have been solved by the host nations accepting and integrating the refugee population into their own. Exchanges of population took place between several nations—including India and Pakistan, and Greece and Turkey—without the need to build permanent refugee camps. Although those exchanges were not without difficulties and some remain controversial, none has created the kind of enduring problems caused by the unwillingness of Arab states to integrate the Palestinian Arab population.

Between 1948 and 1967, tens of millions of other refugees became productive members of their new societies. Yet for the nearly twenty years that Egypt and Jordan controlled the Gaza Strip and the West Bank, the Palestinian refugee population remained in camps, growing in size and desperation. Even King Hussein of Jordan, who could have helped solve the refugee problem, acknowledged that the Arab nations have used the Palestinian refugees as pawns since the beginning of the conflict: "Since

1948 Arab leaders . . . have used the Palestine people for selfish political purposes. This is . . . criminal."[44]

The other major refugee problem that affected the Middle East was the creation of hundreds of thousands of Jewish refugees from Arab and Muslim countries in which they had lived for hundreds or sometimes thousands of years, even before the advent of Islam. Mohammed and his contemporaries created a refugee problem when they banned Jews from Arabia. Then again after the creation of the Jewish state, the situation of Jews in many Arab and Muslim countries became so fraught with risk that many felt they had no choice but to leave. In the years following the establishment of the state of Israel, as many as 850,000 so-called Arab Jews became refugees from the lands in which they had been born. The number of Jewish refugees from Arab lands was slightly more than the number of Arab refugees from Israel.

There was "an exchange of populations," with the Jewish refugees having been forced to abandon far more of their property and wealth than the refugees left behind. Those abandoned assets included large houses, businesses, and cash. The difference is that Israel worked hard (although not always with complete success) to integrate its refugee population into the mainstream, while the Arabs deliberately encouraged Arab refugees to fester by keeping so many of them in camps, where many still remain, and refusing to integrate them into their more homogeneous populations. This was done purely to try to cast doubt on Israel's legitimacy despite the desperate need in some underpopulated Arab countries, such as Syria and Jordan, for more workers to serve the labor-intensive economic needs of those nations. Even after the Palestinian Authority assumed control over all the major cities on the West Bank and in Gaza, following the initial implementation of the Oslo II Agreement in 1995, no serious effort was made to move the refugees from the camps to integrate them into Palestinian society. They remain pawns in the effort to flood Israel with a hostile population designed to destroy its character as a Jewish state.

There are those who argue that the Palestinian refugees were different from the Jewish refugees in another respect: while the Palestinians were forced to flee from their homes, the Jews chose to leave their ancient homelands. We have already seen that the reasons why the Palestinians left are complex and not amenable to such a simple, singular cause. A brief review of the Jewish flight from Arab and Muslim countries demonstrates a comparable complexity and shows that the two refugee problems, although very different in their solutions, were quite similar in their causes. One historian summarized the situation as follows:

> In the years leading up to the establishment of Israel, Jews in many parts of the Arab and Muslim world faced increasing threats to their safety. In

November 1945, the head of the Jewish community of Tripoli (the capital of Libya) described the scene this way:

"The Arabs attacked Jews in obedience to mysterious orders. Their outburst of bestial violence has no plausible motive. For fifty hours they hunted men down, attacked houses and shops, killed men, women, old and young, horribly tortured and dismembered Jews isolated in the interior. . . . In order to carry out the slaughter, the attackers used various weapons: knives, daggers, sticks, clubs, iron bars, revolvers, and even hand grenades."[45]

When the War of Independence began in 1947, the violence intensified. In Aleppo, 300 houses and 11 synagogues were destroyed in a pogrom, and 82 Jews were killed in Aden. Riots in Iraq and Egypt forced Jews out of those countries. The Jews of the Arab world were forced out by fear as political violence spilled onto the streets. In this case, it was fed by official government incitement, as in Iraq, where Zionism could be punished by death.[46]

Sabri Jiryis, a former Arab-Israeli lawyer who left Israel and became a member of the Palestinian National Council, has acknowledged that "the Jews of the Arab states were driven out of their ancient homes [and] shamefully deported after their property had been commandeered. . . . [W]hat happened was a . . . population and property exchange, and each party must bear the consequences. . . . [T]he Arab states . . . must settle the Palestinians in their own midst and solve their problems."[47] Instead, they deliberately exacerbated the problems.

It is important to recall that Israel was not the only country that gained territory as a result of the failed Arab attack. Jordan occupied—indeed annexed—the entire West Bank, while Egypt occupied the Gaza Strip. There were no resolutions demanding an end to these occupations, although they were often quite repressive and brutal. One observer described Gaza as "in effect, a large Egyptian prison camp."[48] The Palestinians did not seem to care that their land, villages, and cities were being occupied as long as they were not occupied by Jews. Nor were there complaints that some Palestinians—especially Christians—became refugees from the Jordanian and Egyptian occupations.[49] The refugee issue of 1947–1948 was deliberately left unresolved by the Arabs as a tactic designed to destroy the new Jewish state.

To understand how different the Arab–Israeli conflict would look if the Arab world including the Palestinian Muslims had accepted the two-state solution when it was first proposed (or even for years thereafter), we must briefly return to the *Peel Commission Report*. If the Arabs had accepted the Peel Commission partition proposal, there would have been a Palestinian state (in addition to Transjordan) in most of what was left of Palestine following the partition of Transjordan. The vast majority of Arabs and Muslims in Palestine would have lived under Palestinian control, and the Arab minority that lived in the land allotted to the Jewish state would have had the choice to move to the Palestinian state or remain as part of the Arab minority in the Jewish state. The same would have been true for the Jews who lived in the Arab state.

The Jewish state would have been open to immigration and could have saved hundreds of thousands, perhaps even more, European Jews from the Holocaust. Although the area allotted to the Jewish state by the Peel Commission was tiny in comparison with that allotted to the Arab state (and comparably even smaller if Transjordan is included), it was large enough to absorb millions of refugees, as evidenced by the fact that millions of people live within that area today.

There would have been no Arab refugee problem had the Arab states accepted the subsequent U.N. partition. But instead, having rejected Jewish self-determination in 1937, the Arab world rejected it once again in 1948 and attacked Israel in an effort to destroy the new Jewish state, exterminate its Jewish population, and drive the Jews into the sea. Then again in 1967, it threatened Israel with destruction and annihilation.

13 Did Israel Start the Six-Day War?

THE ACCUSATION

Israel started the Six-Day War.

THE ACCUSERS

"In 1967 Israel started the Six Day War by launching an air attack on Egypt, Jordan, Syria and Iraq. Israel occupied East Jerusalem, the West Bank and Gaza and 1.5 million Arabs, mostly Palestinians, came under Israeli occupation. More than 300,000 Palestinians were forced to flee. Israel is still occupying the territories." (Eva Bjoreng, secretary general of Norwegian People's Aid, and Steinar Sorlie, secretary general of Norwegian Refugee Council[1])

THE REALITY

Although Israel fired the first shot against Eqypt—although not against Jordon—the war was begun by Egypt's decision to close the Gulf of Aqaba to Israeli shipping and to order the removal of U.N. troops from the Sinai.

THE PROOF

Although Israel fired the first shots, virtually everyone recognizes that Egypt, Syria, and Jordan started the war. The illegal Egyptian decision to

91

close the Straits of Tiran by military force was recognized by the international community to be an act of war. As Egyptian president Nasser himself boasted, "We knew the closing of the Gulf of Aqaba meant war with Israel . . . the objective will be Israel's destruction."[2] The Egyptian commander of Sharm al-Shekh, the point of entry to the straits from which the Egyptians warned they would shoot at any Israeli ship that tried to pass through on the way to or from Eilat, acknowledged that "the closing of the straits was a declaration of war."[3] However, according to Nasser, the war was not to be over the Straits of Tiran but over Israel's "existence."[4] Nor was Israel's surrender contemplated. This, like the 1948 war, was planned to be a war of extermination.

Damascus Radio incited its listeners: "Arab masses, this is your day. Rush to the battlefield. . . . Let them know that we shall hang the last imperialist soldier with the entrails of the last Zionist."[5] Hafiz al-Assad ordered his Syrian soldiers to "strike the enemy's [civilian] settlements, turn them into dust, pave the Arab roads with the skulls of Jews. Strike them without mercy."[6] He characterized the forthcoming attack on Israel as "a battle of annihilation." The Voices of the Arabs in Cairo exhorted its listeners with similar incitements to see that "Israel is liquidated."[7] The prime minister of Iraq predicted, "There will be practically no Jewish survivors."[8] Cairo was filled with anti-Semitic posters "showing Arab soldiers shooting, crushing, mangling, and dismembering bearded, hook-nosed Jews."[9]

Nor was this only rhetoric. Arab armies were massing along Israel's border poised to strike. Egyptian battle plans included the massacre of the Tel Aviv civilian population. Palestinian plans included the destruction of Israel "and its inhabitants." Israeli intelligence reported that the invading Egyptian army was equipped with "canisters of poison gas."[10] The only question was whether the Arab armies would be able to strike the first military blow. As Prime Minister Levi Eshkol told his cabinet on May 21, 1967, "The Egyptians plan to close the straits or to bomb the atomic reactor in Dimona. A general attack will follow. A war would ensue in which the first five minutes will be decisive. The question is who will attack the other's airfields first."[11] After exhausting all diplomatic options[12] and learning that Egypt was preparing an imminent attack and had flown surveillance flights over Israeli territory, the Israeli air force attacked Egyptian, Syrian, and Iraqi military airfields on the morning of June 5, 1967. Would any reasonable nation faced with comparable threats of annihilation have acted differently?

Israel did not attack Jordan, hoping it would stay out of the war, despite its treaty with Egypt. Israel sent several messages to King Hussein promising not to attack Jordan unless it was attacked first. Israel made it clear that it had no designs on the West Bank or even on the Jewish Quarter of

Jerusalem, with its Western Wall, unless it were to be attacked. It was the Arab legion that initiated the hostilities between Jordan and Israel.[13]

Jordan ignored Israel's repeated peaceful overtures and began shelling Jewish civilian population centers in and around Israel's major cities and suburbs. Six thousand shells were fired into Jewish residential areas, wounding 1,000 civilians, many of them seriously. Twenty civilians were killed and 900 buildings were damaged. Long Tom guns targeted the suburbs of Tel Aviv, and Jordanian planes joined Syrian and Iraqi MIGs in bombing civilian population centers in cities, towns, kibbutzim, and moshavim. Damascus Radio proudly reported, "The Syrian Air Force has begun to bomb Israeli cities."[14] It was a repeat of 1948, in which the Arab armies deliberately and unlawfully targeted Israeli civilian population centers, while the Israeli army attacked legitimate military targets.

Despite Jordan's unprovoked attack against Israeli civilians, the Israeli army did not respond, hoping that Jordan would limit its military actions to a few opening salvos, but after Jordan sent its air force into the sky to bomb the residential neighborhoods of Netanya, Kfar Sirkin, and Kfar Saba, the Israeli air forces finally attacked Jordanian military airfields. The Israelis then accepted a cease-fire proposed by the U.N. chief observer, but the Jordanians fought on. Only then did Israel capture the West Bank and the Old City of Jerusalem—plainly in a defensive war against Jordan started by Jordan after Israel made it clear it wanted no military conflict with the Hashemite Kingdom.

The Six-Day War created yet another refugee problem, this one much easier to resolve in the context of a two-state solution. The 200,000 to 250,000 refugees who left Gaza and the West Bank following the Israeli occupation of those areas will surely have a right of return to *those areas* once a Palestinian state is established. (It will be interesting to see how many actually exercise that right, since the exercise of that right—unlike the claimed right of return to Israel—will have no major political or demographic effect on the Jewish state.) Most of the refugees left on their own accord. The definitive history of the 1967 war by Michael Oren states: "Few Israelis even came in contact with civilians, most of whom had fled with the Syrian command, well in advance of the attackers."[15]

In general, the casualties among civilians "were remarkably low" during the Six-Day War because Israel made sure that most of the fighting "took place far from major population centers," Oren reports. Indeed, the major civilian casualties were inflicted by Arab mobs on innocent Jewish civilians in Arab cities that were not involved in the fighting. Oren summarizes the situation:

With news of Israel's victory, mobs attacked Jewish neighborhoods in Egypt, Yemen, Lebanon, Tunisia, and Morocco, burning synagogues and assaulting residents. A pogrom in Tripoli, Libya, left 18 Jews dead and 25 injured; the survivors were herded into detention centers. Of Egypt's 4,000 Jews, 800 were arrested, including the chief rabbis of both Cairo and Alexandria, and their property sequestered by the government. The ancient communities of Damascus and Baghdad were placed under house arrest, their leaders imprisoned and fined. A total of 7,000 Jews were expelled, many with merely a satchel.[16]

This refugee problem has never been addressed by the international community. The other civilian casualties, as we have seen, were inflicted on Jewish residents of cities and towns that were targeted by Arab mortar shells. The tiny number of Arab civilian casualties was lower than in any comparable war in modern history—a fact never mentioned by those who accuse Israel of genocide or the indiscriminate killing of civilians. The major impact of the Six-Day War was the occupation itself.

14 Was the Israeli Occupation without Justification?

THE ACCUSATION

The Israeli occupation of the West Bank, the Gaza Strip, and the Golan Heights following its victory in the Six-Day War is without any justification.

THE ACCUSERS

"[T]here are two crystal-clear facts that can not be obscured by propaganda and bias: in 1948 Israel ethnically cleansed Palestine to make room for itself and as a result took over 78 per cent of Mandatory Palestine; and, secondly, in 1967 Israel imposed a brutal and callous occupation over the remaining 22 per cent of the land, the West Bank and the Gaza Strip." (Ilan Pappe[1])

"Most of the recent killing and destruction [referring to the violence stemming from the second intifada] has taken place in the West Bank and Gaza, territories conquered (along with East Jerusalem) by Israel in the 1967 war. U.N. Resolution 242—which the U.S. voted for—holds that continued occupation of these territories is illegal. That Resolution proclaims the 'inadmissibility of the acquisition of territory by war.'

"But Israel refuses to end its occupation." (Max Elbaum and Hany Khalil, contributing writers to *War Times*, a publication "opposing the war on terrorism"[2])

THE REALITY

Israel was willing to trade land captured in a defensive war for peace, as it eventually did with the Egyptians and Jordanians, but neither the Palestinians nor the Syrians have been willing to offer peace in exchange for land, as required by Security Council Resolution 242.

THE PROOF

Almost immediately upon prevailing over the Arab armies that had pledged and planned to annihilate Israel, the Israeli government agreed to comply with Resolution 242 of the U.N. Security Council, which for the first time in history ordered a nation to return territories lawfully captured in a defensive war. But it ordered this only as part of an overall peace agreement recognizing Israel's right to "live in security." This is what 242 provided:

> [The Security Council] (1) *Affirms* that the fulfillment of Charter principles requires the establishment of a just and lasting peace in the Middle East which should include the application of *both* of the following principles: (i) Withdrawal of Israel armed forces from *territories* occupied in the recent conflict; (ii) *Termination of all claims or states of belligerency* and respect for and *acknowledgement of the sovereignty,* territorial integrity and political independence of *every* state in the area and their right to live in peace within *secure and recognized boundaries* free from threats or acts of force.[3] [emphasis added]

Note that the resolution does not require Israeli withdrawal from *all the* territories, only "territories," thus contemplating some territorial adjustments of the kind proposed by Israel at Camp David and Taba in 2000. (I played a very small and informal consulting role to U.S. ambassador Arthur Goldberg, who played a major role in negotiating the resolution.) The elimination of the definite article *the* was an explicit compromise engineered by the United States in order to permit the retention by Israel of territories necessary to assure secure boundaries.

Israel immediately accepted the principles of Resolution 242. According to Morris, "The Israeli government hoped to convert its stunning military victory into a political achievement: the conquered territories could be traded for peace."[4] Moshe Dayan, who was then defense minister, was quoted as saying that he was "waiting for a telephone call from King Hussein" to discuss an exchange of land for peace.[5] The call did not come until many years later, by which time Hussein had renounced all claim to the West Bank in favor of the Palestinian Liberation Organization. On

June 19, 1967, the Israeli cabinet decided that Israel would "give up Sinai and the Golan in exchange for peace" with Egypt and Syria, writes Morris.[6] "Within days both Egypt and Syria had rejected the overture."[7]

As we shall see, Israel has, in fact, implemented the operative principles of Resolution 242 by eventually returning all the captured territory sought by Egypt when Egypt terminated all claims of belligerency against it. Israel also returned land claimed by Jordan as part of the peace agreement with the Hashemite Kingdom. Finally, it offered to turn over to the Palestinian Authority nearly all of the remaining territory captured from Jordan in exchange for peace, but the Palestinians rejected this offer made at Camp David and Taba as recently as 2000, and instead resorted to increased terrorism.

The major Arab states, along with the Palestinian leadership, on the other hand, categorically rejected the principles of Resolution 242 in 1967 because it required making peace with Israel, which they adamantly refused to do. At a summit in Khartoum, Arab leaders issued their notorious "three no's" statement: "No peace with Israel, no negotiations with Israel, no recognition of Israel." The Palestinians responded to the Israeli peace offer based on its acceptance of Resolution 242 by adopting the Palestinian National Charter, which expressly denied Israel's right to exist and pledged to continue "armed struggle" as the only way to liberate all of Palestine. It defined Palestine to include all of Israel (as well, apparently, as all of Jordan): "Palestine, with the boundaries it had during the British Mandate, is an indivisible territorial unit." In defiance of the United Nations, the Palestinian Charter declared the U.N. "partition of Palestine in 1947 and the establishment of the state of Israel [as] entirely illegal," because they "were contrary to the will of the Palestinian people." And it rejected "all solutions which are substitutes for the total liberation of Palestine" through armed struggle, declaring Zionism and Israel to be racist, colonial, and fascist.

Any possibility of a two-state resolution—along the lines proposed by the Peel Commission in 1937 or the United Nations in 1947, and immediately accepted by Israel—was thus categorically rejected by the Palestinians, who demanded total control over all of Palestine despite their being on the losing side of four wars of aggression (World Wars I and II, the 1947–1948 war against Israel, and the Six-Day War). Abba Eban, the foreign minister of Israel, observed that this was "the first war in history which has ended with the victors suing for peace and the vanquished calling for unconditional surrender."[8] Indeed, the Palestinians were demanding more than Israel's surrender as a nation.

The Palestinian Charter also demanded the *transfer* out of Palestine of every Jew, except those "Jews who had normally resided in Palestine until the beginning of the Zionist invasion." In the view of the Palestinians, since the Zionist invasion had begun many years earlier—at the latest in 1917 and at the earliest in 1882—this formulation would require the transfer of millions of Jews whose parents and grandparents had lived in what was now Israel for generations and in many instances for a much longer time than the Palestinians who would displace them.

Since Jordan, from whom Israel had captured the West Bank in a defensive war, subsequently renounced all claims to that territory in favor of the Palestinian Authority, and since the Palestinian Authority rejected peace in exchange for the West Bank (as contrasted with all of Palestine, including Israel), a stalemate was assured by the Palestinian Charter. There was no entity to which Israel could return the West Bank in compliance with Resolution 242, even if it were so inclined, so long as the Palestinians refused to comply with principle II of Resolution 242 that required "termination of all claims or states of belligerency" and recognition of Israel's right to "sovereignty, territorial integrity and political independence." Along with most Arab nations, the Palestinians rejected Resolution 242, while Israel accepted it, as it had the *Peel Report* and the U.N. partition. Once again, the Palestinians and Arabs rejected the two-state solution, while Israel indicated a willingness to take steps that would have led to such a solution. Notwithstanding this historical reality, anti-Israel academics such as Noam Chomsky mislead their students by telling them that Israel and the United States are "rejectionist" states that have always opposed a political compromise, while the Arab states and the PLO have accepted it.[9]

There were, of course, unilateral actions the Israeli government could have, and in my view should have, taken following the victory in the Six-Day War and the capture of the West Bank and the Gaza Strip, even though such unilateral action was in no way required by Resolution 242 unless it was accompanied by peace and recognition from the Arab states. (I postpone any discussion of the Sinai at this point, because Israel eventually gave that territory back to Egypt in exchange for peace.) Israel could have, and should have, implemented the so-called Alon Plan or some variant thereof. The Alon Plan, proposed by Israeli general Yigal Alon, who was then labor minister and a key adviser to the prime minister, contemplated Israeli withdrawal from the population centers of the West Bank and from all other captured territories except for some unpopulated areas that were deemed necessary to assure Israel's "territorial integrity" within "secure" boundaries, as contemplated by Resolution 242. Alon's plan, unlike Resolution 242, drew an important distinction between occupying *territory* and occupying *populations*.

The Security Council resolution focused exclusively on territories rather than people. But the West Bank comprises cities, towns, and villages, as well as vast expanses of unpopulated land. The Alon Plan would

THE CASE FOR ISRAEL

have implemented a "territorial compromise" under which Israel would "retain a six–seven mile deep strip along the West Bank of the Jordan River" as a "security belt." It would also have made some other minor border adjustments on the road to Jerusalem so as not to return to what Abba Eban, a major dove, had called "the Auschwitz lines" that exposed Israeli population centers to grave risks.

Although in 1967 Israel had no peace partners who were willing to give peace in exchange for territory, it would have been wiser, in my view, for Israel to have withdrawn, unilaterally if necessary, from Palestinian population centers such as Nablus, Ramallah, Jericho, Hebron, Jenin, Bethlehem, and Tulkarm, while maintaining control over largely unpopulated security areas. If Israel had taken that course, its soldiers would not have become an army of occupation over people. The Arabs would still complain that their land was being occupied, but Resolution 242 contemplated territorial adjustments designed to achieve secure borders "free from threats or acts of war." Moreover, the Arabs would have complained that their land was being occupied even if Israel turned over every inch of territory captured in the 1967 war so long as Israel continued to occupy the Jewish city of Tel Aviv or any other area of what had once been Palestine or southern Syria under the British mandate.

Instead of unilaterally withdrawing from Palestinian population centers, Israel maintained control over the entire West Bank, treating it as a bargaining chip for peace with Jordan. But Jordan had no interest in making peace in exchange for a return of the West Bank, perhaps because it did not want to reassume control over more than 600,000 Palestinians, who might destabilize a shaky Hashemite regime, which already had a majority Palestinian population in Jordan proper. For whatever reason, Israel assumed control over Palestinian population centers for 28 years—from June 1967 until December 1995, when Israel turned these cities over to the Palestinian Authority, pursuant to the Oslo II Agreement.

The twenty-eight-year occupation of these population centers contributed to many of the factors that now make peace more difficult to achieve. There is, however, no assurance that if the Palestinian population centers had not been occupied by Israel, peace would have been achieved, since the ending of the occupation of these centers between 1995 and 2001 did not bring the region much closer to peace. Nor was there peace between 1948 and 1967—a period during which there was no Israeli occupation.

The occupation certainly contributed to an increase in the number and lethality of terrorist attacks by Palestinians, though terrorism had been rampant since the 1920s, and the PLO, which was committed to terrorism as the primary means for liberating all of Palestine, had been established before the occupation began.

15 Was the Yom Kippur War Israel's Fault?

THE ACCUSATION

The Yom Kippur War was Israel's fault.

THE ACCUSERS

"The responsibility for the new military flare-up in the Middle-East lies wholly and completely with the Tel Aviv leaders. . . . Israel continues its aggression started in 1967 against the Arab countries." (Soviet general secretary Leonid I. Brezhnev, October 9, 1973.[1])

"Our victory in the war shattered forever the illusion of our neighbours' invincible military prowess. We had proven ourselves their equals, both intellectually and practically. No longer could the rights and duties of the Arabs, and of the individual Arab, be mocked and derided. The October War spelled the end of the racist theory of the inherent superiority of the Israeli people." (Osama El-Baz, Egyptian national security adviser[2])

THE REALITY

The unprovoked attack on Israel was unjustified and in violation of the U.N. charter.

THE PROOF

In October 1973, Egypt and Syria launched surprise attacks against Israel on Yom Kippur, the holiest day of the Jewish year. The attacks also took place during Ramadan, a period when Muslim leaders often claim an attack on *them* would violate religious principles and show disrespect for Islam. No one disputes that the Egyptians and Syrians, who inflicted considerable casualties on the Israelis, started the Yom Kippur War. Their goal was to recover the land lost to Israel from the Six-Day War—the war the Egyptians started, despite the fact that the Israelis fired the first shot. In the end, the Egyptians accomplished that goal and recovered the entire Sinai after making a cold peace with Israel. The Syrians failed in their effort to regain the Golan Heights because they refused to make any kind of peace with Israel.

Israel learned some important lessons from the Yom Kippur War. First and foremost, it learned how vulnerable it was to a surprise attack, even with expanded borders. In preparation for its attack, Egypt had obtained large quantities of Scud missiles that "could reach Israel's population centers."[3] Again, the Arab goal was to kill as many civilians as possible, despite the fact that deliberately attacking civilian targets is a war crime and a violation of international law. Egypt's initial assault included an attempt to drop bombs on Tel Aviv, which was prevented by Israeli air force interceptors.[4]

The Syrian attack also targeted Israeli civilian settlements, and Syrian tank forces almost succeeded in breaking through Israel's thin defense line that protected its northern population centers. As the commander of the unit in charge of defending Israel's northern towns and villages later told the Agranat Commission that was set up to investigate the near disaster, "The feeling was that there was going to be a holocaust."[5] Everyone knew what Syrian soldiers would do to captured civilians, since they had previously murdered and mutilated captured Israelis.

On the Egyptian front as well, there was a genuine fear of a genocidal result. Moshe Dayan, Israel's defense minister, sent a message to the commander of the Israeli air force that "the Third Temple"—his code for the state of Israel—"is in danger." Dayan suggested mobilizing high school students and people who were too old for reserve duty.[6]

Again it was brought home to Israel that its Arab enemies could afford to lose war after war with no threat to their existence and no danger to their civilian populations. But if Israel lost even a single war, it could mean the end of the Jewish state, a massacre of its civilian population, and the transfer of surviving refugees out of the country. Perhaps it has been this reality that has motivated Israeli soldiers to fight so fiercely in defense of their country. What Morris had said about the motivations and incentives of Israeli fighters during the War of Independence was equally true during the Yom Kippur War: They were fighting "in defense of [their] loved ones" who "faced slaughter should they be defeated."[7]

Israel ultimately prevailed in the war but with enormous casualties. Remarkably, the Egyptians and the Syrians, despite their eventual defeat, regarded and still regard the Ramadan War (as they call what the Israelis call the Yom Kippur War) as a victory. In a speech on October 16, 1973, Egyptian president Anwar Sadat told his people, "The Egyptian armed forces have achieved a miracle by any military standard. . . . [T]hese forces took the initiative, surprised the enemy and threw him off balance." Egypt has "restored its honor."[8] Similarly, President Hafiz al-Assad told his people that Syria had "transformed Israel's aggression, since 6th October, to a retreat of the enemy forces" and "inflicted on the enemy losses which deeply shook the Zionist entity." He told the Syrian people how the "ferocious battles waged by our Arab forces" have "restored self-confidence to the Arab individual."[9] To this day, the Arab victory is celebrated in Egypt and Syria, despite the reality that their armies were saved by a cease-fire imposed on Israel by the United States and the Soviet Union.

Morris has described Sadat's and Assad's motives for attacking Israel:

> For both Sadat and Assad, the war promised major gains, beginning with a restoration of Arab pride. (After the war Arab chroniclers would even speak of "the rebirth" of "Egyptian man.") Merely daring to go to war against the invincible IDF would be seen as profoundly courageous; wiping out the shame of 1967, indeed the shame of Arab history since 1948, would bring both regimes rewards in terms of popularity, legitimacy, and longevity, as well as large contributions from the oil kingdoms.[10]

Israel learned another important lesson from this disparity in defining victory in war: any Arab leader who can inflict serious damage on Israel is motivated to do so, even if his nation will ultimately lose the war. This is the sad reality for a couple of reasons. First, the stakes are far lower for Arab countries that lose wars with Israel. They may lose some territory (which they can get back in exchange for offering peace) and some soldiers, but the existence of their nation and the lives of their civilians are not at stake. Second, any Arab leader who has even the slightest possibility of defeating Israel will be praised and rewarded for trying, and condemned, perhaps even overthrown, for not trying. This is why it is so important for the preservation of peace that Israel remains qualitatively stronger militarily than all the combined Arab armies that surround it. If that military superiority were ever to be lost, it is virtually certain that Israel would again be attacked. That is why Nelson Mandela was wrong in suggesting any analogy between Israel's defensive nuclear program and Iraq's efforts to develop weapons of mass destruction for aggressive use.

This is what Mandela said: "But what we know is that Israel has weapons of mass destruction. Nobody talks about that. Why should there be one standard for one country, especially because it is black, and another one for another country, Israel, because it is white."[11]

Israel has had nuclear weapons since the 1960s. It has never used them, even during the Yom Kippur War. It has been said of Israel's nuclear capacity that it will probably never be used because it could only be used too early or too late: If Israel ever employed nuclear weapons to prevent a disaster, it would be universally condemned. If it waited to use them until after a disaster, it would be too late. Israel's nuclear arsenal is the ultimate deterrent against a radical regime that might seek to produce Armageddon (which is literally a small village in Israel called Meggido). The danger is that there may be some radical Islamic leaders more focused on the next world than this one who may not be deterred even by the prospect of mutual nuclear devastation.

Sadat achieved both of his goals in attacking Israel on Yom Kippur of 1973. In addition to restoring Egyptian honor, he also restored the entire Sinai to Egyptian control. As soon as Sadat courageously indicated a willingness to make peace with Israel in exchange for the Sinai, the Israeli government, then under the control of the hawkish Likud Party and its tough-talking leader, Menachem Begin, uprooted the Jewish settlers in the Sinai and returned it, oil fields and all, to Egypt. The decision to make peace, even a cold peace in exchange for the strategically and minerally valuable Sinai, may have cost Sadat his life—as Jordan's King Abdullah's decision to even consider peace with Israel cost him his life a quarter-century earlier. But it paved the way for Jordan's King Hussein, Abdullah's grandson, to make peace with Israel.

Since Jordan had renounced all claims to the West Bank in favor of the Palestinian Authority, there was no land that Israel could exchange for peace. (Actually, Israel did return a small strip of about 300 square kilometers in the Arava.) Had Jordan wanted a return to the status quo before the 1967 war, it is likely Israel would have welcomed such a return, perhaps with some small territorial adjustments. But the last thing Jordan wanted in 1994 was responsibility for the millions of Palestinians then living in the West Bank, especially after the aborted Palestinian civil war led by the PLO against King Hussein in 1970.

Israel repeatedly tried to make peace with Syria in exchange for territory it captured during the Six-Day War, as Morris reports: "In August 1993 a major breakthrough was achieved when Rabin gave Secretary of State Christopher his 'hypothetical' agreement to Israeli withdrawal from the whole of the Golan Heights, should Syria reciprocate with adequate security arrangements and normalization-of-relations measures. However, the Syrians failed to respond with similar largesse."[12]

16 Has Israel Made Serious Efforts at Peace?

THE ACCUSATION

In recent years, Israel has made no serious efforts at peace with the Palestinians.

THE ACCUSERS

"By now it has become clear that, because Western audiences are so poorly informed, Israeli public officials can say anything, including out-and-out lies. Last week a major television debate in the US between PA Minister Nabil Shaath and Knesset Speaker Avraham Burg confirmed this sad fact. . . . Burg sat there and brazenly manufactured one falsehood after another—that as a democrat and a peace lover he was concerned there was no real Palestinian peace camp; that Israel is trying ever so hard to remain calm while Palestinian terrorists (encouraged by the Authority) threatened his daughter, no less, with brutal killing; that Israel has always wanted peace; . . . and on and on. All of it making the point, in the style of classical propaganda (to repeat a lie often enough is to believe it), that Israel is victimized by Palestinians, that it wants peace, and that it is waiting for Palestinians to catch up with its magnanimity and restraint." (Edward Said[1])

"The longer the U.S. and Israel reject a political settlement, the worse it's going to be." (Noam Chomsky[2])

THE REALITY

Israel has offered the Palestinians every reasonable opportunity to make peace, but the Palestinians have rejected every such offer, most recently at Camp David and Taba in 2000–2001.

THE PROOF

Israel did manage to make some halting progress in peace talks with the Palestinians starting in the early 1990s. Even before that time, a number of senior Fatah figures had been preaching a 'two-state' solution, but these individuals had experienced assassination—what George Bernard Shaw had once characterized as "the ultimate form of censorship"—at the hands of other Palestinians. From its founding in 1964 (and even before), the PLO (and its predecessors) had rejected the two-state solution in favor of terrorism, the destruction of Israel, and the transfer out of the Jewish population.

Palestinian terrorism had, however, been quite successful in bringing the grievances of the Palestinians to the attention of the world. Although the Palestinian demand for the destruction of Israel and the transfer of its Jewish population—as articulated in its covenant—is far less compelling from a moral perspective than the complaints of other stateless and occupied people, such as the Tibetans, the Kurds, and the Basques, the PLO's resort to global terrorism has leapfrogged Palestinian claims over the more compelling claims of others.

Between 1968 and 1990, Palestinian terrorists murdered thousands of innocent civilians, including international travelers, Jews at prayer in synagogues throughout Europe, Olympic athletes, nursery school children, diplomats, and Christian pilgrims. They blew up airplanes, planted bombs in shopping markets, threw hand grenades at children, sent letter bombs to businesspeople, and hijacked a cruise liner, including throwing a wheelchair-bound passenger into the sea. Although all of these actions constitute war crimes and violations of international law, the international community—and especially the United Nations—has repeatedly rewarded Palestinian terrorism by according to the PLO far greater recognition than that accorded to other stateless groups that have not resorted to global terrorism.

As the chart that appears in my book *Why Terrorism Works* vividly demonstrates, the more vicious, unlawful, and lethal the Palestinian terrorist attacks against civilians became, the more diplomatic recognition they have been accorded by the United Nations, which singled out the PLO from among all other representatives of stateless groups for special observer status and other diplomatic privileges. This was done at a time when the PLO rejected the U.N. partition of Palestine, rejected the existence of the

U.N. member nation Israel, rejected Security Council Resolution 242, and demanded control over all of Palestine and the transfer of most Jews out of all of Palestine. No wonder the PLO maintained its central reliance on terrorism as the way to achieve its demands. Terrorism was working for it not only at the United Nations but also in European and other capitals, in the Vatican, and among some academics and public opinion makers in many parts of the world.

But it was not working for the Palestinians in regard to Israel or the United States. Terrorism had only strengthened the resolve of these two democracies not to reward the murder of innocent civilians lest it encourage more to resort to this immoral and unlawful tactic. Despite their diplomatic gains at the United Nations and elsewhere, the Palestinians were no nearer to statehood or the end of the occupation. If anything, Israel was allowing more settlements on the West Bank and justifying them on security grounds, though the reality was that most had little to do with security. Indeed, in the view of most Israelis, many of the settlements had an adverse effect on Israeli security.

The situation, for both Israelis and Palestinians, was growing progressively worse, especially after the first intifada began in the late 1980s, resulting in increased violence against Israelis and increased restrictions on Palestinians. Islamic fundamentalism was growing, and Hamas—which was more uncompromising in its fundamentalist zeal but less corrupt than the PLO—was increasing its influence among Palestinian Muslims. Its charter, adopted in August 1988, is even more extremist and overtly anti-Semitic than the PLO charter. It calls for the "reinstitution of the Muslim state" in "every inch of Palestine," and the raising of the "banner of Allah" over all of Palestine, which it described as an "Islamic Waqf." It proclaims that any compromise, even if every Arab and Palestinian leader were to accept it, would be in violation of Islamic law. All peace initiatives or "so called peaceful solutions are contrary to the beliefs of the Islamic Resistance Movement." And "renouncing any part of Palestine means renouncing part of the religion." It proclaims that neither Jews nor Christians, who it characterized collectively as "the unbelievers," can be trusted, and declares, "There is no solution to the Palestinian problem except by Jihad."

The charter then becomes overtly and crudely anti-Semitic in describing the "Nazism of the Jews" and claiming that "Israel, by virtue of its being Jewish and having a Jewish population, defiled Islam and the Muslims." It falsely claims that "when the Jews occupied Holy Jerusalem in 1967, . . . they shouted with joy, 'Muhammad is dead, he left daughters behind,'" implying that the Jews want to rape Muslim women and girls. It then invokes the anti-Semitic czarist forgery, *The Protocols of the Elders of Zion,* and argues that their "present [conduct] is the best proof of what is said there [in the *Protocols*]."

The Hamas Charter also blames the Jews for the French and Russian Revolutions, World Wars I and II, and the creation of the United Nations "in order to rule over the world."[3] Calling the arrival of Jewish refugees in Palestine "this despicable Nazi–Tartar invasion," the charter—in a burst of irrationality exceeding even that which came previously—casts some of the blame on "the Freemasons, Rotary Clubs, Lions Clubs [and other] secret organizations [which] act for the interests of Zionism and under its directions, strive to demolish societies" and to distribute "drugs and toxics of all kinds in order to facilitate its control and expansion." The charter ends by demanding that all Muslims resist this new Crusade by "Jews, the merchants of war," as they resisted the Christian Crusades. Describing Judaism as a "false and falsified faith," it confidently predicts victory over the "Nazi Zionists."[4]

The Hamas Charter condemned Egypt for making peace with Israel and condemned the PLO for "adopting secular thought" and advocating secular solutions. Only a purely Islamic state, with no Jews, and all Christian Arabs in a subordinate status, would be acceptable to Hamas. A few months later, a Muslim Brotherhood pamphlet characterized the Jews as "the dirtiest and meanest of all races," and Hamas handbills called "the Jews brothers of the apes, the murderers of the prophets."[5] This kind of racist rhetoric also permeates Palestinian school curricula throughout the West Bank and Gaza. One high school examination asked the following question: "Explain the reasons that made the Europeans persecute the Jews." The answer, as provided in the schoolbook text, included the "facts" that Jews are "self-centered," that their Torah promotes "religious and racial fanaticism [and] malice towards other nations," that they hold "anti-Christian beliefs" and cause "massacres," that they control the "economy," that they feel "superior," are "money changers," and crucified Jesus. The text also tells the students not to sympathize with Jews because "persecution [is] desired by the Jews" so that it can be "exploited for the realization of material . . . gain" and to help "Zionize" the Jews of the world.[6]

Not surprisingly, the intifada took on an overtly anti-Semitic tone, as evidenced by the weekly Friday sermons in defense of the violence aired by the Palestinian Authority media.[7] It also directed extreme violence against Palestinians who were believed to be cooperating with Israel. Morris writes, "By the end of 1989, about ninety Arabs who had given intelligence to the Israelis or had helped sell them land had been killed, many savagely tortured before being dispatched."[8] By the end of the intifada in 1993, almost 400 Palestinians had been murdered by other Palestinians—nearly as many as had been killed by Israeli defense forces.[9] In an incredible display of chutzpah, some Palestinian spokesmen counted *these* murders when providing the media with a list of Palestinians killed during the intifada![10]

The intifada probably pushed both the Israeli government and the PLO (which was losing control over the Palestinian street to more radical Islamic groups) toward some kind of rapprochement. The United States had been gently pushing in this direction for several years, as had some Israeli doves.

When the Oslo peace process began in the early 1990s, Israel was willing to accept the Palestinian Authority as an equal negotiating partner so long as the Palestinian Authority was willing to accept Israel's right to exist. Never before in history had the winning side of defensive wars been willing to negotiate with the losing side that had started the wars being treated as equals. To regard those who have initiated aggressive wars and lost as equal bargaining partners is to encourage the waging of war as an adjunct to negotiation. There must be a price paid for starting and losing wars. That price includes a diminished status in the postwar peace negotiations.

If a people are free to initiate warfare, sue for peace when they lose, then expect to be treated at the negotiating table as the moral equals of those they attacked, there will be little disincentive to aggression. Why not start a war? If that fails, initiate negotiations, insisting on parity as a condition for not starting war once again. After the defeat of Germany and Japan in World War II, just imagine how the world would have reacted if some Germans and Japanese had employed terrorism against the victorious powers, then demanded equal status as bargaining partners in the postwar negotiations!

Treating the Palestinians as equal negotiating partners risks sending the wrong message about aggressive war. The Palestinians should be treated as aggressors who lost. They should be treated fairly but without moral claims to equal partnership in the negotiating process. Disagreements about security should be resolved against those who started the wars and in favor of those who successfully defended against aggression. Disputes about control of holy places should also be resolved against those who seized these places, as the Arabs did in 1948, and denied access to those from whom they were seized. Aggressors should be made to absorb refugees created by their aggression.

In the end, however, compromises have to be reached to assure peace, and compromises cannot always be based on pure principle. But at least the principle being compromised should remain clear, and that principle is that no one should benefit from having waged aggressive war and lost. The principal reason that the Palestinians were accorded equal status in these negotiations was that most Israelis want peace more desperately than do most Palestinians. Public opinion polls demonstrate this reality beyond any doubt. Most polls show that an overwhelming majority of Israelis want peace and will give up much in an effort to secure it,[11] while as many as 87 percent of Palestinians want terrorism to continue until all of

Palestine is liberated.[12] Accordingly, Israel has long been prepared to give more in the hope of achieving a lasting and secure peace.

This attitude is surely commendable, but there are even larger issues at stake than peace in the Middle East. Other nations and people must not be encouraged to pursue the aggressive path of war and terrorism that has led the Palestinians to being given equal status in the negotiating process. If the Palestinians succeed in getting everything they have sought by this path, it will only be a matter of time before other nations and people who believe themselves to be aggrieved will pursue aggressive warfare and terrorism as a first option. The world will be a far more violent and dangerous place if that is the lesson of the Israeli–Palestinian negotiations. Thomas Friedman of the *New York Times* has warned that if terrorism is rewarded in the Middle East, it will "be coming to a theatre near you."[13]

The end result of these negotiations has been an ongoing start-and-stop and restart-and-restop process that has held much promise followed by much disappointment for a resolution of the Palestinian–Israel, and perhaps even the Arab–Israel, conflict. The Oslo peace process ultimately led to an end of the Israeli occupation of Palestinian cities, towns, and villages (with a few exceptions). On September 25, 1995, Israel and the Palestinian Authority signed an agreement under which Israeli troops were to withdraw from most of the populated areas of the West Bank and Gaza.[14] Palestinian Authority police, numbering 30,000, assumed control over these Palestinian population centers. Although Israel still maintained control over substantial areas of the West Bank with few or no Palestinian residents, the occupation of Palestinian population centers was substantially ended in 1995. It had lasted twenty-eight years. Israel did not reoccupy any of these population centers until 2001, approximately a year after an epidemic of Palestinian suicide bombings began, and even then it only reoccupied on a temporary basis those places that were being used as launching pads for terrorist attacks. Jericho, for example, has not been reoccupied, since it has not served as a base for terrorism.

During the nearly six years of Palestinian control over its population centers, some progress was made toward resolving outstanding issues. The PLO, although not Hamas and the other radical Islamic groups, appeared to be moving toward accepting a two-state solution to the Palestinian–Israeli conflict.

By the early summer of 2000, it looked as if peace might actually be at hand. Terrorism had abated somewhat over the previous several years, and now a dovish Israeli government headed by Ehud Barak was actively seeking peace. Bill Clinton, serving his last year as president, was determined to leave a legacy of peace in the Middle East. The Israelis and the PLO agreed to meet beginning July 11, 2000, under the auspices of the United

States. In the course of these meetings, which lasted until January 2001, Barak startled the world by offering the Palestinians nearly all the territory they were seeking. By the time the negotiations ended, Barak had accepted Clinton's even more generous proposal and was offering the Palestinians "between 94 and 96 percent of the West Bank" and all of the Gaza Strip.[15] In exchange for the 4 to 6 percent that Israel would retain for security purposes, it would cede 1 to 3 percent of its land to the Palestinians. This would plainly have satisfied Security Council Resolution 242, which mandated return of "territories," not all territories, captured in Israel's defensive war with Jordan. Few, if any, Palestinian *people* would remain under Israeli occupation.

In addition, Barak offered the Palestinians a state with Arab Jerusalem as its capital and complete control over East Jerusalem and the Arab Quarter of the Old City, as well as the entire Temple Mount, despite its historic and religious significance to Jews. Israel would retain control over the Western Wall, which has no significance for Muslims.

On the refugee issue, Israel would "acknowledge the moral and material suffering caused to the Palestinian people as a result of the 1948 war and the need to assist the international community in addressing the problem."[16] Israel would accept some of the refugees on humanitarian and family unification grounds, but most would live in the Palestinian state; $30 billion in compensation would be agreed to for those who did not move to Israel. No compensation was offered for the Jewish refugees from Arab states following the 1948 and 1967 wars. As far as the Jewish settlements were concerned, Barak agreed to the "dismantling of most of the settlements and the concentration of the bulk of the settlers inside" the small percentage of the West Bank to be annexed by Israel.[17]

Yasser Arafat rejected the Barak proposal, making it clear that he would never surrender the right of more than 4 million Palestinians to return to Israel rather than live in the Palestinian state with compensation. This would, of course, quickly turn Israel into yet another Palestinian state, in addition to Jordan and the new West Bank–Gaza Strip state. The Palestinian refugee issue has always been a ploy designed to turn Israel into a Palestinian state, and Arafat's rejection of the generous Barak offer demonstrated this with little ambiguity.

It is only natural that most Palestinians would ordinarily prefer to live in a Palestinian state under Palestinian control than in a Jewish state under Israeli control—this is certainly what the Palestinians have been demanding for years. But if the goal is to flood Israel with millions of Arabs in order to turn it into another Palestinian state, many refugees might decide—or be persuaded—to do their duty and move to Israel, if given that choice. The dovish Israeli newspaper *Ha'aretz* editorialized the following after Barak made his offer:

The Palestinians could not ask for a better time to get the best possible peace treaty than right now. But they want more. . . . More than anything else, they want the right of return to be recognized and fulfilled. The Palestinian refugee problem was not caused by Israel; it was caused by Arab states, which have tried, time and again, to use brute force to wipe us off the map. . . .

Fulfillment of the right of return would mean the end of Israel as a Jewish state, and thus Israel will never agree to this demand.

If the Palestinians have included the clause on the right of return as a ploy intended simply to enhance their bargaining position, they would be wise to withdraw it right now—because time is running out. Even the most patient suitor gives up trying to capture a hard-to-get virgin. Arafat lost his virginity a long time ago, and we've had it with his game playing and with his arm-twisting attempts. . . .

If they fail to grab hold of these offers now, instead of Barak, they'll get Sharon.[18]

Some Palestinian leaders complained that the offered land was not all contiguous. The Gaza Strip, for example, is separated from the West Bank. Israel offered some land bridges and permanent leasing arrangements, but the Palestinians demanded contiguity. It should be recalled that the land offered to Israel in 1937 by the Peel Commission and by the United Nations in 1947 was also noncontiguous. Israel accepted those offers anyway.

Moreover, some of the major terrorist groups, such as Hamas, Islamic Jihad, and Hezbollah, oppose the existence of Israel and reject the creation of a Palestinian state on the West Bank and Gaza. They have pledged to continue terrorism against Israel's Jews until all of Palestine is liberated and not one inch of it is under Jewish control. For them mere contiguity is irrelevant. They want everything.

The real reason why Arafat turned down Barak's offer is that he was afraid to make peace with Israel, regardless of what Israel offered, short of ending its own existence. He knew that the radical Islamic groups representing a growing number of Palestinians reject the two-state solution and would regard anyone who accepted it as a traitor, deserving the death that had been meted out to so many others—from Abdullah to Sadat to moderate Palestinians—who had previously accepted Israel's right to exist. It was safer for Arafat to find excuses not to accept a peace offer than to provoke the potentially lethal enmity of those who reject Israel's right to exist.

There are some who place the blame for the renewal of the terrorism following the Arafat rejection of the Israeli peace offer on the decision by Ariel Sharon—before he became prime minister—to visit the Temple

Mount on September 28, 2000. But the evidence plainly shows that the violence had been carefully planned well before Sharon's visit. As the communications minister of the Palestinian Authority candidly acknowledged:

> The PA had begun to prepare for the outbreak of the current Intifada since the return from the Camp David negotiations, by request of President Yasser Arafat, who predicted the outbreak of the Intifada as a complementary stage to the Palestinian steadfastness in the negotiations, and not as a specific protest against [Ariel] Sharon's visit to Al-Haram Al-Qudsi [Temple Mount]. . . . The Intifada was no surprise for the Palestinian leadership. The leadership had invested all of its efforts in political and diplomatic channels in order to fix the flaws in the negotiations and the peace process, but to no avail. It encountered Israeli stubbornness and continuous renunciation of [Palestinian] rights. . . . The PA instructed the political forces and factions to run all materials of the Intifada.[19]

The Mitchell Commission, headed by former Senate majority leader George Mitchell—himself a descendant of Lebanese Christians—came to a similar conclusion: "The Sharon visit did not cause the Al-Aksa Intifada." Indeed, there were no deaths and few Palestinian injuries on the day of the Sharon visit, although twenty-eight Israeli policemen were injured by rock throwers. The deaths and injuries came shortly after an orchestrated attack by Palestinians against Jews praying at the Western Wall.

Ariel Sharon's visit to the Temple Mount was negotiated in advance with Palestinian leaders. Nonetheless, in my view it was a wrong-headed provocation that provided an excuse—even a trigger—for the violence, but the gun had already been loaded in anticipation of an inevitable provocation of some sort.

A real peace in the Middle East must be able to endure the kind of symbolic verbal provocation represented by Ariel Sharon's visit to the Temple Mount. Any enduring peace should expect these kinds of provocations on both sides. What cannot be tolerated are violent responses to these provocations, especially if the violence is orchestrated or even accepted at the top levels. This is a major lesson that was misunderstood during the bloody days following Sharon's visit.

The Israelis are provoked daily by similar verbal and symbolic actions, ranging from the teaching of Holocaust denial and anti-Judaism in state-run Palestinian schools to a provocative visit to the Western Wall by Arab legislators. The appropriate response to verbal and symbolic provocation is political protest, including demonstrations and perhaps even work stoppages. But throwing rocks and bombs and shooting guns is utterly unacceptable and should not be encouraged by the international community.

Yet the world, including many in the media, academia, and even diplomacy, seems to accept Palestinian violence as cultural. On the other hand, something different is expected from Israelis. This is cultural relativism bordering on racism. To expect less of Palestinians, regardless of their grievances, is to diminish their humanity.

The point is that provocations will occur, especially in a democracy where Sharon, like any Israeli citizen, is entitled to visit a site open to the public that is holy to both Jews and Muslims. The mindset of Palestinians must change if peace is to become a reality. They must learn that proportionality, which they appropriately demand from the Israeli military, must also be demanded of them by their leaders. Verbal and symbolic provocations are part of a democracy. Sharon, in his own inartful way, was making a relevant point: when the Old City of Jerusalem was controlled by the Jordanian government and the Palestinian imams, no Jew was allowed to visit the Temple Mount or to pray at the Western Wall. After Israel defended itself from Jordanian attack during the Six-Day War and captured Jerusalem, the holy sites were opened to all.

Sharon was seeking to demonstrate that if the Temple Mount were returned to Palestinian control, he and other Jews would not be welcome there. There may have been better ways to make that point, but governments in a democracy may not generally restrict the manner by which political points are made so long as it is nonviolent. To allow a rock-thrower's veto is to undercut freedom of expression. Had the Israeli government prevented Sharon from entering the Temple Mount, that, too, would have weakened the peace process by giving ammunition to the Israeli extreme right.

When the two sides move back to the negotiating table, they must take into consideration the likelihood—indeed, the inevitability—that similar and even worse provocations will occur on both sides. No provocateur, whether a symbolic one like Sharon or a violent terrorist on either side, should be able to put an end to the peace process. It will take wise minds and accepting hearts to build a peace that can endure provocations. The Egyptian–Israeli peace, as well as the Jordanian–Israeli peace, have been able to endure terrorist attacks by individual Egyptians and Jordanians against Israeli citizens, including children. The Palestinians must learn to endure verbal and symbolic provocations, just as the Israelis must learn to respond to violence in a manner that minimizes injury and escalation. But instead, in the fall of 2000, the Palestinians decided to use the Sharon visit as an excuse to accelerate the terrorism.

As we will see in detail in the next chapter, the outbreak of terrorism that followed Arafat's rejection of the Barak offer was carefully "planned in advance,"[20] because Arafat knew that by playing his tried-and-true terrorism card, he could once again influence public and diplomatic opinion in his favor. When Arafat walked away from Barak's generous offer, the international community initially turned against him in favor of Israel. But after the well-planned resumption of terrorism against Israeli civilians and the entirely predictable Israeli overreaction to the murder of youngsters and families in pizza parlors, discotheques, and Passover seders, much of European public opinion once again turned against Israel.

Understanding this dynamic, some Palestinians "almost welcomed the Israeli attacks," according to the *New York Times*.[21] It was part of their strategy to regain international support. As one diplomat told the *New York Times*, "The Palestinians have mastered a harsh arithmetic of pain. . . . Palestinian casualties play in their favor and Israeli casualties play in their favor. Non-violence doesn't pay."[22] Terrorism is a tactic selected by elite leaders because it works, not because it is a desperate reaction to oppression. Thomas Friedman of the *New York Times* observed that

> The world must understand that the Palestinians have not chosen suicide bombing out of "desperation" stemming from the Israeli occupation. That is a huge lie. Why? To begin with, a lot of other people in the world are desperate, yet they have not gone around strapping dynamite to themselves. More important, President Clinton offered the Palestinians a peace plan that could have ended their "desperate" occupation, and Yasser Arafat walked away.[23]

A survey of the research on who becomes a suicide bomber puts the lie to the claim that terrorism is the inevitable consequence of hopelessness, poverty, and disenfranchisement. "As logical as the poverty-breeds-terrorism argument may seem, study after study shows that suicide attackers and their supporters are rarely ignorant or impoverished." Many were raised "in relatively prosperous circumstances, and attended college." One study of nearly 250 aspiring Palestinian suicide bombers found that "none were uneducated, desperately poor, simple-minded or depressed." Other studies found that these mass murderers "were not ignorant, destitute or disenfranchised." They held "normal, respectable jobs" and seemed "to be entirely normal members of their families." They do not "express hopelessness or a sense of 'nothing to lose.'"[24]

Desperation may explain how easy it has been for elite leaders to persuade impressionable youngsters to become suicide bombers, but desperation alone is not the complete explanation even for that form of Palestinian child abuse. Glorifications of the suicide bomber coupled with dehumanization of his victim are essential contributing factors to why children are willing to blow themselves up. An example of the political glorification of suicide bombing is the statement made by Yasser Arafat's wife, who is living in luxury with her daughter in Paris. Although far from desperate, she said that she "hates" Israel and if she had a son there would be "no greater honor" than for him to become a suicide bomber who killed Jews. She did not say whether she wanted her daughter to become a martyr.[25]

Islamic religious and political leaders make it easier for these suicidal killers to engage in the mass murder of civilians by dehumanizing Israelis and Jews in their schools, mosques, and media. As Charles Krauthammer wrote in the *Washington Post*, "Arafat has raised an entire generation schooled in hatred of the 'Judeo-Nazis.'" This indoctrination includes "the rawest incitement to murder, as in this sermon by Arafat-appointed and Arafat-funded Ahmad Abu Halabiya broadcast live on official Palestinian Authority television early in the Intifada. The subject is 'the Jews.'" (Note: not the Israelis, but the Jews): "They must be butchered and killed, as Allah the Almighty said: 'Fight them: Allah will torture them at your hands.' . . . Have no mercy on the Jews, no matter where they are, in any country. Fight them, wherever you are. Wherever you meet them, kill them."[26]

Palestinian educators, too, incite their students to murder by racist rhetoric. An end-of-the-year ceremony for 1,650 kindergarten students run by Hamas "included a skit by children that encouraged the murder of Jews as a religious commandment."[27] This combination of religious, political, and media messages helps explain why, among the many desperate peoples in the world, only Palestinian children are lining up to commit suicide and homicide.[28]

It may seem ironic that so soon after Israel offered the Palestinians nearly everything they and the international community wanted—a Palestinian state with Arab Jerusalem as its capital, return of the entire Gaza Strip and almost the entire West Bank, a fair and practical resolution of the refugee issue, and an end to Jewish settlements—it is now a pariah of the international community, European public opinion, and large segments of the American academic and religious left. Israel has become the object of divestiture and boycott campaigns and other efforts at demonization, while the Palestinians—who rejected the peace offer and responded with the systematic and deliberate murder of Israeli civilians—have become the darlings of the same groups.

But it is no irony at all. It is the result of deliberate calculations made by Palestinian leaders who understand how easy it is to provoke democracies into overreaction by murdering their most vulnerable civilians. France, England, Russia, the United States, and Canada have been similarly provoked, but only Israel has been so unfairly condemned for its entirely understandable, if sometimes disproportionate, efforts to protect its civilian population from terrorism. The Palestinian leadership well understands the eagerness of many groups to criticize for diverse reasons the Jewish state for actions that do not produce equivalent criticism when engaged in by other nations or groups. The reasons for this double standard lie deep within the psyche and history of the selective critics, but the double standard is undeniable and demonstrable. It is also eagerly exploited by the Palestinians.

The tragedy is that by applying this double standard, those who are too hard on Israel, while being too soft on the Palestinians, actually encourage the Palestinians to opt for terrorism over compromise and peace. They too share some of the complicity for the Palestinian reliance on terrorism—and for the resulting deaths.

17 Was Arafat Right in Turning Down the Barak–Clinton Peace Proposal?

THE ACCUSATION

Arafat was right in turning down the Barak–Clinton peace proposals of 2000–2001, and the fault for the breakdown of the peace talks is either all on the Israeli side or shared by Barak and Arafat.

THE ACCUSERS

"In the wake of the collapse of the Camp David Summit in July 2000, the finger of blame was instantly pointed at the Palestinian President, charging him with willful sabotage of the peace process by repudiating Ehud Barak's 'generous offer,' by indirectly espousing the liquidation of the Jewish state and then by launching a violent uprising to this end. He has been reviled as an unrepentant terrorist and an inveterate liar, who could no longer suppress his true aims. Even US President Clinton and many self-proclaimed supporters of the Israeli peace camp—nursing a deep sense of trust betrayed—joined the orgy of defamation." (Tony Klug, former head of international development at Amnesty International[1])

"The Israeli Government called off the Taba negotiations." (Noam Chomsky[2])

THE REALITY

Not only have Presidents Clinton and George W. Bush placed all of the blame on Arafat but so have many of Arafat's closest advisers. And now even Prince Bandar of Saudi Arabia, who played a central beyond-the-scenes role in the peace negotiations, has called Arafat's rejection of the Barak offer "a crime against the Palestinians—in fact against the entire region." Prince Bandar's assessment of Arafat's rejection of the peace proposal and of the resulting widespread support for the Palestinians provides a case study of how Arafat's use of terrorism is encouraged by the double standard under which Israel is blamed for offering peace and the Palestinians are rewarded for rejecting peace.

THE PROOF

Virtually everyone who played any role in the Camp David–Taba peace process now places the entire blame for its failure on Arafat's decision to turn down Barak's offer. President Clinton, who was furious at Arafat and has called him a liar, has blamed the failure completely on Arafat. Dennis Ross, who was the chief U.S. negotiator, has said that Arafat was unwilling to accept any peace proposal, because for Arafat "to end the conflict is to end himself."[3] The best proof of Ross's point is that Arafat did not even offer a counterproposal to Israel's offer. He simply rejected it and ordered preparation for renewed terrorism. President Bush, according to *The New Yorker*, also "places all the blame for the increase in violence on Arafat."[4]

Even some of Arafat's most trusted advisers and senior associates are now regretting the decision, and Arafat himself has let it be known that if the same offer would now be made, he might accept it—after approximately 3,000 entirely avoidable deaths. Of course, no one in Washington or in Israel takes Arafat's promises seriously after he lied both to President Clinton at Camp David and to President George Bush when he denied knowledge of the boatload of Iranian arms destined for use by Palestinian terrorists, despite an admission by the ship's captain that his orders came directly from Arafat.[5] Nor is Arafat trusted by the most dovish members of the Israeli peace camp, many of whom feel absolutely betrayed by his rejection of an offer that they pressed Barak to make and that they assured Barak that Arafat would accept. They blame Arafat for Barak's electoral loss to Sharon following the rejection of what many Israelis now regard as a naive and overgenerous offer. If Arafat was unwilling to accept *that* offer, they believe he will be unwilling to accept any peace offer that leaves Israel in existence.

In a remarkable series of interviews conducted by Elsa Walsh for *The New Yorker*, Prince Bandar of Saudi Arabia has publicly disclosed his behind-the-scenes role in the peace process and what he told Arafat. Bandar's disclosures go well beyond anything previously revealed by an inside source to the negotiations and provide the best available evidence of how

Arafat plays the terrorism card to shift public opinion not only in the Arab and Muslim worlds but in the world at large.

Bandar, who has been a Saudi diplomat in Washington for twenty years and is a high-ranking member of the royal family, served as a crucial intermediary between Arafat and the Clinton administration. He, like nearly everyone else, was surprised at Barak's "remarkable" offer that gave the Palestinian state "about 97% of the occupied territories,"[6] the Old City of Jerusalem other than the Jewish and Armenian Quarters, and $30 billion in compensation for the refugees. Arafat asked Crown Prince Abdullah, the acting monarch of Saudi Arabia, for Bandar's help with the negotiations. Bandar agreed but told Abdullah that "there's not much I can do unless Arafat is willing to understand that this is it." No better offer from Israel was possible.

On January 2, 2001—just weeks before the end of Clinton's term—Bandar picked Arafat up at Andrews Air Force Base, went over the Barak proposal, and asked Arafat whether he could ever get "a better deal." He also pointedly asked him whether he preferred to deal with Sharon rather than Barak. Arafat agreed, since "Barak's negotiators are doves." Bandar then reviewed the history of missed opportunities with Arafat: "Since 1948, every time we've had something on the table we say no. Then we say yes. When we say yes, it's not on the table any more. Then we have to deal with something less. Isn't it about time we say yes?" Bandar emphasized that the Arabs had always told the Americans that if "[y]ou get us a deal that's O.K. on Jerusalem and we're going, too." Bandar laid out the options to Arafat: "Either you take this deal or we go to war. If you take this deal, we will all throw our weight behind you. If you don't take this deal, do you think anybody will go to war for you?"[7]

Shortly thereafter, Bandar sternly warned Arafat: "I hope you remember, sir, what I told you. If we lose this opportunity, it is not going to be a tragedy, it is going to be a crime." Despite Arafat's promises that he would take the deal if Saudi Arabia and Egypt gave him cover, and despite Egyptian and Saudi assurances and Bandar's threats, Arafat rejected the deal and flew home without offering any counterproposals or amendments. As the negotiations faltered, Arafat ordered his terrorist leaders to ratchet up the violence. He had a plan for how to turn a public relations disaster and a crime against the Palestinian people into a public relations bonanza. It was a tried-and-true plan; it worked even more effectively this time than it had in the past.

But first, back to Prince Bandar, who was privately furious at Arafat because he had lied to him. He was, however, not surprised, as Walsh reports, "Bandar told associates that it was an open secret within the Arab world that Arafat was not truthful." In private, Bandar blamed everything on Arafat. "Clinton, the bastard, really tried his best," Bandar told Walsh on the record. The most critical of his comments regarding Arafat were apparently made off the record, again as reported by Walsh:

> Bandar believed that Arafat's failure to accept the deal in January of 2001 was a tragic mistake—a crime, really. Yet to say so publicly would damage the Palestinian cause. . . .
>
> Bandar was particularly angry with Arafat because if he publicly defended Barak's account, it would make him sound like an apologist for Barak and Israel. "I was there. I was a witness, I cannot lie," he said privately.[8]

But he was willing to make the following damning statements on the record:

> "I still have not recovered, to be honest with you, inside, from the magnitude of the missed opportunity that January," Bandar told me at his home in McLean, Virginia. "Sixteen hundred Palestinians dead so far. And seven hundred Israelis dead. In my judgment, not one life of those Israelis and Palestinians dead is justified."[9]

But this is not the end of the story. Now we go back to Arafat's grand plan for getting Bandar, the Arab countries, and most of the rest of the world back on his side. The plan was simple: start murdering Jews at prayer, Israeli teenagers at pizza parlors and discos, pregnant women in shopping malls, workers taking a falafel break, and university students sipping soda in a student lounge. You can count on an Israeli overreaction, especially after you helped elect a hawkish general as prime minister, who promised to be tough on terrorism. Even if there is no overreaction, there will surely be *some* reaction that you can characterize as an overreaction. Even an underreaction to terrorism will produce some civilian casualties, especially if you are careful to locate your bomb-making factories alongside kindergartens and to use women (including pregnant women) and children as human shields, bomb- and rock-throwers, and even suicide bombers.

The plan worked, even with Bandar, who knew exactly what Arafat was doing. Walsh describes how the crown prince was watching television and saw an Israeli soldier shoving a Palestinian woman. The prince phoned Bandar: "This is it. Those bastards! Even women—they're stepping all over them."[10]

Bandar described the anger of the prince, especially at the Israeli practice of destroying the houses of family members of terrorists: "We wonder how the American people would have accepted the President of the United States ordering all the McVeigh family houses to be destroyed or burning their farms," he said, referring to the Oklahoma City bomber Timothy McVeigh.[11]

Abdullah failed to mention that McVeigh's family did not praise their son's actions. Nor did they assist him and encourage him to become a martyr. Moreover, he was not part of an ongoing effort that continues to terrorize civilians.

As a result of Israel's response to the calculated Palestinian terrorism, Abdullah ordered Bandar to meet with President Bush. In one such meeting, Bandar showed Bush photographs of dead Palestinian children. He did not show Bush photographs of the *many more* Jewish children who have been *deliberately* killed by Palestinian terrorists than Palestinian children (some of them suicide bombers) who have been *accidentally* killed by Israeli soldiers. But a photograph of a dead child is certain to invoke sympathy, and as Walsh reports, Bush's "eyes seemed to well up."

Similar one-sided pictures were being telecast to the Arab and Muslim street, creating tremendous sympathy for the Palestinians and hatred toward the Israelis, which was precisely the goal of the Arafat plan. Terrorism works better on the Arab street than negotiations, especially if it produces the intended double benefit: the "courageous" martyrdom actions of the suicide bombers who kill hated Israelis, followed by the Israeli reaction, which provides new Palestinian martyrs. The effect on the Arab street quickly translated into pressure on Arab governments, which in turn put pressure on the United States. In this case, Bandar pressed the Americans to control the Israelis "even if they didn't trust Arafat."

> It did not help Bush in the Arab world that he seemed to place all the blame on Arafat. In May, Crown Prince Abdullah publicly declined an invitation to the White House. "We want them to look at the reality and to consider their conscience," he said to a reporter for the *Financial Times*. "Don't they see what is happening to Palestinian children, women, the elderly—the humiliation, the hunger?"[12]

The result of all this pressure was a statement by President Bush in favor of a Palestinian state—the first time a U.S. president has officially endorsed this outcome. I personally favor the creation of a Palestinian state as a consequence of making best efforts to end terrorism, not as a reward for increasing terrorism as a carefully calculated tactic to achieve statehood. The real point is how Arafat manipulates public opinion by turning the terrorism spigot off and on. Even those who know *intellectually* what Arafat is doing—like Prince Bandar—and that he is entirely to blame for the collapse of the peace process, are now *emotionally* compelled to support the "victims" of Israeli overreaction to terrorism, even though the terrorism was calculated to cause this response and the world's emotional reply to it. Terrorism works, and Arafat exploits this reality.

The Palestinian leadership made a tragic mistake in rejecting the

Barak–Clinton peace offer of 2001–2002. Yet, most Palestinians blame Israel for their own leader's mistakes. This is part of a long pattern, as described by the historian Benny Morris in an article in April 2003:

> [O]ne of the characteristics of the Palestinian national movement has been the Palestinians' view of themselves as perpetual victims of others— Ottoman Turks, British officials, Zionists, Americans—and never to appreciate that they are, at least in large part, victims of their own mistakes and iniquities. In the Palestinian Weltanschauung, they never set a foot wrong; their misfortunes are always the fault of others. The inevitable corollary of this refusal to recognize their own historical agency has been a perpetual Palestinian whining—that, I fear, is the apt term— to the outside world to save them from what is usually their own fault.[13]

18 Why Have More Palestinians Than Israelis Been Killed?

THE ACCUSATION

The fact that more Palestinians than Israelis have been killed during the recent spate of terrorism (September 2000 to present) proves that Israel's response is worse than the Palestinian terrorism.

THE ACCUSERS

"I can't believe that as a man of the cloth, you're not alarmed by the use of American attack helicopters, bombers, tanks, attacking the Palestinian defense police force with pistols, with young suicide bombers. You know, maybe more Palestinians have died in this than the Israelis. Aren't you appalled as a man of the cloth of the use of American weapons taking so many civilian lives?" (Bob Novak, political commentator[1])

"Abbas Hamideh said he was upset by media reports that depict Israelis as victims when more Palestinians have died since the second intifada began in September 2000." (Ernie Garcia, journalist[2])

THE REALITY

There are several important reasons why this comparison is misleading. These include the fact that Palestinians count the suicide bombers themselves as victims and ignore the large number of foiled and prevented terrorist attacks against Israelis.

THE PROOF

The Palestinians have willfully tried to kill many more Israelis than they have succeeded in doing, whereas the deaths attributable to Israel have mostly been caused accidentally in a legitimate effort to try to stop terrorism. For example, during the first two months of 2003, there were no successful terrorist attacks against Israeli civilians. This was not because Palestinian terrorists did not make considerable efforts to commit lethal acts of terrorism. Israeli authorities prevented *hundreds* of attempted terrorist attacks during that time period alone. An attempted terrorist attack carries the same moral culpability as a successful one. If each of these intended and well-planned attacks had been successful, perhaps as many as a thousand Israeli citizens would have been killed during these two months of "quiet" and tens of thousands more since the suicide bombings resumed in 2000.

In one planned attack alone—the thwarted bombing of the Shalom Towers (Israel's equivalent of the World Trade Center)—hundreds of civilians might have been killed. In another, the thwarted attack on the Pi Glilot gas and fuel storage facility in Tel Aviv, thousands more might have been killed. Between September 2000 and August 2002 "approximately 14,000 attacks have been made against the life, person and property of innocent Israeli citizens and residents, the elderly, children, and women."[3] Many have occurred since. Thousands more were thwarted or prevented.[4] A conservative estimate of the number of Israelis who might have been killed if all or most of these attempts had succeeded is at least ten times higher than the more than 800 who have actually been killed.

The number of Israeli citizens killed, as compared with the number of Palestinian citizens killed, also reflects different priorities in the allocation of medical care to the injured. Israel has allocated very substantial resources to its medical response to terrorism. It has developed a medical specialty of treating victims of terrorist attacks and has managed to turn hundreds of what would otherwise have been lethal results into very serious, often permanent, but nonlethal injuries. The number of very seriously injured Israelis with permanent disabilities or wounds is in the thousands. Many of these victims would have died if the Israeli medical response had not been so extraordinary.

The *New York Times* has reported, "Research published this year [December 2002] suggests that the most significant factor in keeping the homicide rate down is . . . faster ambulances and better care in the emergency room."[5] The research concluded, "The murder rate is being artificially suppressed because thousands of potential homicide victims . . . are now receiving swift medical attention and surviving." The lethality rate is dropping by as much as 70 percent. Assailants "aren't any less murderous—it's just getting harder to kill." The same is true for Palestinian terrorists: they are not any less murderous—it's just getting harder for them to kill Israelis because of the excellent medical response.

Israel's medical response to terrorism must be contrasted with the Palestinian response. The Palestinian Authority has decided no longer to transfer wounded Palestinians to Israeli hospitals, despite the fact that Israeli hospitals are completely nonpolitical in their treatment of patients, triaging them by reference to the seriousness of their injuries rather than by which side of the conflict they happen to be on.[6] Israel's health minister "has several times offered to treat all Palestinians wounded in the current Intifada at Israeli hospitals and at Israel's expense." The minister noted that "Palestinian medical facilities are unable to treat many of the wounded adequately." The Palestinians rejected the offer, according to the health minister, "because they prefer that we don't know the truth about the number of their wounded."[7] Whatever the reasons, the reality is that significantly fewer Palestinians would have died of their injuries if their leaders had been willing to have them treated by Israel's excellent first responders rather than by often incompetent Palestinian doctors and inadequate Palestinian hospitals.

Even as far back as 1994, when there was considerably less violence, Palestinian hospital administrators allowed "4 injured Palestinians [to die] from a lack of blood while being sent from Hebron to Mohassed Hospital in Jerusalem by ambulance. This occurred while [Israel] offered helicopters to transport the injured to Israeli hospitals for free medical attention." A Supreme Court justice appointed to investigate this tragedy "was furious" with the Palestinian administrators, declaring that he does not "understand the idea of refusing to accept medical aid on political grounds."[8] The refusal of Palestinians to take their wounded to the best available medical facility has certainly contributed to the number of preventable Palestinian deaths.

Moreover, despite the enormous personal wealth accumulated by Palestinian leaders through personal corruption—Arafat's personal wealth according to *Forbes* magazine is in excess of $300 million—very little money has been allocated to upgrading the Palestinian Authority's primitive emergency medicine system. This too has contributed to the number of nonlethal wounds that have proved fatal.

Some Palestinian spokespersons count among the Palestinian dead some or all of the following: the suicide bombers themselves; armed Palestinian fighters; leaders of terrorist groups, including those like the Engineer, who had operational responsibility for bomb-making; terrorists shot in self-defense while planting or throwing bombs; bomb-makers (and their neighbors) who have been killed when the bombs they were making accidentally blew up; collaborators who have been killed by other Palestinians; even people who have died as a result of the absurd and dangerous practice of shooting live ammunition in the air at Palestinian funerals and protests. The very idea that *anyone* would count suicide bombers and other terrorists who have been killed *as victims* to be compared with the innocent civilians who were their targets is so absurd and immoral that it defies explanation as to how the media could present these figures as comparative casualties with a straight face. Yet many newspapers, and television and radio accounts, continue to provide these asymmetrical and biased comparisons.

The Palestinians also count innocent people caught in crossfire between Palestinian and Israeli fighters, even in situations where it cannot be known which side fired the fatal shot. For example, the child who was filmed by French TV being shot in his father's arms may well have been shot by Palestinian gunmen, according to a German TV investigative report comparing the angle of the bullets with the location of Palestinian and Israeli fighters: "The extensive evidence points, with high probability, to the fact that the Israelis did not do it."[9] Moreover, Palestinian spokespersons blatantly exaggerate the number of victims, as they did following the fighting in Jenin in 2002. Palestinians initially claimed that Israel had "massacred" 3,000 civilians. Then they reduced their number to 500. The U.N. secretary general found the total number of Palestinians killed to be 52, many of whom were armed combatants. There is no evidence that Israeli soldiers deliberately killed even a single civilian, despite the fact that armed fighters shooting from among civilians in Jenin and booby-trapping civilian homes killed 23 Israeli soldiers. This willful exaggeration is all too typical, even among Palestinian academics. Professor Edward Said has written that "hundreds of thousands [have been] killed . . . by Israel with U.S. support."[10] This is simply a lie. One more polite critic called it "a preposterous claim."[11]

Even with all of these distortions and exaggerations, the actual number of innocent Palestinian civilians killed by Israelis is considerably lower than the number of innocent Israelis killed by Palestinians. The vast majority of Palestinians who were killed were directly involved in terrorist activity. Those who were not directly involved were killed accidentally in the course of legitimate military actions against terrorists. According to an internal analysis by the IDF, as reported in the *Boston Globe* in April 2003, "18 percent of the nearly 2,000 Palestinians killed by Israeli forces since the uprising began in September 2000 were civilians with no connection to acts of terror."[12] This comes to approximately 360 innocent civilians killed in the course of legitimate self-defense.

In my view this number and proportion is too high and Israel must bear some responsibility for the dead and injured Palestinians. But Israel's moral responsibility for these accidental, although often foreseeable, casualties of war, is in no way comparable to the responsibility of Palestinian terrorists who have deliberately targeted every single Israeli civilian victim. Of the more than 800 Israeli deaths, approximately 567 have been innocent civilians, many of these children, women, and the elderly.[13] Every such killing is an act of first-degree murder. To compare the accidental killing of civilians during legitimate self-defense against terrorism with the targeted murder of innocent civilians is like comparing medicine to poison. Both can result in death; but with the former, it is a tragic, if sometimes foreseeable, side effect, whereas with the latter it is the direct intended effect.

The number of Israeli women and children killed and injured is well in excess of the number of Palestinian women and children killed and injured—as many as three times more according to one study.[14] A prominent feminist writer has observed,

> On the Israeli side, 80 percent of those killed were noncombatants, most of whom were women and girls. *Israeli female* fatalities far outnumbered *Palestinian female* fatalities by either 3 to 1 or 4 to 1. (So far, I have heard no feminist complaints about this; have you?) Israeli women and girls constituted almost 40 percent of the Israeli noncombatants killed by Palestinians. Of the Palestinian deaths, over 95 percent were male. In other words, Palestinians purposefully went after women, children, and other unarmed civilians and Israelis fought against armed male soldiers who were attacking them."[15]

Even when men—who are more likely to be combatants—are included, the number of *innocent* Israelis killed and injured exceeds the number of innocent Palestinians killed and injured, and the reasons should be obvious to anyone who bothers to think about it for even a moment.

Terrorists try everything possible to maximize deaths, even sometimes reportedly soaking the nails they use in their antipersonnel bombs in rat poison to prevent coagulation of blood. Recently, Israeli doctors expressed concern that the blood of some of the suicide bombers, which splatters all over the scene and is touched by medical personnel, as well as their bones, which penetrate the bodies of the victims, might contain hepatitis or the AIDS virus, raising the fear that terrorist leaders could be turning suicide bombers into biological warfare carriers either by injecting them or selecting carriers as suicide bombers. The first such case was documented in the July 2002 issue of the *Israel Medical Association Journal.* Doctors at the Hillel Yaffe Medical Center in Hadera extracted bone fragments from the neck, breast, and groin of a woman who had been the victim of a suicide bombing. The bone fragments were sent to the Institute of Forensic Medicine in Tel Aviv and tested positive for hepatitis B.[16] The authors of the medical journal said: "Human bone fragments, which act as foreign bodies and are of biologic infected origin, are a new concept in blast injuries."[17] The doctors "theorized that suicide bombers might carry a number of infectious diseases including the hepatitis strain, HIV, syphilis, dengue fever, Creutzfeld-Jacob disease or malaria."[18] Theory turned to practice when the victims of the Hebrew University cafeteria bombing had to be given massive doses of antibiotics because "Israeli doctors have learned that many of the suicide bombers are infected with diseases ranging from hepatitis to HIV."[19]

Whether this turns out to be an isolated situation or a gruesome escalation in the methodology of terrorism remains to be seen. In the meantime, Israeli hospitals must prepare for the worst-case scenario. Israeli medical journals are discussing these problems. Indeed, the entire July 2002 issue of the *Israeli Medical Association Journal* was devoted to the subject of "Terror and Medicine." First responders have been equipped with test kits, vaccines, and antibiotics to confront this potential new threat. And it will not be easy, because "test kits are designed for blood. It is very hard to test bone, especially for a fragile virus like HIV."[20] Moreover, the new danger requires the surgical removal of bones that could otherwise be left in the victim's body. Terrorists succeed whenever they make the job of those trying to save lives more difficult. By that standard, the new threats posed by infected suicide bombers represent a victory for terrorism.

In distinct contrast to the modus operandi of Palestinian terrorists—to kill as many innocent Jews as possible by any available means—the innocent Palestinian civilians who have been killed by Israelis were not the intended targets of Israeli counterterrorism efforts. Israel tries to use rubber bullets and other weapons designed to reduce fatalities, and aims at the legs whenever possible. When Israelis accidentally kill a civilian, there is internal criticism, boards of inquiry, and sometimes even punishment.[21] When Palestinian terrorists murder schoolchildren, there is widespread cheering and adulation of the killers. Israel has nothing to gain and everything to lose by killing innocent Palestinians. The opposite is true for Palestinian terrorists, who deliberately target the most innocent Israeli civilians.

By deliberately hiding in and operating out of civilian population centers such as refugee camps, Palestinian terrorists use their own civilians as shields. It is a violation of international law to use civilians as shields, and under international law a civilian who is killed while being used as a shield is counted as a casualty caused by those using him as a shield, not by those who were legitimately trying to attack an appropriate military target such as an armed terrorist. To repeat what a diplomat told the *New York Times,* "The Palestinians have mastered a harsh arithmetic of pain. . . . Palestinian casualties play in their favor, and Israeli casualties play in their favor."[22]

Hamas leader Ismail Haniya told the *Washington Post,* "Palestinians have Israelis on the run now because they have found their weak spot:

Jews . . . love life more than other people, and they prefer not to die. So suicide bombers are ideal for dealing with them." This view of life and death may be "really sick," as Thomas Friedman has characterized it,[23] but it is part of the Palestinian terrorist arithmetic. Those who make the argument that Israel should be condemned because more Palestinians than Israelis have been killed actually encourage this cruel calculus of death.

No one claims that "Arabs and Muslims have terrorism in their genes," as Edward Said accuses pro-Israel advocates of believing.[24] Said's genetic straw man should not, however, blind us to the sad reality that much of the Palestinian leadership—both political and religious—have adopted terrorism as a first recourse and glorified it as part of their culture and religion. They are responsible for its proliferation.

Palestinian leaders are also responsible for the large number of Palestinian children and young adults killed and injured by Israeli gunfire. It was the Palestinian leaders who changed the rules of engagement by deliberately using children and young adults as aggressive weapons. These young people—some as young as eleven—have been recruited as suicide bombers, bomb-throwers, and rock-throwers. Salah Shehadeh, a leader of Hamas in Gaza, said in a May 26, 2002, interview that children were being recruited into a special branch of Hamas. In an interview on Al-Jazeera television, a prominent Muslim professor defended the use of what he called callously "the children bomb."[25]

A poll conducted by Islamic University of 1,000 youngsters between the ages of 9 and 16 showed that 49 percent said they had participated in anti-Israel violence and 73 percent expressed a desire to die martyrs. Not surprisingly, some children have been blown up in the process of detonating or planting bombs. Israeli soldiers or civilians who were targeted by the young terrorists have shot others in self-defense. For example, the *New York Times* of March 8, 2003, reported, "Youths threw stones and firebombs at troops throughout the day. At one point, soldiers fired and hit a youth who had thrown a firebomb," according to officials at an Arab hospital in Gaza.[26] Other examples include the following:

- On July 6, 2002, two eleven-year-olds were caught trying to plant a bomb near an Israeli outpost, and one of them said he hoped to become a martyr.

- On April 23, 2002, three students, ages twelve, thirteen, and fourteen, were killed while trying to infiltrate the town of Nitzarim in order to precipitate a suicide attack. They each left a will emphasizing their wish to die as martyrs. The three dead youths are now held up as examples of martyrs.

- A fourteen-year-old was killed while trying to enter an Israeli outpost carrying two pipe bombs.

- A sixteen-year-old was killed as he threw a hand grenade at Israeli soldiers.

- A fifteen-year-old girl was arrested after confessing that her uncle, a senior Tanzim operative in Bethlehem, had recruited her to become a suicide bomber and she had agreed to recruit additional girls from her school.

- On March 31, 2002, a sixteen-year-old carried out a suicide bombing at a Magen David Adom (Israeli Red Cross) station, killing six Israeli civilians and himself.

- A sixteen-year-old high school student was arrested on his way to committing a suicide bombing of a crowded bus after he announced in front of his entire class that he would not be returning because he was becoming a martyr.

Yet, despite these well-documented cases, a spokesperson for Amnesty International told a gathering at the U.N. Human Rights Commission in 2003 that "to my knowledge, there has never been a Palestinian minor involved in a suicide bombing."[27] She should tell that to the families of the six Israelis murdered by the sixteen-year-old Palestinian suicide bomber at the Israeli Red Cross station!

The University of Chicago philosopher Jean Bethke Elshtain, in her book *Just War against Terror,* compares Islamic terrorist leaders who claim that "Islamist young people are in love with death" to Nazi leaders who sent "5,000 children between the ages of 8 and 17" to near certain death in the last days of the siege of Berlin:

> Only five hundred survived. What was astonishing to observers was the determination of these children to "do their duty until they were literally ready to drop. They had been fed on legends of heroism for as long as they could remember. For them the call to 'ultimate sacrifice' was no empty phrase."[28]

No one blamed the Allied troops for killing the armed children who were trying to prevent them from capturing Berlin and ending the war. Citing the work of theologians H. Richard Niebuhr and Paul Tillich, Elshtain offered the following analysis:

> A willingness to sacrifice children is one sign of a culture of death. One is reminded not only of the drive toward death lauded by bin Laden and extolled by Islamist radicals everywhere, but specifically of how thousands of Iranian children were thrown into the horror of the eight year war between Iran and Iraq from 1980 to 1988. These children were dec-

imated: sent out as human minesweepers, they were either killed outright or left limbless and scarred. Yet families spoke of the honor of being parents of such martyrs. Contrast this hideous will to sacrifice children with the ethic of training adult soldiers to fight in a manner that preserves as many lives as possible, both of their own number and of noncombatants.[29]

The more that Palestinian leaders break the taboo against using youths as terrorists, the more youths will be injured and killed. Such deliberate misuse of children is an extreme form of child abuse, and it is entirely the fault of the abusers, not those who legitimately defend themselves against fire bombers and suicide bombers who happen to be youths. As Golda Meir, former prime minister of Israel, once said, "We can perhaps forgive them for killing our children, but we can never forgive them for forcing us to kill their children."

The same is true for Palestinian women, even pregnant women, who have now been recruited to become suicide bombers. Women have carried out more than twenty suicide attacks since 2001. Some of these women have been recruited by the use of emotional and cultural blackmail. For example, terrorist operatives deliberately seduced Andalib Suleiman, a twenty-one-year-old woman from Bethlehem. When she became pregnant, she was told that the only way to avoid the shame was to die a martyr's death. She then agreed to blow herself up in a Jerusalem shopping market, killing six civilians, including two workers from China. A similar example is Ayat al-Ahras, an eighteen-year-old woman from Dehaisi, who blew herself up in a supermarket, killing two civilians, after having been seduced and made pregnant.

This method of terrorist abortion is a despicable example of creating new life in order to generate death. There are other examples of young women being raped in order to turn them into shamed women whose only means of restoring family honor is martyrdom. In one case, the family learned of the attempt by Tanzim operatives to blackmail their daughter and smuggled her out of Bethlehem. She is now living in hiding.[30] Hamas has even obtained a legal religious ruling about what a female suicide bomber is permitted to wear as she goes about the business of killing Jewish civilians:

Question: "Must the female suicide seeker about to execute an operation dress in accordance with Sharia [Muslim religious law] knowing that if the operation is to be in an Israeli area . . . the woman will be exposed?"

Answer: "The question of the hijab [woman's head covering] is not open to discussion. This is a commandment and obligation a Jihad warrior may not forgo. A second point is that in our streets and cities occupied by the

Jews [all of Israel is considered 'occupied'], our sisters may walk about dressed in their Sharia clothes even with veils on their faces and wearing gloves. The third point, and it is very significant, is that our sisters, the Jihad warriors, can deceive the Jews by wearing clothes of the type worn by the so-called religious Jewish women which is acceptable under the Sharia. Onward the Shahid [Death for Allah] convoy!"[31]

A recent ruling by "an influential cleric based in Qatar" said that a Palestinian woman "could reach paradise through suicide bombings" and that she could remove her veils and go without a chaperone to kill Jews, because she is going to "die in the cause of Allah, and not to show off her beauty."[32]

Appropriate rules of engagement require a response to anyone engaged in potentially lethal activity against the armed forces or civilians of a nation. An apt analogy is to the recent recruitment by international drug smugglers of young children to carry the drugs—sometimes inside their bodies by swallowing condoms filled with heroin and cocaine. As a result of this change in the age of drug carriers, the customs authorities have had to begin searching children, giving rise to some complaints.

But the fault lies with those who have decided to use children as drug smugglers, just as the fault lies entirely with those who have decided to use children as carriers of deadly explosives. A 13-year-old suicide bomber is just as dangerous as a 25-year-old, and Israel has the same right of self-defense against both. The only way to end the killing of youths and women by Israeli soldiers and police is for the Palestinians to stop using them as terrorists. But this is unlikely, because the terrorist leaders have made a cruel calculation: their cause benefits every time an Israeli soldier kills a Palestinian child or woman. They have even gone so far as to place their bomb-making factories adjacent to kindergartens and elementary schools so that if Israel were to attack the factories, they would kill children. The placement of these dangerous factories also exposes the children to the risk of accidental death.[33]

The United States too had to change its rules of engagement after the Iraqis used an apparently pregnant woman as a terrorist. United States soldiers had to begin checking women more intrusively and occasionally shooting at cars that were running checkpoints. These are the tragic but unavoidable costs of protecting people against terrorism, especially when women and children are used as human bombs.

Those well-intentioned people who loudly criticize Israel whenever a Palestinian child is killed in self-defense by Israeli soldiers actually encourage the recruitment of more children as terrorists—and victims. Palestinian propagandists understand and exploit the reality that decent people become outraged at the killing of a child and often do not pause to move the blame beyond the side that fired the fatal shot toward the side that deliberately placed the child in harm's way.

Palestinian propagandists also understand that they receive more benefits from Palestinians killed by Israelis (even in self-defense) than from Palestinians killed by Arabs (even in cold blood). Thomas Friedman of the *New York Times* put it this way:

> Why is it that when Hindus kill hundreds of Muslims it elicits an emotionally muted headline in the Arab media, but when Israel kills a dozen Muslims, in a war in which Muslims are also killing Jews, it enflames the entire Muslim world?
>
> . . . This is a serious issue. In recent weeks, whenever Arab Muslims told me of their pain at seeing Palestinians brutalized by Israelis on their TV screens every night, I asked back: "Why are you so pained about Israelis brutalizing Palestinians, but don't say a word about the brutality with which Saddam Hussein has snuffed out two generations of Iraqis using murder, fear and poison gas? I got no good answers."[34]

Even though many more Arabs and Palestinians have been killed by fellow Arabs than by Israelis, the loudest and most effective complaints arise when a Palestinian is killed by a Jew. This too is a form of racism.

There are loud complaints as well, when Americans kill Arab civilians, as we did in Afghanistan and Iraq, but the shrill cries of "genocide," "Nazi tactics," and "holocaust" are generally reserved for Israel. On June 10, 2003, the Associated Press released the findings of its five-week investigation into the number of Iraqi civilians killed during the recent fighting. After examining hospital and other records, it concluded that "at least 3,240 civilians died throughout the country, including 1,896 in Baghdad." The report emphasized that the "count is still fragmentary, and the complete number—if it is ever tallied—is sure to be significantly higher."[35]

The reasons these figures are so high for so brief a war is that Iraqi soldiers—like Palestinian terrorists—dressed as women, hid among civilians, and even hid in ambulances, thus making it difficult to distinguish between combatants and noncombatants. Many of the Iraqi civilians had been victims of Saddam Hussein's brutal regime and were not, in any way, supporting his army. Many of the civilian victims among the Palestinians who were killed by Israeli troops were, on the other hand, complicit in and supportive of the terrorists. Yet the criticism directed against American troops has been nowhere near the level of criticism directed at Israeli soldiers.

Body counts alone do not determine the morality or legality of a military operation. Yet opponents of Israel tend to focus on the misleading "fact" that more Palestinians than Israelis have been killed.

19 Does Israel Torture Palestinians?

THE ACCUSATION

Israeli law authorizes the torture of Palestinian detainees, and Israeli authorities persistently engage in torture.

THE ACCUSERS

"[I]t is a well-documented, and easily verifiable fact that Israeli law officially authorizes the use of torture on detainees." (John Ihnat, North American coordinating committee for NGOs on the question of Palestine, in a statement issued in 2001, nearly two years *after* the Supreme Court of Israel officially outlawed all forms of physical pressure[1])

THE REALITY

Israel is the only country in the world whose judiciary has squarely faced the difficult issue of whether it is ever justified to engage in even a modified form of nonlethal torture—akin to the tactics currently being used by the United States on captured al-Qaeda prisoners—in order to obtain information deemed necessary to prevent a ticking bomb from killing dozens of civilians. On September 6, 1999, the Israeli Supreme Court decided that not only is torture absolutely prohibited but even the types of physical pressure currently being used by the United States—sleep deprivation, forced uncomfortable positions, loud music, shaking, hoods over the head—are prohibited by Israeli law, even in cases in which the pressure is used not to elicit a confession but rather to elicit information that could prevent an imminent terrorist attack. Prior to this decision, the Israeli security services did sometimes employ physical measures similar to those now being used by U.S. authorities against suspected terrorists.

This contrasts sharply with the situation in Egypt, Jordan, Morocco, Saudi Arabia, the Philippines, and other Muslim countries, where torture—including the lethal torture of purely political prisoners—is common and approved at the highest levels of government. It also contrasts sharply with the situation in the United States, where modified forms of torture that include physical and psychological components are practiced and are not easily subject to judicial review. Indeed, the leading case in the American courts seems to regard nonlethal torture as reasonable and necessary when its purpose is not to elicit a confession for use in a prosecution but rather to gain information to save a single life.[2]

A debate about this difficult issue is currently under way in Germany following the threat to use torture on a kidnapper in an effort to save the life of his victim.[3] Other countries, such as France, publicly condemn all forms of torture while quietly tolerating some of its worst forms. England employed tactics similar to those used by Israel—uncomfortable positions, loud music, hoods, and so forth—when interrogating suspected terrorists in Northern Ireland. But only Israel has been so repeatedly and viciously condemned for a practice that their current law does not even permit.

THE PROOF

The issue of torture, perhaps better than any other, illustrates the hypocritical double standard applied against Israel. Israel's record on the issue of torture is far better than that of any other Middle Eastern or any Muslim nation, and better than that of most democracies, including the United States, France, and Germany, but only Israel is repeatedly condemned for engaging in torture. For example, one of the four items comprising the complaint and demand portion of the divestiture petition that is currently circulating around university campuses includes the following: "We also call on [universities] to divest from Israel [until] Israel is in compliance with the United Nations Committee Against Torture 2001 Report, which recommends that Israel's use of torture be ended." This petition began circulating in 2002, three years after the Israeli Supreme Court rendered its decision prohibiting the use of physical pressures even short of what most countries, including the United States, regard as torture. The interrogation techniques explicitly prohibited by the Israeli Supreme Court include the following:

1. Making the suspect "crouch . . . on the tip of his toes for five minute intervals"

2. Making the suspect sit, handcuffed to a low chair in the uncomfortable "Shabach position" ("the suspect is cuffed with [one hand] placed inside the gap between the chair's seat and back support, while the other is tied behind him, against the chair's back support")

3. Covering the suspect's head with a "ventilated sack"

4. Playing "powerfully loud music"

It is worth reading the decision by Professor Aharon Barak, the president of the Israeli Supreme Court, which includes the following:

> The facts presented before this Court reveal that one hundred and twenty one people died in terrorist attacks between 1.1.96 to 14.5.98. Seven hundred and seven people were injured. A large number of those killed and injured were victims of harrowing suicide bombings in the heart of Israel's cities. Many attacks—including suicide bombings, attempts to detonate car bombs, kidnappings of citizens and soldiers, attempts to highjack buses, murders, the placing of explosives, etc.—were prevented due to the measures taken by the authorities responsible for fighting the above described hostile terrorist activities on a daily basis.[4]
>
> [The decision proceeds to prohibit all forms of physical pressure, then summarizes its holding as follows:]
>
> This decision opens with a description of the difficult reality in which Israel finds herself security wise. We shall conclude this judgment by readdressing that harsh reality. We are aware that this decision does not ease dealing with that reality. This is the destiny of democracy, as not all means are acceptable to it, and not all practices employed by its enemies are open before it. Although a democracy must often fight with one hand tied behind its back, it nonetheless has the upper hand. Preserving the Rule of Law and recognition of an individual's liberty constitutes an important component in its understanding of security. At the end of the day, they strengthen its spirit and its strength and allow it to overcome its difficulties.
>
> Consequently, it is decided that the order nisi be made absolute, as we declare that the GSS does not have the authority to "shake" a man, hold him in the "Shabach" position . . . force him into a "frog crouch" position and deprive him of sleep in a manner other than that which is inherently required by interrogation. Likewise, we declare that the "necessity" defense, found in the Penal Law, cannot serve as a basis of authority for the use of these interrogation practices, or for the existence of directives pertaining to GSS investigators, allowing them to employ interrogation practices of this kind.[5]

I know of no other Supreme Court decision acknowledging that the restrictions it imposes on interrogation will almost certainly cost the lives of its civilians, yet nonetheless prohibiting the use of effective but inhumane tactics.

In light of this courageous decision, it is ironic that in May 1999 the Dutch sections of Amnesty International publicly opposed the awarding of a human rights prize to the author of that, and many other, human rights rulings supporting Palestinian claims on the ground that "the Israel Supreme Court's decisions with regard to human rights . . . have been devastating." Amnesty International specifically claimed that "Israel is the only country in the world to have effectively legalized torture."[6] It should not be surprising that so many human rights advocates have lost faith in Amnesty International's objectivity when it comes to reporting on Israel.

Contrast the Israel Supreme Court decision with a decision of the U.S. Court of Appeals for the Eleventh Circuit in a case involving two kidnappers who were holding an adult victim for ransom. One of the kidnappers came to the family home of the victim to collect the ransom, and the police arrested him and demanded that he tell them the whereabouts of his confederate and the victim. When he refused, the policed "choked" the suspect and twisted his arm "until he revealed where [the victim] was being held." One judge characterized the police action as "rack and pinion techniques." Nonetheless, the Court of Appeals approved the actions as necessary for "a group of concerned officers acting in a reasonable manner to obtain information they needed in order to protect another individual from bodily harm or death."[7] The Supreme Court of Israel would not have approved this police action either in an ordinary criminal case or in a terrorist prevention situation.

The practice outlawed by the Israeli Supreme Court was similar both in kind and degree to that being used by the United States following September 11, 2001. On March 9, 2003, the *New York Times* reported on the pattern being followed by American interrogators. It includes forcing detainees to stand naked, with "their hands chained to the ceiling and their feet shackled." Their heads are covered with "black hoods"; they are forced "to stand or kneel in uncomfortable positions in extreme cold or heat," which can quickly vary from "100 to 10 degrees." The detainees are deprived of sleep, "fed very little," exposed to disorienting sounds and lights, and, according to some sources, "manhandled" and "beaten." In one case involving a high-ranking al-Qaeda operative, "pain killers were withheld from Mr. [Abu] Zubaydah, who was shot several times during his capture."[8]

A Western intelligence official described these tactics as "not quite torture, but about as close as you can get." There have been at least two deaths and seventeen suicide attempts attributed to these interrogation tactics. When Israel has employed similar although somewhat less extreme tactics, they were universally characterized as torture without even noting that they were nonlethal and did not involve the infliction of sustained pain.[9] This is what the U.N. Committee Against Torture concluded in 1997:

> The Committee Against Torture today completed its eighteenth session—a two-week series of meetings marked, among other things, by a spirited debate with Israel over Government-approved use during interrogations of what it termed "moderate physical pressure" in efforts to elicit information that could foil pending terrorist attacks. This morning the Committee said in official conclusion that such interrogation methods apparently included restraining in very painful conditions; holding under special conditions; sounding of loud music for prolonged periods; sleep deprivation for long periods; threats, including death threats; violent shaking; and use of cold air to chill—and that in the Committee's view, such methods constitute torture as defined by Article 1 of the Convention against Torture, especially when they were used in combination, which it said appeared to be the standard case.
>
> It called, among other things, for Israel to "cease immediately" the use of those and any other interrogation procedures that violated the Convention, and emphasized that no circumstances—even "the terrible dilemma of terrorism" that it acknowledged was faced by Israel—could justify torture.
>
> . . . Members of a Government delegation appearing before the Committee contend that such methods had helped to prevent some 90 planned terrorist attacks over the last two years and had saved many civilian lives, in one recent case enabling members of the country's General Security Service to locate a bomb. The delegation repeatedly denied that the procedures amounted to torture.[10]

Whether the procedures previously used by Israel and currently used by the United States did or did not constitute torture, the Supreme Court of Israel has now outlawed them.

Intelligence officials "have also acknowledged that some suspects have been turned over [by the United States] to security services in countries known to employ torture."[11] These countries include Egypt, Jordan, the Philippines, Saudi Arabia, and Morocco. Turning captives over to countries for the purpose of having them tortured is in plain violation of the 1984 International Convention Against Torture, to which we, and the countries to which we are sending the captives, are signatories.

An Egyptian government spokesman "blamed rogue officers" for any abuse in his country and said "there was no systematic policy of torture." He went on to argue, "Any terrorist will claim torture—that's the easiest thing. Claims of torture are universal. Human rights organizations make their living on these claims." The spokesman went on to brag that Egypt had "set the model" for antiterrorism initiatives and the United States is seemingly "imitat[ing] the Egyptian model."[12] When Israel too has claimed that allegations of torture made by some detainees who have provided information may be self-serving and exaggerated, Egyptian and other authorities have insisted that the detainees must be believed.

The *Wall Street Journal* reported that a U.S. intelligence official said that detainees with important information could be treated roughly:

> Among the techniques: making captives wear black hoods, forcing them to stand in painful "stress positions" for a long time and subjecting them to interrogation sessions lasting as long as 20 hours.
>
> U.S. officials overseeing interrogations of captured al-Qaeda forces at Bagram and Guantanamo Bay Naval Base in Cuba can even authorize "a little bit of smacky-face," a U.S. intelligence official says. "Some al-Qaeda just need some extra encouragement," the official says.
>
> "There's a reason why [Mr. Mohammed] isn't going to be near a place where he has Miranda rights or the equivalent of them," the senior federal law enforcer says. "He won't be someplace like Spain or Germany or France. We're not using this to prosecute him. This is for intelligence. God only knows what they're going to do with him. You go to some other country that'll let us pistol whip this guy." . . .
>
> U.S. authorities have an additional inducement to make Mr. Mohammed talk, even if he shares the suicidal commitment of the Sept. 11 hijackers: "The Americans have access to two of his elementary-school-age children," the top law enforcement official says. "The children were captured in a September raid that netted one of Mr. Mohammed's top comrades, Ramzi Binalshibh."[13]

There is no doubt that these tactics would be prohibited by the Israeli Supreme Court, but the U.S. Court of Appeals for the District of Columbia recently ruled that American courts have no power to even review the conditions imposed on detainees in Guantanamo or other interrogation centers outside the United States.[14]

Yet on university campuses across the world, not a word of criticism is heard about the widespread use of torture by any countries other than Israel. Certainly there is no criticism of Muslim countries and other countries that torture political dissidents routinely while facing far lesser threats than Israel faces. This double standard began at the United Nations, where far more time, attention, and condemnation have been directed at Israel's former use of nonlethal physical pressure to elicit lifesaving information than at lethal torture currently employed by many regimes, including the Palestinian Authority, against mere political opponents, dissidents, and collaborators. Those who accuse only Israel of using torture, without condemning the far more brutal and less justifiable practices of Middle Eastern nations, have the burden of justifying their palpable double standard.

20 Has Israel Engaged in Genocide against Palestinian Civilians?

THE ACCUSATION

Israel is guilty of genocide against the Palestinians and Arabs.

THE ACCUSERS

"I would like to propose publicly here in Gaza, Palestine—where the Intifadah began ten years ago at this time—that the Provisional Government of the State of Palestine and its President institute legal proceedings against Israel before the International Court of Justice (ICJ) in The Hague (the so-called World Court) for violating the 1948 Convention on the Prevention and Punishment of the Crime of Genocide. I am sure we can all agree that Israel has indeed perpetrated the international crime of genocide against the Palestinian People. The purpose of this lawsuit would be to demonstrate that undeniable fact to the entire world. These World Court legal proceedings will prove to the entire world and to all of history that what the Nazis did to the Jews a generation ago is legally similar to what the Israelis are currently doing to the Palestinian People today: genocide. . . . Certainly, Palestine has a valid claim that Israel and its predecessors-in-law—the Zionist Agencies and Forces—have committed genocide against the Palestinian People that actually started in 1948 and has continued apace until today in violation of Genocide Convention Article II(a), (b), and (c), inter alia.

"For at least the past fifty years, the Israeli government and its

140

predecessors-in-law—the Zionist Agencies and Forces—have ruthlessly implemented a systematic and comprehensive military, political, and economic campaign with the intent to destroy in substantial part the national, ethnical and racial group known as the Palestinian People. This Zionist/Israeli campaign has consisted of killing members of the Palestinian People in violation of Genocide Convention Article II(a)." (Francis Boyle, international law professor at the University of Illinois, presented in Gaza on December 13, 1997, in honor of the tenth anniversary of the first intifada[1])

THE REALITY

All nations must be judged in comparison with other nations facing comparable threats. Context is essential to any fair evaluation of a nation's behavior. Judged in this manner, Israel's action in its war against terrorism and external attack receives relatively high grades. Indeed, no other nation faced with comparable threats, both external and internal, has ever been more protective of enemy civilians, more willing to take risks for peace, and more committed to the rule of law.

THE PROOF

For three-quarters of a century, the Arab–Israeli war has been between Arab nations dedicated to genocidal aggression against civilians on the one hand and the Jewish state determined to protect its civilian population by taking defensive actions directed against military targets on the other hand. This war, in which the Arab side has consistently, illegally, and aggressively targeted civilians, and the Israeli side has consistently, lawfully, and defensively responded by attacking military targets, began in 1929 with the well-planned and carefully coordinated massacre of sixty Jewish children, women, old people, and other unarmed civilian residents of the biblical city of Hebron, in which Jews had lived peacefully and continually from time immemorial. The victims of this crime against humanity included many Jews who were not Zionists or settlers. The 1929 massacre was a harbinger of civilian massacres to come—much like Kristallnacht nine years later, which portended the Holocaust. It was also the first instance in Palestine of "ethnic cleansing," as all the Jews of Hebron were either murdered or transferred out of the city in which Jews had lived for millennia.

Prior to the establishment of the state of Israel, dissident groups—not under the control of the Jewish Agency (the pre-Israel government) or the Haganah (the pre-Israel official army)—did blow up the headquarters of the British colonial government located in a wing of the King David

Hotel, killing ninety-one people, many of whom were Jews and British colonial officials. The Irgun claimed that warnings had been called in before the King David was blown up. Dissident groups also killed civilians at Deir Yassin (see chapter 12) and some other locations, but these deviations were firmly condemned by the Jewish Agency. As soon as Israel became a state, its prime minister, David Ben-Gurion, disarmed these dissident groups by force, even sinking a ship loaded with weapons purchased by the Irgun. Sixteen Jews were killed by Haganah forces during the battle over the *Altalana*. No further acts of terrorism were committed by the Irgun or Lechi. Ben-Gurion also dismantled the Palmach—the permanently mobilized commando force loyal to Ben-Gurion's own party—and merged it into the IDF, which was and remains under civilian control.

Between 1948 and 1967, Palestinian fedayeen sponsored by Egypt and Syria murdered Israeli civilians in hundreds of cross-border raids. These murders took place before Israel occupied any Palestinian land or built any settlements outside of the area it controlled pursuant to the U.N. partitions and the cease-fire that followed the 1948 attack against the newly established Jewish state.

In the 1967 war, every single Arab army—including the Egyptian, Syrian, Palestinian, Jordanian, and Iraqi armies—targeted Israeli civilian population centers in violation of the laws of war. As previously documented, Syrian artillery and MIGs opened fire on Israeli towns, kibbutzim, and moshavim, including Degania. Jordan rained 6,000 shells on western Jerusalem and the suburbs of Tel Aviv, while its Hawker Hunter fighters dropped bombs on Netanya, Kfar Sirkin, and Kfar Saba. Iraqi planes strafed Nahalal, Afula, and civilian communities in the Jezreel Valley.

Damascus radio bragged that the Syrian air force was bombing Israeli cities. Jordanian forces were instructed to "destroy all buildings and kill everyone present," including civilians, if they captured portions of Jerusalem. Palestinian battle plans included the destruction of Israel and its inhabitants. Egyptian battle plans included the massacre of Tel Aviv's civilian population as the first step toward "the destruction of Israel." Posters in Cairo showed "Arab soldiers shooting, crushing, strangling and dismembering bearded, hook-nosed Jews."[2] As Nasser put it, "If war comes it will be total and the objective will be Israel's destruction."[3]

In sharp contrast, Israel did not target innocent civilians, although it certainly had the capacity to retaliate against the bombing of its civilian population centers. Israel threatened to bomb Amman and Damascus during the 1967 war if Jordanian and Syrian forces persisted in bombing Israeli cities, but it never did so. It bombed air bases, tank convoys, and other legitimate military targets, despite its enemies' targeting of Israeli civilians throughout the short war. In Oren's definitive account of the 1967 war, he concluded that the number of casualties among Arab civilians was "remarkably low" because Israel's military actions were conducted "far from major population centers."[4]

Since the end of the 1967 war, the entire focus of Palestinian aggression has been on civilians, both inside Israel and around the world. Global terrorism began in 1968 not as a last resort against a long occupation but as a first resort—really as a continuation of an illegal and immoral tactic that had been continuously used by the Arabs against the Jews since the beginning of the conflict. Targeting civilians was not a result of the occupation. To the contrary, the occupation was the result—at least in part—of a long Arab history of massacring civilians.

If occupation were to justify terrorism, then the post–Civil War Ku Klux Klan and the Night Riders who terrorized blacks during Reconstruction—which included the military occupation of the defeated Confederacy—would be seen as freedom fighters. Yet these terrorist groups have been relegated, quite deservedly, to the dustbin of history and are glorified only in racist films like *Birth of a Nation*. Many of those who march in support of Palestinian terrorists would be outraged if *Birth of a Nation* were to be shown on a college campus, or if the Klan were to be invited to recruit members, despite the reality that Palestinian terrorists have lynched and blown up more people—including hundreds of people of color[5]—than the Klan managed to kill in its century-long reign of terror. Those who praised and supported the murderers who dynamited the black church in which four girls were killed are now regarded as moral monsters. Yet those, such as the poet Tom Paulin, who praise and support terrorists who murder Jews are invited to speak on college campuses as honored guests.

To be sure, Palestinian civilians have died in the seventy-three-year-long war, but their numbers have been infinitesimal in comparison with the number of Palestinians and Arabs killed by Jordan, Syria, Iraq, and Iran during this same period. Even comparing innocent Israeli civilian casualties with Palestinian civilian casualties reveals that Israel has acted with restraint. And this does not take into account the reality that many of the so-called Palestinian civilians were not-so-innocent harborers and supporters of terrorists.

Moreover, the Palestinian deaths have resulted primarily from terrorists hiding among their own civilians, as in Lebanon, whereas the Israeli deaths have resulted from innocent civilians being specifically targeted. When Palestinians have been accidentally killed in a legitimate effort to prevent terrorism, Israel has expressed genuine regret. The murder of innocent Israelis, on the other hand, has generated celebration among Palestinians.

In 1994, Baruch Goldstein, a deranged Jewish doctor from Hebron, machine-gunned 29 Muslims at prayer. His family claimed that the repeated terrorist attacks against Jews made him snap. It is interesting that the same people who have always claimed that suicide bombers—and those who send them—were provoked by Israeli repression into their murderous acts quickly reject this claim when it is made by a Jewish family. In any event, Goldstein's individual terrorist attack against Palestinian civilians was strongly condemned by the Israeli government and the overwhelming majority of Israelis and Jews throughout the world. This is in sharp contrast to the Palestinian reaction to their "martyrs" who blow up innocent Israelis and Jews. These people are praised and their families are rewarded for their well-planned crimes.

In April 2002, following hundreds of suicide bombings that culminated in the Passover seder massacre of twenty-nine Jewish women, children, and men at prayer, the Israeli army entered the Jenin refugee camp, which has become a bomb-making factory and terrorist center. Instead of bombing the terrorists' camp from the air, as the United States did in Afghanistan and as Russia did in Chechnya, with little risk to their own soldiers but much to civilians, Israeli infantrymen entered the camp, going house to house in search of terrorists and bomb-making equipment, which they found. Twenty-three Israeli soldiers and fifty-two Palestinians, many of whom were combatants, were killed. This is now called a massacre by Palestinian propagandists. *By Israeli standards,* the deaths of fifty-two Palestinians, some of whom were not combatants, were a deviation from the norm, even though they placed their own soldiers at risk to minimize Palestinian civilian casualties. But *by Palestinian terrorist standards,* the killing of only a few handfuls of noncombatants is just another average day for their terrorism! Yet the hypocritical Palestinian cry of a Jenin massacre persists, and it is supported by the head of the United Nations Refugee Agency (UNRWA), Peter Hanson, a longtime apologist for, and facilitator of, terrorism. He characterized Israel's actions in Jenin as a "human rights catastrophe that has few parallels in recent history."

Not only was Jenin not a massacre or an unparalled catastrophe but it is regarded by many as a model of how to conduct urban warfare against terrorists hiding among civilians. A *New York Times* story of April 1, 2003, reported that the U.S. military has studied Israel's experience "in close-quarter fighting":

> United States Army officials have said they were particularly interested in how the Israeli Army used specially loaded tank rounds to blast holes through walls, without collapsing buildings, during fighting last year in the Jenin refugee camp. In Jenin, Israel also used bulldozers and wire-guided missiles fired from helicopters to overwhelm about 200 gunmen holed up inside the camp.[6]

The *Times* story quoted Israeli military historian Martin van Creveld stating that when he visited an American military camp, the Marines were "interested in what it would be like fighting a guerrilla war, especially urban warfare of the kind we were conducting in Jenin."

Professor van Creveld focused on bulldozers, helicopters, and "the moral and ethical problems that were sure to come" from fighting among noncombatants.[7]

An op-ed article in the *New York Times* on April 3, 2003, urged American commanders to "take a close look at the hard-learned lessons of Israel's experience with urban combat," because it provided "a good model for military tactics."

The piece went on to say:

> Twenty-nine Israeli soldiers were killed in these battles, all but six of them in the battle for the Jenin refugee camp. Although the number of Palestinian deaths is, of course, hotly debated, the Israeli estimate is 132 killed in Nablus and Jenin. Compared with casualty figures from urban combat in recent years—such as the fighting in Chechnya, where Russia's army lost at least 1,500 soldiers during its first assault on Grozny—these numbers are astonishingly low.[8]

A cover story in the June 2003 issue of *Atlantic Monthly* by a leading terrorist expert for the Rand Corporation also focused on the "lessons" America must learn from how Israel deals with terrorism.

A lead story in the "Ideas" section of the *Boston Globe* analyzed the ethical training received by Israeli soldiers and concluded, "The IDF army offers a model for us and other coalition forces."[9] It described the Israeli concept of "purity of arms," which "requires that soldiers put their own lives at stake in order to avoid harming non-combatants." It also requires them to respond only with "proportional force." The IDF's ethical code, which is "incorporated into the training of all Israeli soldiers," was compiled "with the assistance of some of the country's leading moral philosophers" and "enjoys widespread support among an otherwise divided citizenry." It requires every soldier to act "out of a recognition of the supreme value of human life" and commands them to "do all in [their] power to avoid causing harm to [noncombatants'] lives, bodies, dignity and property; and refrain from obeying blatantly illegal orders."

One of the members of the team who drafted the code is a well-known peace advocate, Professor Moshe Halbertal, who supports unilateral Israeli withdrawal from the territories. He recognizes that the strategy of the Palestinians in the recent intifada has been "to erase the distinction between combatants and noncombatants on both sides" by targeting Israeli civilians and having Palestinian terrorists blend into the

Palestinian civilian population. Nonetheless, he sees the challenge to Israel as directing its defensive measures "against those who insti-gate"[10]—a daunting challenge indeed with a Palestinian population that contains thousands upon thousands of instigators, facilitators, harborers, and supporters.

Israel has met that challenge better than any nation that has faced com-parable dangers. According to IDF figures compiled between September 2000 and March 2003, "18 percent of the nearly 2,000 Palestinians killed by Israeli forces . . . were civilians with no connections to acts of terror." This is a considerably lower ratio of civilian deaths than those achieved by other armies. Professor Michael Walzer of Princeton University, a strong critic of the Israeli occupation and the author of the 1977 classic *Just and Unjust Wars,* has noted that

> in battle, the Israeli army regularly accepted risks to its own men in order to reduce the risks that it posed on the civilian population. The contrast with the way the Russians fought in Grozny, to take the most recent example of large-scale urban warfare, is striking, and the crucial mark of that contrast is the very small number of civilian casualties in the Pales-tinian cities despite the fierceness of the fighting."[11]

This situation also compares favorably with the way we sometimes fought in Iraq, as we shall soon see.

Three stories illustrate the Israeli commitment to proportionality and to avoiding unnecessary civilian casualties. The first involves an Israeli attack directed against Salah Shehadeh, a leading Hamas commander who was responsible for hundreds of terrorist bombings. On several occasions, the army passed up opportunities to attack him "because he was with his wife or children. Each time Shehadeh's life was spared, he directed more suicide bombings against Israel." In other words, Israel was prepared to risk the lives of its own civilians in order to spare the lives of Palestinian civilians, including the wife of a major terrorist.

The second story was related by the chief of staff of the IDF, Moshe Ya'alon. It involves

> an intelligence officer who has prevented the air force from attacking a Palestinian target by withholding necessary information. The officer had believed, mistakenly, that the operation would put civilians at risk. "From the moral point of view, he deserves a commendation," commented Ya'alon. "From the operational one, he deserved to be removed from his post." The chief of staff added that he was "proud that we have officers" who take their moral responsibility so seriously.

The third story involves an Israeli infantry officer named Ze'ev who described

> a two-month stakeout of a Palestinian village in the West Bank. "Every night there was a shooting from the village, heavy gunfire. When you see a person with a gun, there's no question what you have to do. But when you see not three or four, but rather 40 people, with a single rifle, which moves around, you have to pick your targets carefully."
>
> Ze'ev recounts an incident in which a comrade had his commander's authorization to shoot an armed combatant below the knees—to wound, not to kill. The soldier shot twice, the second time after the enemy had fallen to the ground, and ended up killing a young boy with a rifle.

The soldier, according to Ze'ev, was "sent to jail, and thrown out of his unit"—a claim that could not be independently corroborated because only first names were given. It can be corroborated that violations of the code have been investigated and even prosecuted, although not in large numbers. According to the *Boston Globe* account,

> Ze'ev says that behaving with restraint under fire "is not a mission impossible." He adds, "If you have any sense of moral behavior, and you think for a second, there shouldn't be any problem sticking to the things that are in the code."
>
> But not everyone in the IDF thinks it's that simple. Elazar Stern, a brigadier general and chief of the IDF Education Corps, is aware of the moral ambiguities inherent in a soldier's job. "Part of what the nation demands of us," he says, "is a willingness to have our heads toss and turn on the pillow several times at night. And, if you're lucky, in the end you'll know that you did the right thing."[12]

This kind of tossing and turning is typical of Israeli soldiers who must make life-and-death decisions constrained by a rigid code of conduct. Their decisions are not always the right ones; mistakes inevitably occur in the fog of war, especially when terrorists deliberately hide behind civilians in order to provoke mistakes that add to the body count—a count that is central to their cruel arithmetic of death. Although Israeli soldiers make mistakes and overreact like soldiers in every army, at least there is an ethical code against which their actions can be judged. Palestinian terrorists have no similar constraints. Their orders are to kill and maim as many innocent civilians as possible, and they do so with zeal and with a promise of a heavenly bounty for every Jewish child and woman who is murdered.

The United States also has a code, but it is far more general than Israel's, emphasizing honor and tradition. American soldiers carry "Rules of Engagement" cards that instruct them to spare civilian targets unless they must be attacked in self-defense.[13] As with Israeli soldiers, these codes and cards do not resolve life-and-death decisions that must be made in the midst of combat. A dramatic and moving battlefield account of the Iraq war by Peter Maas in the *New York Times Magazine* of April 20, 2003, describes a situation faced by American marines that was similar to those frequently experienced by Israeli soldiers. Two American marines had been shot by Iraqis firing from moving trucks. The American commander instructed his forces

> to fire warning shots several hundred yards up the road at any approaching vehicles. As the half-dozen vehicles approached, some shots were fired at the ground in front of the cars; others were fired, with great precision, at their tires or their engine blocks. . . .
>
> But some of the vehicles weren't fully disabled by the snipers, and they continued to move forward. When that happened, the marines riddled the vehicles with bullets until they ground to a halt. . . .
>
> The vehicles, it only later became clear, were full of Iraqi civilians. These Iraqis were apparently trying to escape the American bombs that were landing behind them, farther down the road, and to escape Baghdad itself; the road they were on is a key route out of the city. The civilians probably couldn't see the marines, who were wearing camouflage fatigues and had taken up ground and rooftop positions that were intended to be difficult for approaching fighters to spot. . . . In the chaos, the civilians were driving toward a battalion of marines who had just lost two of their own in battle that morning and had been told that suicide bombers were heading their way.
>
> One by one, civilians were killed. Several hundred yards from the forward marine positions, a blue minivan was fired on; three people were killed. An old man, walking with a cane on the side of the road, was shot and killed. [O]ver a stretch of about 600 yards nearly a half dozen vehicles were stopped by gunfire. When the firing stopped, there were nearly a dozen corpses, all but two of which had no apparent military clothing or weapons.
>
> A squad leader, after the shooting stopped, shouted: "My men showed no mercy. Outstanding."
>
> I counted at least six vehicles that had been shot at. Most of them contained corpses or had corpses near them. The blue van, a Kia, had more than 20 bullet holes in its windshield. Two bodies were slumped over in the front seats; they were men in street clothes and had no weapons that I could see. In the back seat, a woman in a black chador

had fallen to the floor; she was dead, too. There was no visible cargo in the van—no suitcases, no bombs. . . .

A journalist came up and said the civilians should not have been shot. . . .

"How can you tell who's who?" said Corporal Ventura. He spoke sharply, as though trying to contain his fury. "You get a soldier in a car with an AK-47 and civilians in the next car. How can you tell? You can't tell."

He paused. Then he continued, still upset at the suggestion that the killings were not correct.

"One of these vans took out our tank. Car bomb. When we tell them they have to stop, they have to stop," he said, referring to civilians. "We've got to be concerned about our safety. We dropped pamphlets over these people weeks and weeks ago and told them to leave the city. You can't blame marines for what happened. It's bull. What are you doing getting in a taxi in the middle of a war zone?

"Half of them look like civilians," he continued. He was referring to irregular forces. "I mean, I have sympathy, and this breaks my heart, but you can't tell who's who. We've done more than enough to help these people. I don't think I have ever read about a war in which innocent people didn't die. Innocent people die. There's nothing we can do. . . ."

[T]he destroyed cars were several hundred yards from the marine positions that fired on them. The marines could have waited a bit longer before firing, and if they had, perhaps the cars would have stopped, or perhaps the marines would have figured out that the cars contained confused civilians. The sniper knew this. He knew that something tragic had happened at the bridge. And so, as we spoke in Baghdad, he stopped defending the marines' actions and started talking about their intent. He and his fellow marines, he said, had not come to Iraq to drill bullets into women and old men who were just trying to find a safe place. . . .

The civilians who were killed—a precise number is not and probably never will be available for the toll at Diyala bridge, or in the rest of Iraq—paid the ultimate price. But a price was paid, too, by the men who were responsible for killing them. For these men, this was not a clean war of smart bombs and surgical strikes. It was war as it has always been, war at close range, war as Sherman described it, bloody and cruel.

Although many innocent civilians were tragically killed in this single-day battle—probably more than in the week-long house-to-house warfare in Jenin—no one called it a massacre. It was an increasingly typical battle between a regular army and terrorists who hide among civilians. Israel, like America, is trying to fight these battles by striking an appropriate balance between self-defense and undue risk to innocent civilians.

In addition to the Code of Ethics by which all Israeli soldiers are trained, the Supreme Court of Israel—unique among the world's judiciaries—exercises control over military decisions that are challenged under the rule of law as creating undue risks to civilians. Consider, for example, the following choice-of-evils conundrum faced by the Israeli military when it is seeking to apprehend an armed terrorist who is holed up in a home. If the soldiers approach the home and knock down the door, they risk being shot by the terrorist, as many soldiers have been. So the army devised a tactic called the neighbor procedure, pursuant to which they first demanded the surrender of the terrorist over a loudspeaker. If that produced no results, they sent a Palestinian neighbor to the house bearing a message to the terrorist asking him to surrender.

According to the IDF this neighbor procedure worked effectively for more than twenty years, saving the lives of many Israeli soldiers, as well as of Palestinians who were being held in the house with the terrorist. In the summer of 2002, the procedure resulted in the first casualty of a Palestinian man named Nidal Abu M'Khisan, who was shot and killed by a terrorist who mistook him for an Israeli soldier. The Israeli army had given M'Khisan a bulletproof vest, but it did not save him.

As a result of this tragedy, in which a Palestinian civilian took a terrorist bullet intended for an Israeli soldier, several Israeli rights organizations brought a lawsuit seeking to have the Supreme Court enjoin any further use of the neighbor procedure. No other Supreme Court in the world would even hear such a case, especially not during an ongoing war. The Supreme Court of Israel not only heard the case but issued the injunction prohibiting the IDF from using this procedure in the future, even when the field commander believes that it poses little risk to the civilian and could save the lives of his soldiers.

The point is not whether this decision is right or wrong—I personally believe it is right—but rather that the Supreme Court of Israel is ordering the military to make its time-tested procedures comply with the rule of law, even if that means risking the lives of its own soldiers. From an objective view of the facts in context, it becomes eminently clear that no country in the modern history of warfare has been more protective of the rights of innocent noncombatant enemies than Israel. I challenge anyone to name a country that has faced comparable attacks on its civilian population and has responded with more solicitude toward its enemy civilians at such great risk to its own soldiers. Certainly not Great Britain or the United States, which bombed enemy cities, or France, or Russia, which did worse.

Israel is the only country in the history of modern warfare that has never dropped bombs indiscriminately on an enemy city in an effort to kill innocent civilians in retaliation for the deliberate bombing of its own civil-

ians. Even when it attacked those parts of Beirut that were home to terrorists, the Israeli air force made great efforts—although not always with
success—to avoid unnecessary civilian casualties.

Recall that when Israel sought to protect itself against Beirut-based
terrorism in 1982, it sent in a team of soldiers—led by then Major General
Ehud Barak, dressed as a woman—to target the terrorists themselves in a
building then being used as their base, instead of bombing the building
from the air, which would have resulted in many more casualties. This is
typical of the Israeli "retail," rather than "wholesale," approach to targeting terrorism. One can be critical of the Israeli air attacks on Beirut—as I
was and as many Israelis were—but to characterize Israel's self-defense
actions (even overreactions) as genocide and to compare them to Nazi
atrocities is to engage in a not-so-subtle form of international anti-
Semitism against the Jewish nation. It is interesting and significant that
Israel's enemies never compare the Jewish state to Mussolini's Italy, or
Stalin's Soviet Union, or Hirohito's Japan—only to Hitler's Nazi Germany. The comparison is obscene and anti-Semitic in intent as well as in
effect.

In fact Israel should be compared with the United States, in that both
countries make significant efforts to train their troops to avoid civilian
casualties and do not always succeed. In her book *Just War against Terror,*
University of Chicago philosopher Jean Bethke Elshtain sharply contrasts
the training films shown to U.S. soldiers (similar ones are shown to Israeli
soldiers) with a training film being widely used to recruit Islamic terrorists:

U.S. military training films include generous helpings of "what went
wrong" in various operations. "Wrong" refers not only to U.S. military
losses but also to operations that led to the unintentional loss of civilian
life. These films ask: How can such losses be prevented in the future in a
theatre of war? No one is encouraged, or even allowed, to call the killing
of civilians "God's will" or, even worse, an act carried out in God's name.

The [Islamic terrorist] video [which is "routine fare" in many radical
mosques, including the one attended by Zacarias Moussaoui and Richard
Reed] shows enemies being decapitated with knives after they are disarmed—something strictly forbidden by the laws of war. The film's nar-
rator intones: "You have to kill in the name of Allah until you are killed.
Then you will win your place forever in Paradise. The whole Islamic
world should rise up to fight all the sick unbelievers. The flag of Jihad
will be forever held high. Our enemies are fighting in the name of Satan.
You are fighting in the name of God."

The viewer is subject to "excited shouting as the militants notice that
one soldier is still alive. 'He is moving,' calls out a fighter. A militant
calmly bends down and runs a knife across the wounded conscript's

throat. The image of the blood pumping from his severed carotid artery is shown five times during the video."[14]

Since September 11, and especially during the war against Iraq, the United States government has committed virtually all of the wrongs for which Israel has been condemned. Indeed, many of the wrongs committed by Israel—and then replicated by the United States—were condemned by the United States itself in its annual State Department reports on human rights. For example, U.S. soldiers shot into a crowd of demonstrating Iraqis, killing more than a dozen, including two children under the age of 11.[15] Our troops claimed, as the Israeli troops have claimed in similar situations, that they were fired upon first by people in the crowd. The American government also pointed out, as the Israeli government has similarly pointed out, that combat troops are not trained to perform riot control and will occasionally overreact to provocations from an undifferentiated crowd of protesters, rock throwers, bomb throwers, and shooters. American soldiers have also been accused of shooting first and asking questions later when their checkpoints are approached by unidentified vehicles that fail to comply with an order to stop. The United States points to situations in which individuals and vehicles approaching a checkpoint have caused the deaths of U.S. soldiers. After an apparently pregnant woman blew herself up, killing and injuring Americans, our soldiers responded more aggressively to similar approaches. United States authorities have engaged in administrative detention of hundreds of suspected terrorists, Islamic militants, and others for long periods of time. American authorities have employed pressure tactics, bordering on nonlethal torture, in an effort to elicit information deemed necessary to prevent future acts of terrorism. By making these comparisons, I do not mean to single out the United States for criticism, as so many have done with regard to Israel. Indeed, both the United States and Israel have conducted themselves far better than other countries confronting terrorism and urban warfare. Comparisons with the Russians in Chechnya and the French in Algeria favor the United States and Israel. Nor do I mean to suggest that two wrongs make a right. Both the United States and Israel are justly criticized when they do wrong, as are all other nations. My point goes back to the international community's willingness—indeed, eagerness—to portray Israel as a unique or "prime" violator of human rights, when any objective comparative assessment will prove that although Israel has made mistakes and overreacted, its overall record is among the best in the world, perhaps *the* best in the world when the circumstances they face are taken into account.

Professor Francis Boyle, the American law professor who has become a spokesperson for Palestinian terrorist groups, is right about one thing: one side has attempted genocide during the Arab–Palestinian–Israeli conflict.

The self-proclaimed Arab War of Extermination in 1948, the targeting of Israeli cities by Arab armies during the 1948, 1967, and 1973 wars, and the continuous terrorist attacks that have killed thousands of Israeli, Jewish, and other civilians can be characterized as attempted genocide. Israel's efforts to protect its citizens from these mass murders by attacking Arab military targets can only be labeled as genocide by a bigot willing to engage in Orwellian turnspeak against a people that was truly victimized by the worst form of genocide.

Perhaps nothing more can be expected of Professor Boyle, who has long been a one-sided propagandist for Palestinian terrorism, but more is certainly expected of a Nobel Prize–winning author such as Jose Saramago, who recently characterized Israeli efforts to defend its citizens against terrorism as "a crime comparable to Auschwitz." When Saramago was pressed about "where . . . the gas chambers" are, he responded, "Not here yet."[16] This revolting comment is nothing short of obscene, and can only be explained by abysmal ignorance or a deep-seated and irrational hatred for the Jewish state. But ignorance alone cannot explain the alleged "reporting" of a "journalist" like Chris Hedges, who claimed to have personally observed Israeli soldiers "entice children like mice into a trap and murder them for sport."[17] This sort of reporting belongs alongside the report that appeared in the Saudi newspaper *Al-Riyadh* on March 10, 2002, describing the "well established fact" that the Jews use "the blood of Christian and Muslim children under the age of 10" to "prepare pastries for their holidays."[18]

21 Is Israel a Racist State?

THE ACCUSATION

The fact that Israel is a Jewish state with a law of return that entitles Jews and their families to become Israeli citizens only proves that it is a racist state.

THE ACCUSERS

"Israel, moreover, is the only country in the world today that has adopted, as a matter of official policy, the pursuit of a certain racial makeup of its citizenry: i.e., maintaining a Jewish majority. This policy, as is well known outside of the United States, is of course in direct violation of The International Convention on Elimination of All Forms of Racial Discrimination, which explicitly prohibits 'any distinction, exclusion, restriction or preference based on race, color, descent, or national or ethnic origin.'" (Ahmed Bouzid, president of Palestine Media Watch[1])

"Israel's Law of Return is another racist law. By it the state must accommodate any Jews from anywhere in the world that might, at any time, migrate to Israel. If four million Jews suddenly emigrate to Israel/Palestine, the Israeli government will accommodate them. In contrast, four million Palestinians that were dispossessed of their land and forced into exile when Israel was formed have no right of return because—in Ehud Barak's words—it would be 'national suicide.'" (Na'eem Jeenah, Islamic Association for Palestine[2])

"Of all the discriminatory laws and practices of Zionism, none can match the Israeli Law of Return for its inequity. This law which was enacted on 5th July 1950 affords to every member of the 'Jewish people' born anywhere in the world the right to immigrate to Israel and become a citizen upon arrival. At the same time, it denies this right to Palestinian Muslims and Christians who were born in Palestine and expelled during the successive wars of occupation." (Dr. Daud Abdullah, Palestinian Return Centre[3])

THE REALITY

Every other state in the area, including the Palestinian Authority, has an officially established religion, Islam, and discriminates both in law and in fact against non-Muslims, especially Jews. Israel, in contrast, is in practice a secular state that is religiously and racially pluralistic with freedom of religion for all. Moreover, several other states and the Palestinian Authority have laws of return, and Jordan has a law explicitly prohibiting Jews from becoming citizens, but only Israel—whose law grew out of a history of Jews being slaughtered because no other state, or Palestine under the British mandate, would accept Jewish refugees—is condemned for its law of return.

THE PROOF

Although Israel is a Jewish state, it is largely secular and accords complete freedom of religion to Muslims, Christians, and other religious groups. The only religious groups that are in any way discriminated against in Israel are Jewish groups that do not conform to the strictures of Orthodox Judaism. Conservative Jews, Reform Jews, and secular Jews are less than equal when it comes to issues such as marriage, conversion, and governmentally supported education. Put another way, there is freedom *of* religion for all in Israel, but there is less than complete freedom *from* religion for non-Orthodox Jews. I have been long critical of the Israeli government's policy toward Conservative, Reform, and secular Jews, although I understand that its sources lie in the quixotic nature of the Israeli political system, which gives the Orthodox disproportionate power because of the need to include them in coalitions of both the right and the left. But even with regard to non-Orthodox Jews, significant progress has been made in recognizing their rights both to practice a form of Judaism different from Orthodoxy and to practice no religion at all.

Despite the imperfections of the Israeli government's approach to religion, it is far more accepting of religious pluralism than any other country in the Middle East, any Muslim state in the world, and most Christian states throughout history, even today. To single out Israel for criticism because it is a Jewish state is clearly a form of international anti-Semitism, especially when the criticism is not coupled with comparable, or more severe, criticism of Muslim states that practice a far more discriminatory form of state-sponsored religion. Even the Palestinian Authority, which has long advocated a secular binational state in Israel (clearly as a ploy) and has been extremely critical of Israel as a Jewish state, recently declared Islam to be its official and sole state religion.[4] I have heard no criticism of this move by those who are so quick to condemn Israel for any deviation from an unrealistic perfection that no country has ever achieved.

With regard to Israel's law of return, there has been continuing controversy about whether it is primarily a religious law, a family reunification law, a reaction to ethnic discrimination, or some combination of these historical factors. More than any of these, it should be viewed as a humanitarian law. It followed the immigration waves during Israel's first years that brought Holocaust survivors along with refugees forced out of Arab countries. Since its passage, Jews have been rescued from the repression and anti-Semitism of the Communist bloc, from "disappearances" under Argentine dictators, and from famine in Ethiopia.

Some critics of the law characterize it as "racist." Aside from the obvious falsehood of this claim—which I will discuss in a moment—these critics are guilty of their usual double standard: Israel is far from the only country—and far from the only democracy—with comparable laws. Since the breakup of the Soviet Union, Russia has welcomed thousands of ethnic Russians from the former republics. Since 1945, millions of ethnic Germans have come to Germany from all over central and eastern Europe and the former Soviet Union. For almost fifty years, German immigration law even followed the official definition that "members of the German people are those who have committed themselves in their homelands to Germanness (Deutschtum), in as far as this commitment is confirmed by certain facts such as descent, language, upbringing or culture."[5] Other states, too, have similar laws and similar connections with their diasporas. Yet only Israel is attacked as racist for its nonracial law of return.

Although Jews (and certain of their relatives) are entitled to citizenship (subject to certain disqualifications for criminal activities), non-Jews may also seek citizenship, and many have, in fact, been welcomed by Israel as first-class citizens with all the rights accorded to Jewish citizens. In April 1999, Israel airlifted more than 100 Albanian refugees from Kosovo and invited them to live in Kibbutz Maagan Michael. These non-Jewish refugees joined a previous group of Muslims who escaped from the Bosnian Civil War in 1993. The refugees were given the choice to remain in Israel permanently or to return to Kosovo after the fighting.[6] Israel had previously offered asylum to non-Jewish refugees from other parts of the world embroiled in conflict. Many of those who escaped Soviet repression by emigrating to Israel were not Jewish (although most were related to Jews). The law of return was clearly a response to historic discrimination by other nations against Jews. It is surely understandable why Israel, as soon as it became a state, responded to that discrimination by opening its doors to every Jew, as well as to others seeking refuge or a better life.

There is, in fact, some discrimination against Arab citizens of Israel. Most cannot serve in the army, but few would choose to fight against fellow Arabs if given that option. Until recently, Arabs could not buy homes in certain Jewish areas, just as Jews cannot buy homes in Arab villages. A decision by the Israel Supreme Court in 2002 ruled that the government may not allocate land based on religion or ethnicity and may not prevent Arab citizens from living wherever they choose: "The principle of equality prohibits the state from distinguishing between its citizens on the basis of religion or nationality," Chief Justice Aharon Barak wrote. "The principle also applies to the allocation of state land. . . . The Jewish character of the state does not permit Israel to discriminate between its citizens."[7] It is fair to say that Israel, led by its progressive Supreme Court, is making considerable progress in eliminating the vestiges of anti-Arab discrimination that were largely a product of the refusal of the Arab world to accept a Jewish state. It is also fair to say that despite some lingering inequalities, there is far less discrimination in Israel than in any Middle Eastern, Arab, or Muslim nation.

The most primitive apartheid against non-Muslims is still openly practiced in some Arab countries.[8] Moreover, Jordan has a law of return that explicitly denies citizenship to all Jews, even those who lived there for generations. Its laws provide that citizenship is open "to any person who was not Jewish" and who meets certain other criteria.[9] Saudi Arabia similarly bases eligibility on religious affiliation. Germany long had a law of return, as do China and many other countries. Yet only Israel, which has citizens of virtually every religion, ethnicity, race, and national origin, is characterized by its enemies as racist or apartheid.

22 Is the Israeli Occupation the Cause of All the Problems?

THE ACCUSATION

The Israeli occupation is the longest and most brutal in modern history.

THE ACCUSERS

"Al Nakba [the original sin] is the largest, most carefully planned and longest ethnic cleansing operation in modern history. The population of 530 towns and villages have been expelled in 1948, removing 85 per cent of the Palestinians in the land that became Israel. Those who did not suffer this fate in the remaining part of Palestine are now in the grip of the most brutal, longest and only occupation in the world." (Salman Abu Sitta[1])

"The life of the ordinary Palestinian has been one long journey of misery and humiliation. Colonized, dispossessed, occupied and collectively punished and enduring ethnocide and starvation and further robbed of their homes and land for a crime committed by Europeans against Jews 50 years ago, the Palestinians no longer care what the West, or the Arabs for that matter, think. Suffering under the brutal Israeli regime and under the longest military occupation in recent history, they have, reluctantly, resorted to the "martyrdom operation"—in reaction to continued Israeli repression and carnage." (Article at www.mediareviewnet.com, in reaction to a photograph showing a Palestinian baby dressed as a suicide bomber[2])

THE REALITY

Other occupations, such as the Chinese occupation of Tibet, have been longer and less justified, and Israel ended its occupation in 1995, only returning to *some* areas to prevent terrorism. It has again offered to end the occupation in exchange for best efforts by Palestinian authorities to end the terrorism.

THE PROOF

As previously documented, the Palestinians have been offered a homeland on three separate occasions—in 1937, 1947, and 2000–2001—and each time have rejected the offer and responded with increased terrorism. It is quite remarkable that the Palestinians were offered anything after the Second World War, considering the fact that their leadership actively sided with the losing Nazis. Supporting the losing side generally does not result in offers of statehood. The Jews got the Balfour Declaration for supporting the right side in World War I. The Palestinians got a generous offer of partition after siding with Hitler.

I know of no situation in history where a state has twice rejected generous offers of statehood, responded with the massacring of civilians, then been rewarded for its rejectionism and crimes against humanity by still another offer of statehood. In 2000, the Palestinians were again offered statehood, this time quite understandably with a reduction in territory but with no reduction in control over the Palestinian population. For the third time, Palestinians responded with violence.

By any standard of morality and justice, the case for Palestinian independence and statehood is far weaker than the case for the independence and statehood of numerous other people seeking autonomy over their lives. The occupation of Tibet by China has been longer and more brutal and less justified by protective or military considerations, and there are many more Tibetans than there are Palestinians. Moreover, there exists no other state with a majority Tibetan population, whereas the Jordanian population is at least two-thirds Palestinian. The Chinese government has built far more settlements in Tibet than Israel has in the West Bank and Gaza. While Jewish settlers constitute a tiny minority in Palestinian areas, the Chinese have flooded Tibet with so many ethnic Chinese that Tibetans have become a minority in their own land:

> One policy has become increasingly prominent and may prove to be the most effective over time: the policy of population transfer of Chinese citizens into Tibet. Population transfer has made Tibetans a minority in Tibet, has damaged the Tibetan environment and facilitated human rights abuses.[3]

The Dalai Lama summarized the situation in 2000:

> After 50 years of Chinese rule, Tibet seems no closer to freedom. Although human rights appeals have had little effect thus far, these appeals will no doubt continue to be made; this may eventually help the Tibetans in their fight for self-determination and an end to population transfers. . . . In 1999 alone there have been six known cases of deaths resulting from torture and abuse. Authorities have expelled a total of 1,432 monks and nuns from their monasteries and nunneries. . . . There are 615 known and documented Tibetan political prisoners. . . . Since 1996, a total of 11,409 monks and nuns have been expelled. . . . Even today the present young reincarnate Panchen Lama is under virtual house arrest, making him the youngest political prisoner in the world. I am deeply concerned about this.[4]

A recent article in an international law review added the following:

> The rights denied to the Tibetans include: 1. Life, liberty and security have been violated. 2. Forced labour has been inflicted on the Tibetans. 3. Torture and cruel and degrading treatment have been inflicted. 4. Rights of home and privacy have been violated. 5. Freedom of movement within a state, and the right to leave and return to Tibet have been denied. 6. Marriages have been forced upon unwilling parties. 7. Property rights have been arbitrarily violated. 8. Freedom of religion and worship have been systematically denied. 9. Freedom of the expression and communication of ideas is totally lacking. 10. Freedom of association is denied. 11. The right to representative government is denied. 12. There is a wanton disregard for the economic rights of man in relation to his country's resources. 13. The right to a free choice of employment is denied. 14. Conditions of labour do not conform to minimum standards in respect of rest and limitations of hours. 15. The right to an adequate standard of living is denied. 16. The right to a liberal and efficient, non-discriminatory educational system is denied. 17. The right to participate in the cultural life of the community is denied. 18. The limitations imposed on the rights of the Tibetans far exceed any which are reasonably referable to the requirements of public morality, public order and the welfare of society.[5]

Despite this horrendous record, the United Nations has never condemned China or recognized the rights of Tibetans to self-determination. To the contrary, the international community rewarded China with the 2008 Olympics, and few who demand Palestinian statehood are ever heard on the far more compelling issue of Tibetan independence. Why? The same question can be asked about the Kurds, the Armenians in Turkey, the Chechens, the Basques, and dozens of other stateless groups, none of which have observer status at the United Nations or recognition by so many states or religious groups as the Palestinians do. Moreover, none of these other groups have been offered statehood and have rejected it on multiple occasions.

Israel has offered statehood to the Palestinians in exchange for a commitment by the Palestinian Authority to make its best efforts to end terrorism, and the Palestinian response has been an escalation of terrorism. The Palestinians will eventually have a state, but it should not come as a reward for terrorism.

I have strongly opposed the occupation of Palestinian population centers since 1967, but Israel's actions have been far more justified militarily, legally, and morally than other longer occupations that have not been the object of nearly as much condemnation. Moreover, the Israeli occupation, unlike any of the other current occupations, has brought considerable dividends to the Palestinians, including significant improvements in longevity, health care, and education. It has also brought about a reduction in infant mortality. Between 1967 and 1994, when Israel was responsible for health and medical services, more than 90 percent of infants and schoolchildren were immunized, there was an increase in control of childhood contagious diseases, and the infant mortality rate declined from 100 to 150 deaths per 1,000 live births in the years during which the West Bank and Gaza were occupied by Jordan and Egypt to 20 to 25 deaths per 1,000 live births by the end of the Israeli occupation in 1994.[6] Ironically, being occupied by Israelis as distinguished from Jordanians and Egyptians also promoted Palestinian nationalism. None of these dividends alone or in combination justify an unwanted occupation, but they do place a burden of justification on those who condemn *only* the Israeli occupation without even expressing concern for other far more brutal and less justified occupations.

Nor would Palestinian terrorism necessarily end if Israel gave back every inch of land it occupied in defending itself against Jordanian and Egyptian aggression in 1967. In the first place, Palestinian terrorism preceded the occupation as the tactic of choice. Beginning in the 1920s, terrorist attacks targeted Jews—Zionists and non-Zionists alike. Terrorism got worse in the 1930s and continued after Israel became a state but before it occupied the West Bank and Gaza. Between 1951 and 1955, nearly a thousand Israeli civilians were killed by fedayeen in cross-border attacks. Among the terrorist attacks conducted against Israeli civilians *before* the occupation of the West Bank and Gaza Strip were the following: the mass murder of eleven bus passengers returning from vacation in Eilat in 1954 (the terrorists first killed the driver and then boarded the bus and shot each passenger), and the 1955 shooting of children and teenagers in a synagogue, in which four were killed and five wounded. This latter attack was similar to the Ku Klux Klan bombing of a black church in Alabama in which four children were killed.

Hamas, Hezbollah, and other rejectionist groups have vowed to continue terrorism even if the occupation were to end. A recent poll taken at Najah University in Nablus found that "87% of Palestinians surveyed were in favor of continuing terror attacks" and "87.5% were in favor of 'liberating all of Palestine.'"[7] If terrorism succeeds in securing a Palestinian state in the West Bank and the Gaza Strip, why should it not continue to be used to secure what the vast majority of Palestinians say they want? As Thomas Friedman put it in a column shortly after the poll,

> Palestinians who use suicide bombers to blow up Israelis at a Passover meal and then declare "Just end the occupation and everything will be fine" are not believable. No Israeli in his right mind would trust Yasser Arafat, who has used suicide bombers when it suited his purposes, not to do the same thing if he got the West Bank back and some of his people started demanding Tel Aviv. The Palestinians cannot yet be trusted to control these areas on their own if Israel withdraws.[8]

Friedman concluded with a rhetorical question that all non-Israelis should ask themselves: "Would you trust Yasser Arafat to police your neighborhood?"[9]

23 Has Israel Denied the Palestinians Statehood?

THE ACCUSATION

Israel has denied statehood to the Palestinian people, who deserve statehood more than any other stateless and occupied group.

THE ACCUSERS

"The aims of Israel are clear, for, as Zionist and Israeli leaders have been saying candidly for several generations, Palestinian national claims are neither admissible nor valid. . . . With Israel, the U.S. has resolutely opposed the idea of national self-determination." (Edward Said and Christopher Hitchens[1])

"Why aren't Europeans as sympathetic with the Tibetans, Chechens or Kurds as they are with the Palestinians?

"This is another perverse lapse, because were the West to do for the Palestinians what it did for the Iraqi Kurds, Yasser Arafat would be a very happy man indeed. Besides, neither does Saddam Hussein nor the Chinese Communist Party come to Western capitals every other month begging (using blackmail would be more accurate) for funds to subsidize their machines of oppression and dispossession against Kurds and Tibetans.

"But even if this argument were valid, and the West was silent about the crimes against other oppressed peoples, does this make what Israel does less of a crime?

"There is a paradoxical invitation to immorality inherent in this perverse logic. Supporters of Israel acknowledge that Israeli society is engaged in an immoral endeavor to subjugate, dispossess and oppress the Palestinians. They know that what they are doing is immoral and illegal, and they have chosen to be led by a notorious war criminal who has made no secret of his intention to use only violence to impose his will on a captive population.

"When these simple facts are pointed out, supporters of Israel cry 'racism!' Criticizing these crimes becomes perverse racism, while acquiescing in them, even defending them, becomes the correct attitude. Immorality turns into moral rectitude, and the whole world becomes the 'underworld,' a fraternity of crime and in crime." (Abdelwahab el-Affendi, Senior Research Fellow, Center for the Study of Democracy, University of Westminster[2])

THE REALITY

The Palestinians never sought statehood when they were occupied by Jordan and Egypt. Historically they wanted to be part of Syria. The claim of Palestinian statehood began as a tactic to eliminate the Jewish state of Israel. Moreover, the Palestinian claim to statehood and independence is no stronger, and in some cases far weaker, than the claims of the Tibetans, the Kurds, the Basques, the Chechens, the Turkish Armenians, and other stateless groups.

Yet the Palestinian claim has been leapfrogged over other more compelling claims for one major reason: the Palestinians have attracted worldwide attention by murdering thousands of innocent people, whereas the Tibetans have never resorted to terrorism, and the other groups have employed only episodic local terrorism, which has not been rewarded by the international community in the way that Palestinian terrorism has been so richly rewarded. The Palestinian success in bringing their cause to the attention of the world has not, however, brought them a state, because neither Israel nor the United States has been willing to reward terrorism in the way that the United Nations, the European Community, the Vatican, and others have.

THE PROOF

On the merits, the Palestinian cause is far weaker than that of many other stateless people. Why then does the extreme left, particularly the European left, along with the extreme right, champion the cause of the Palestinians, while largely ignoring the far more meritorious causes of the Tibetans, the Kurds, and other stateless peoples? By any objective standard of morality, the claims of the Tibetans and Kurds—to focus on only two stateless groups—are far more compelling than the claims of the Palestinians. There are many more stateless Tibetans and Kurds than there are stateless Palestinians. The Tibetans and the Kurds have been treated far more brutally by their occupiers than have the Palestinians. There is already one state where a majority of the population is Palestinian, whereas neither the Tibetans nor the Kurds have any state of their own.

The Tibetans have employed only lawful and legitimate means of seeking redress, and the Kurds have relied primarily on such means, whereas from the very beginning the Palestinians have employed crimes against humanity, targeting the most vulnerable of civilians. The Tibetans and the Kurds have always sought independence and statehood, whereas the Palestinians have had many opportunities to achieve statehood, beginning with the *Peel Report,* the U.N. partition, the Jordanian and Egyptian occupations, and the offers made at Camp David and Taba. The Palestinians never sought statehood, except as a tactic to destroy Israel.

The claims of the Kurds and the Tibetans under international law are far superior to those of the Palestinians. The Palestinians supported the losing side in every war of the twentieth century, including the First World War, the Second World War, the Israeli War of Independence, and the Gulf War, whereas the Tibetans and the Kurds have not aligned themselves with the evils of Nazism, terrorism, and Saddamism. A majority of Palestinians support the destruction of a U.N. member state, whereas neither the Tibetans nor the Kurds seek the destruction of any state.

Yet despite the significantly more compelling claims by the Tibetans and the Kurds, neither group has ever received any recognition from the United Nations, the European community, the Vatican, or any other official body. Moreover, intellectuals of the extreme right and the extreme left have largely ignored their causes. A heavy burden falls upon those selective moralists who champion a weaker cause while neglecting stronger ones.

Palestinians have been denied statehood by their own leaders, who have rejected—time after time—offers that would have led to statehood. The historian Benny Morris writes of the "instinctive rejectionism that was like a dark thread through Palestinian history."[3] Israel has stood ready—and stands ready today—to offer the Palestinians statehood, in exchange for the Palestinian Authority's making genuine best efforts to stop terrorism by those Palestinian groups committed to continuing their crimes against humanity until Israel is destroyed. That is a perfectly reasonable condition that any democratic nation, faced with comparable dangers, would demand.

24 Is Israel's Policy of House Destruction Collective Punishment?

THE ACCUSATION

The Israeli policy of house destruction is collective punishment prohibited by international law.

THE ACCUSERS

"The demolition of [empty] houses by Israeli tanks in the Rafah Refugee Camp is not much different from the scene of the World Trade Center [in which more than 2,500 people were killed] which was destroyed by the terrorists whom we have agreed here to combat and eliminate.

"The Security Council 'is practicing a double standard in not denouncing Israeli actions' while 'denouncing the perpetrators of the September 11th destruction.'" (Statement by the Syrian representative to the Security Council[1])

THE REALITY

Whether it is wise or unwise, the Israeli policy of demolishing houses that were used to facilitate terrorism or owned by people who assisted terrorists is an economic penalty for complicity with murder. It is not particularly effective, since the houses are rebuilt with money provided by sympathizers, but so long as it is limited to houses that are owned by accessories to terrorism it is not collective punishment. Moreover, the concept of collective accountability for terrorism that is widely supported by the vast majority of Palestinians and their leadership is entirely consistent with law and morality.

THE PROOF

Terrorism against innocent civilians is, of course, the ultimate form of collective punishment. Every Israeli—regardless of his or her support for or opposition to particular governmental policies—is targeted for death just for being Israelis or Jews. Yet those who support Palestinian terrorism complain most loudly when a home used by a terrorist is destroyed as an economic deterrent against those who harbor terrorists.

Because of the impossibility of deterring the terrorists themselves, especially suicide bombers, it is important to direct deterrence at those who send them, those who facilitate their actions, and those who can have some influence over them. Whenever a deterrent is directed against anyone other than the immediately culpable actor, it can be deemed a form of collective punishment. Although collective punishment is prohibited by international law, it is widely practiced throughout the world, including by the most democratic and liberty-minded countries. Indeed, no system of international deterrence can be effective without some reliance on collective punishment. Every time one nation retaliates against another, it collectively punishes citizens of that country. The American and British bombings of German cities punished the residents of those cities. The atomic bombings of Hiroshima and Nagasaki killed thousands of innocent Japanese for the crimes of their leaders. The bombing of military targets inevitably kills civilians.

Beyond the killing and wounding of nonculpable individuals, there is collective economic punishment, such as U.N.-approved sanctions and the bankrupting of an enemy nation's economy, which is a common weapon of both hot and cold wars. Nations that wage aggressive war and are defeated often lose territory, and such a loss may well punish innocent residents of that territory. Many ethnic Germans, some of whom did not support Hitler, were forced to relocate following Germany's defeat in World War II. Collective punishment is a matter of degree, with the Nazi concept of Sippenhaft—the murder of kin or townsfolk—at one end of the continuum and economic consequences of aggression at the other. Calling something collective punishment is often a political or public relations tactic calculated to confuse rather than to clarify. There is much wrong with certain types and degrees of collective punishment. But there is little wrong—and often something very right—about some kinds of collective accountability for the actions of leaders.

For example, it was right for the entire German people to suffer for what their elected leader had unleashed on the world. The few Germans who fought against Hitler should have been rewarded, but the vast majority of Germans should have been held accountable for their complicity with evil. In a perfect world, the accountability would have been imposed in direct proportion to personal complicity, with those most directly involved being imprisoned and those less directly involved being made to suffer economic deprivation. The German people were promised that they would benefit from a Nazi victory, which is part of the reason so many supported Hitler. Therefore, it was just for them to suffer from a Nazi defeat, even though some among the sufferers were less culpable than others. That is part of what it means to be a nation or a people. Those who start wars and lose them often bring suffering to their people. That is rough justice. It is also a deterrent to unjust wars.

Applying this principle to terrorism, it is not unjust to make the cause itself suffer for terrorist actions committed on its behalf, especially if there is widespread support for the terrorism within the cause. Consider, for example, a group of extremist antiabortionists, some of whose members murder abortion doctors, blow up abortion clinics, and threaten pregnant women seeking abortions. It would be absurd to reward their terrorism by restricting a woman's right to choose abortion. It would be justified to set back their cause if they persisted in or increased their terrorism, especially if the terrorism were widely supported by rank-and-file members of the group.

In this context, recall the 2002 poll described earlier that found 87 percent of Palestinians supported continuing terrorist attacks. Since these supporters hope and expect to benefit collectively from the terrorism, it is just (albeit imperfectly just) to hold the cause collectively accountable for the murderous acts perpetrated in its name and under its ultimate control. If this benign form of collective accountability can effectively save innocent lives by deterring terrorism, the balance of justice weighs in its favor.

The kind of suicide terrorism practiced by Palestinians—mass murder of perfectly innocent civilians with the widespread logistical, financial, religious, political, and emotional support of a large majority of the civilian population—challenges us to rethink the classic bright-line distinction between combatants and noncombatants. This line, which lies at the core of the international law of war, has been exploited in the interest of terrorism. Palestinian terrorists have learned how to use civilians as both swords and shields: they target Israeli civilians, then hide behind Palestinian civilians when the Israeli military comes after them. They use noncombatants as shields for combatants. They deliberately place their bomb-making factories adjacent to schools, hospitals, and other civilian buildings.

The result is that Israel must choose between employing wholesale self-defense tactics such as air strikes that risk killing large numbers of noncombatants among whom the combatants are hiding and employing retail tactics such as house-to-house combat that risk the lives of Israeli soldiers, as they did in Jenin. There is no precise formula for calculating the appropriate combatant/noncombatant ratio even in conventional warfare.

A moral nation must be prepared to place *some* of its own soldiers at risk to prevent the collateral killing of enemy civilians, but it need not risk the lives of *many* of its own combatants to achieve this salutary aim. The proper moral ratio should depend, at least in part, on the complicity of the noncombatants. If many of them willingly allow combatants to hide among them, if they provide support for the combatants, if they make martyrs of the murderers, their own complicity increases and they move closer to combatant status on what has become a continuum rather than a bright line separating civilians from combatants. An army of liberation whose purpose is to rescue nonconsenting citizens from human rights abuses committed against *them* by their unelected *leaders* should employ a different moral ratio than that used by an army fighting against a mixed group of civilians and combatants who mutually support each other in committing crimes against humanity.

How far then along the continuum of collective accountability would it be just to move in order to combat terrorism? Certainly not to the point of deliberately targeting completely innocent people for murder. Indeed, that is precisely what the terrorists do. But economic sanctions imposed on supporters of terrorism are fair and may be effective. Even if some people who do not support terrorism feel some economic impact, it seems a small moral price to pay for saving many innocent lives, especially since those who support the terrorists expect to reap the benefits of the terrorism.

Whenever collective economic punishment is imposed on those who support terrorism, I am always flabbergasted to hear the protestations made in high moral dudgeon by those who themselves support lethal terrorism, such as Yasser Arafat. Equally hypocritical are those academics who support the boycotting of every Jewish Israeli scholar, regardless of their individual views of Israeli policy, then complain about collective punishment of Palestinians who are themselves complicit in terrorism. A boycott of all Israeli scholars and divestment from all companies that do business with Israel are, of course, acts of collective punishment.

The debate over collective punishment of those who are complicit in terrorism reminds me of the infamous Fall River rape case (fictionalized in the film *The Accused*), in which there were several categories of morally and legally complicit individuals: those who actually raped the woman; those who held her down; those who blocked her escape route; those who cheered and encouraged the rapists; and those who could have called the police but did not. No rational person would suggest that any of these people were entirely free of moral guilt, although reasonable people might disagree about the legal guilt of those in the last two categories. The objection to imposing legal responsibility on people in these two categories would be diminished if the only sanction against them were economic—a fine, say, or civil liability. Their accountability for rape is surely a matter of degree, as is the accountability for terrorism of those who cheer the terrorists, make martyrs of them, encourage their own children to become terrorists, or expect to benefit from terrorism. There is nothing morally wrong with holding such complicitors accountable so long as the consequences imposed on them are proportional to their complicity.

The U.S.-led economic sanctions against Iraq, Libya, and Cuba are collective punishments imposed on large populations for the deeds of their leaders. So were the sanctions and boycotts imposed against Israel by the Arab League. Israel's policy of demolishing the homes of terrorists or those who harbor them is a soft form of collective punishment directed against the property of those who are deemed somewhat complicit. That it occasionally has an impact on innocent people detracts from its moral purity, but to a considerably lesser degree than widespread economic sanctions directed against entire nations. Yet the United Nations has supported such economic sanctions even as it has condemned Israel's policy on punishing those who assist terrorists.

The U.S. policy of confiscating cars, boats, airplanes, and homes used to facilitate the drug trade is also a form of collective accountability designed to deter people from allowing their property to be used by drug smugglers. It may well be a questionable policy, but it has not incurred the kind of condemnation to which Israel has been subjected for taking far less questionable actions to protect against a far more serious evil.

Israel empties the homes, of course, before bulldozing them, but on a couple of occasions people have been killed, including a protester who threw herself in front of the bulldozer and was apparently not seen by its operator. Although she was characterized by the media as a peace activist—implying that she was a nonpartisan supporter of peace—nothing could be farther from the truth. She belonged to a radical pro-Palestinian group of zealots—some from the extreme left, others from the extreme racist "right wing"[2]—who are one-sided supporters of Palestinian terrorism. Members of the International Solidarity Movement are taught to "be sensitive" to suicide bombers, because "they are giving their lives for their land and their people." They are directed "to consult with the Palestinians" before they do anything. They serve as human shields, working closely with Palestinian terrorist groups and protecting *only* Palestinians from Israeli soldiers. They have never offered to serve as shields protecting Israeli civilians against Palestinian terrorism. They do not support peace.

Instead, these zealots advocate the victory of Palestinian terrorism over

Israeli self-defense. They receive "funds from both the Palestinian Authority and Hamas, and Shadi Sukiya, a senior member of Islamic Jihad in Jenin who was involved in the planning of several thwarted suicide bombing attacks was arrested by I.D.F. troops while hiding in the offices of the International Solidarity Movement" in March 2003.[3] And in April 2003 two suicide bombers from England hid among the group, even attending a service conducted by it, just days before one of them blew himself up along with three Israelis.[4] The "solidarity" group then condemned Israel for its response to the murders.

The media should stop referring to these people as peace activists and should call them what they are: active supporters and facilitators of Palestinian terrorism. Nevertheless, there is no excuse for the kind of negligence by those responsible for house demolitions that resulted in the death of the zealot, but absent physical harm to individuals, the economic sanction of home destruction is entirely moral if it is limited to those who bear some moral complicity in the terrorism that is sought to be deterred.

The major problem with the destruction of houses involved in terrorism is not with its morality. A nonlethal approach like this is among the most moral and calibrated responses to terrorism—far more so than massive military retaliation, which inevitably produces collateral deaths of noncombatants (especially when combatants blend in with noncombatants and when noncombatancy is often a matter of degree). The problem with destruction of houses is that it plays poorly on television. Indeed, in some Muslim countries viewers are led to believe that the houses are destroyed with people still in them!

Even when it is clear that no one is inside, the inevitable picture of the crying woman bemoaning the loss of her home creates sympathy, even if that same woman was yesterday encouraging her son to become a martyr and tomorrow will be cheering at the news of an Israeli restaurant being blown up with a dozen teenagers inside. (If the terrorists would agree to give advance warning that they were going to blow up a building, the way the Israelis do, then there might be some argument for moral equivalency.)

House destruction is also ineffective because Hamas continues to pay people whose houses are destroyed enough money to build a bigger house. (Saddam Hussein had announced in April 2002 that he would pay the family of any suicide bomber who killed Jews $25,000 in cash, but that stream of payment ended after he was toppled.) Under U.S. law, anyone who agrees in advance to pay the family of suicide bombers is a conspirator in terrorism and murder.

The international community must come to accept the justice of directing proportionate, nonlethal deterrents against those who support and benefit from terrorism, rather than threatening meaningless sanctions against the suicide terrorists themselves. This is both fair and potentially effective as a deterrent against many types of terrorism, especially those that rely on suicide bombers. The Associated Press reported on May 21, 2003, that Palestinians whose houses were destroyed by the Israeli military have expressed anger at Palestinian terrorists who they say invited attack by firing rockets from their town. According to Mohammed Zaaneen, one of the Palestinian farmers, "[The terrorists] claim they are heroes [but they] brought us only destruction and made us homeless. They used our farms, our houses and our children . . . to hide."[5]

As we will see in chapter 28, the Israeli Supreme Court recently ruled that only people directly involved in acts of terrorism may be moved from one part of the occupied territories to another part. This important decision will surely be cited as a precedent for those arguing that house destruction may be used only against people who are complicit in terrorism.

In a detailed analysis of Israeli responses to suicide bombings, the *New York Times* concluded that Israel had achieved considerable success in stemming many attacks—but at a cost. It described one case in which a man named Ali Ajouri had dispatched two suicide bombers who had killed five civilians. The Israeli army blew up Ajouri's family home and charged his sister with "sewing bomb belts for the attackers" and his brother with assisting the murderers. Then they shot Ali Ajouri himself while he was trying to escape. He was a member of the Al-Aksa Martyrs Brigade, which specializes in suicide bombing.

Palestinians—70 to 80 percent of whom still support suicide bombing, according to opinion polls cited by the *New York Times* on April 5, 2003[6]—have criticized these tactics, although "the militants themselves concede that the measures have made it harder to stage attacks."[7] The Ajouri home "has been largely rebuilt." The lives of his victims cannot be rebuilt. While civil libertarians may disagree about whether the measures taken by Israel are or are not excessive, no reasonable person of goodwill can plausibly claim they constitute gross violations of human rights or are in any way comparable to the acts of terrorism they are trying to prevent—or to Nazi tactics, or even to the tactics currently being used by the most "progressive" Arab regimes, such as Jordan or Egypt. They are, in fact, comparable to measures taken by other democracies such as the United States and Great Britain.

25 Is Targeted Assassination of Terrorist Leaders Unlawful?

THE ACCUSATION

The Israeli policy of targeted assassination of terrorist leaders is murder prohibited by international law.

THE ACCUSERS

"Assassinations have been part of Israel's security policy for many years. Israel is the only democratic country which regards such measures as a legitimate course of action. This policy is patently illegal, according to both Israeli and international law, a policy whose implementation involves a high risk of hurting bystanders and from which there is no turning back even if errors are uncovered after the fact. Israel must cease assassinating Palestinians immediately." (Yael Stein of the Israeli human rights organization B'Tselem[1])

THE REALITY

Targeting the military leaders of an enemy during hostilities is perfectly proper under the laws of war, which is what Israel—as well as the United States and other democracies—has done.

THE PROOF

In one sense, the polar opposite of collective punishment is targeted assassination. This tactic seeks to prevent future terrorism by incapacitating

173

those who are planning to carry it out but are beyond the reach of other methods of incapacitation, such as arrest. Tyrannical regimes have widely employed an extreme form of targeted assassination against perceived enemies at home and abroad. Hitler had his rivals murdered with impunity. Stalin took his campaign of targeted assassination around the world, even to Mexico, where his operatives murdered Leon Trotsky.

The United States has certainly tried to assassinate foreign leaders over the years. Its hit list has included Fidel Castro, as well as Patrice Lumumba, Muammar el-Qaddafi, and Saddam Hussein. Although the United States did not directly murder Salvador Allende or Ngo Dinh Diem, it certainly played an active role in helping others to dispatch them. Recently, it again targeted Saddam Hussein, his children, and his generals, and has put bounties on the heads of Osama bin Laden and Mullah Mohammad Omar. Other democratic nations have also given their agents a "license to kill" in extreme situations.

Targeted assassination, like collective punishment, operates along a continuum. At the hard end is the widespread targeting of all perceived political opponents, as Hitler and Stalin practiced it. At the soft end is what the United States and Israel currently do: targeting specific terrorist leaders who are actively involved in planning or coordinating terrorist attacks and who cannot be arrested. An example of such a target was Yehiya Ayash, known as "the Engineer," the chief bomb maker for Hamas, whom Israeli agents killed in January 1996 by placing explosives in his mobile phone. Another example was the April 2003 Israeli rocket attack on a car that killed the leader of Islamic Jihad, Mahroud Zatme. His organization issued a statement "condemning the killing" but boasting that "the martyr was the engineer of bombs and explosive belts that killed tens and wounded hundreds of Zionist occupiers,"[2] meaning Jewish children and other civilians. No one else was killed in the attack on Zatme.

The vice of targeted assassination is that those who authorize the hit are prosecutor, judge, and jury—and there is no appeal. In Israel, the decision regarding who is an appropriate target is generally made by high-ranking government officials with political accountability. The virtue of targeted assassination, if the targets are picked carefully and conservatively, is precisely that it is targeted and tends to avoid collateral damage and collective punishment. Albert Camus's "just assassin" was employing targeted assassination against an evil wrongdoer, and he refused to proceed in the face of collectively (or collaterally) punishing the evildoer's young niece and nephew. Even where there are collateral victims, there are fewer of them than in typical military reprisals.

Under international law and the laws of war, it is entirely legal to target and kill an enemy combatant who has not surrendered. Palestinian terrorists—whether they are the suicide bombers themselves, those who recruit them, those in charge of the operation, or commanders of terrorist groups—are undoubtedly enemy combatants, regardless of whether they wear official uniforms or three-piece suits. It is lawful to kill an enemy combatant even when he is sleeping, as the United States tried to do with Saddam Hussein, so long as he has not surrendered. Nor need he be given an opportunity to surrender. He must take the initiative; otherwise the soldier on the other side will risk being fired upon. The Israeli government generally targets only terrorists, not political leaders, as evidenced by the fact that it has repeatedly protected the life of Yasser Arafat, who is both a political leader and a terrorist. Israel has also announced that it will stop targeting Hamas terrorists if the Palestinian Authority would start arresting them.

The key issue in evaluating targeted assassination is whether the targeting is sufficiently focused on the terrorist without unduly risking the lives of innocent (and sometimes not-so-innocent) civilians. For example, when the United States targeted Qaed Salim Sinan Al-Harethi—al Qaeda's top man in Yemen—for assassination in Yemen, it blew up the car in which he was traveling, killing him and other occupants of the car. The only real question was whether those occupants were themselves appropriate targets. Similarly, when Israel bombed a terrorist headquarters in Gaza, targeting Mohammed Deif, a leading Hamas terrorist, the appropriate criticism—in which I joined—was that the action was not sufficiently targeted, in light of the fact that several innocent bystanders were killed or injured. Many Israelis shared my criticism of that particular assassination, and the Israeli military acknowledged that the intelligence on which that action was based was flawed. When the United States targeted Saddam Hussein and in the process killed many civilians, the issue was the same.

I believe that targeted assassination should only be used as a last recourse when there is no opportunity to arrest or apprehend the murderer (although this is not required by the law of war if the murderer is a combatant), when the terrorist is involved in ongoing murderous activities, and when the assassination can be done without undue risk to innocent bystanders. Proportionality is the key to any military action, and targeted assassination should be judged under that rubric. Under any reasonable standard, Israeli policy with regard to targeted assassinations of "ticking-bomb terrorists" does not deserve the kind of condemnation it is receiving, especially in comparison with other nations and groups whose legal actions are far less proportionate to the dangers they face.

26 Is Settlement in the West Bank and Gaza a Major Barrier to Peace?

THE ACCUSATION

The Jewish settlements in the West Bank and Gaza are the major barrier to peace.

THE ACCUSERS

"Why is it so hard to make peace in the Middle East? The greatest barrier is the Israeli settlements—these are both the motivation and engine of the Israeli occupation of the Palestinian territories. Three decades of objections from the United States and Europe have achieved nothing. The rapid expansion of Israeli settlements—all illegal—has undermined Palestinian attempts at nation building. If they continue to spread, they will end the Israel that its founders envisioned." (Marwan Bishara, professor of international relations at the American University in Paris[1])

THE REALITY

The Arabs and Palestinians refused to make peace before there was a single settlement, and the Palestinians refused to make peace when Ehud Barak offered to end the settlements. Moreover, when Egypt offered to make peace, the Sinai settlements were not a barrier; they were immediately uprooted. Although I am personally opposed to the settlements, I do not believe that they are the real barrier to peace. The real barrier has been the unwillingness of many Palestinians, and many Palestinian terrorist groups and nations, to accept the existence of a Jewish state in any part of Palestine. If these groups would accept a two-state solution, the settlements would be uprooted (with some territorial adjustments).

A recent poll showed that a large number of the settlers themselves would be willing to abandon their homes if the Palestinians were to agree to peace. And Prime Minister Ariel Sharon announced in April 2003 that Israel would be willing to make "painful concessions" regarding the settlements in exchange for peace with the Palestinians: "I know that we will have to part with some of these places. As a Jew this agonizes me. But I have decided to make every effort to reach a settlement."[2]

Even after years of terrorist murders, according to polls taken in late April 2003, the Israeli public supports the American- and European-sponsored "road map" which requires Israel to make significant concessions and contemplates the establishment of a Palestinian state by 2005.[3]

THE PROOF

From a purely legal and moral point of view, there is no good reason why ancient Jewish cities like Hebron should be Judenrein. The Jews who were forced out of Hebron by religiously inspired massacres and their descendants should have the same right of return or compensation as the Arab refugees are claiming. Moreover, the return of a few thousand Jews to Hebron would not affect the demographics of that Arab-controlled area, whereas the return to Israel of the millions of Palestinians who claim refugee status would quickly turn Israel into a third Palestinian state.

Nevertheless, for pragmatic reasons, these Jewish refugees from Hebron and other Jewish areas in the biblical provinces of Judea and Samaria should be denied their right to return in the interests of peace and compromise. A two-state solution presupposes one state with a predominantly Jewish character and population and another state with a predominantly Palestinian character and population. In an ideal world, Jews should be able to live as a minority in a Palestinian state, just as Palestinians have lived as a minority in Israel since its establishment. The world we live in is, however, far from ideal, and if the price of peace is a Judenrein Palestine (along with a Judenrein Jordan), it is a price worth paying—but it is a price, and the world should recognize that Israel is willing to pay it for peace.

27 Is Terrorism Merely Part of a Cycle of Violence?

THE ACCUSATION

Israel's policy of aggressive retaliation against terrorism—including assassination, home destruction, bombings that kill civilians, and reoccupying Palestinian cities and refugee camps—promotes a cycle of violence.

THE ACCUSERS

"What Israel is doing is increasing the amount of hatred toward Israelis, and making it much easier for civilians to be recruited as militants who would willingly give their lives to cause some sort of damage to Israel and the innocent Jews who represent it." (Ash Pulcifer, columnist, Yellowtimes.org[1])

THE REALITY

While reasonable people might disagree about the effectiveness of aspects of Israeli counterterrorism tactics, the history of Palestinian terrorism clearly shows that terrorism increases whenever Israel offers peace or is involved in an election in which a dovish candidate is running. Terrorism has been used as a deliberate tactic to derail any movement toward peace and a two-state solution. For example, on the very day Mahmoud Abbas was sworn in as the Prime Minister of the Palestinian Authority, and just hours before the peace roadmap was to be unveiled, a Palestinian suicide bomber set off a deadly explosion at a café near the U.S. embassy in Tel Aviv. Radical Palestinian groups took credit for the murders and said that they would continue with their terrorism in order to prevent the peace plan, which contemplates a two-state solution, from succeeding. As the *New York Times* editorialized:

> It was hardly a coincidence that the explosion came just after the new Palestinian prime minister delivered an inaugural speech decrying terrorism. The extremists behind the Tel Aviv attack were undoubtedly aiming their violence at their own leadership as well as the Israelis. They cannot be allowed to succeed. There will be enormous obstacles to peace. All those involved—Israelis, Palestinians, Americans and Europeans—must be prepared to show determination, courage, and energy. The terrible attack yesterday will be only the first test.[2]

There is nothing Israel can do to stop terrorism other than taking actions to prevent determined terrorists from succeeding. A cycle of violence presupposes that one side can voluntarily stop the cycle if it simply does not respond to the other side's violence. Experience shows that when Israel did not respond firmly to Palestinian terrorism, more terrorism followed, and when Israel took appropriate military steps, the number and severity of terrorist attacks were reduced.

THE PROOF

The assumption underlying the cycle of violence argument is that terrorism is an emotionally motivated act of revenge engaged in by frustrated individuals who have no other recourse. The history of terrorism against Israel undercuts this assumption and proves that Palestinian terrorism is a rational tactic selected by leaders because it has proven effective.

It may be easier to *recruit* suicide bombers from a population of frustrated individuals seeking revenge, but individual suicide bombers and other terrorists do not send themselves on missions of death. They are sent by elite leaders who are making a rational calculation based on costs and benefits. The costs are quite low, since the radical terrorist groups benefit from every death of both Israelis and Palestinians. The Palestinians are treated as martyrs and their families are honored and paid handsomely.

One of the goals of the terrorists is to provoke an overreaction by the Israelis so as to generate support for the terrorists' cause. This was certainly the motivating consideration in the well-planned escalation of suicide bombing following Arafat's rejection of the Barak–Clinton offers at Camp David and Taba in 2000–2001. The international community, which was

turning against Arafat for rejecting these reasonable offers, quickly turned
against Israel following the Israeli response to the suicide bombings.

Another goal—particularly of the radical rejectionists like Hamas—is to
drive the Israeli electorate to the right so as to reduce the prospects for a
negotiated peace that would leave Israel as a Jewish state. This was certainly an important effect of the escalated suicide bombings, which
helped assure the election of Sharon, much to the satisfaction of Hamas
and others who reject Israel's right to exist.

A third goal is to kill as many Israelis as possible and to try to frighten
Israel into submission. A fourth goal is to satisfy the Arab street, which has
too often been taught in the classrooms, in the mosques, and in the media
that the spilling of Jewish blood is an obligation. Only the first of these
goals might be influenced by more moderate Israeli responses, but at a
high price. Israel should be moderate and proportionate in its response to
terrorism because that is the right thing to do. But to believe that Israeli
moderation would significantly reduce terrorism is to falsely assume that
terrorism is part of a cycle of violence rather than a tactic of first choice
that has worked for the Palestinians.

28 Is Israel the Prime Human Rights Violator in the World?

THE ACCUSATION

Israel is "the prime example of human rights violators in the world."[1]

THE ACCUSERS

"The World Conference Against Racism was preceded by four Regional Conferences whose task it was to draft a composite Declaration against Racism and a Plan of Action. Israel was excluded from the last of the regional conferences in Teheran, which issued the most scurrilous indictment against Israel since the Second World War. There were seven components to the 'indictment':

- Occupation is a crime against humanity, a new form of Apartheid, a threat to international peace and security;
- Israel is in essence an Apartheid State;
- Israel is a meta–Human Rights violator (in a world in which human rights constitutes a new secular religion, Israel becomes the new 'Anti-Christ' of our time);
- Israel is the perpetrator of international crimes—war crimes, crimes against humanity, genocide—hence the right to 'armed struggle' and 'resistance' against this 'criminal' state;
- Israel (as a Jewish state) is an 'original sin' established through 'ethnic cleansing' of Mandatory Arab Palestine;

181

- The reference to 'holocausts' is, in the plural and in lowercase, with Israel an example of a 'holocaust' against Arabs;
- Zionism is declared to be not only a form of Racism, but Zionism itself was declared to be 'antisemitic.'" (Professor Irwin Cotler, describing the accusations[2])

"Every day of the UN Commission on Human Rights' six-week session, which has now finished its second week, begins with a violation of the UN Charter's most basic principle of international relations, 'the equality of all nations large and small.' One UN member is left standing in the halls every morning from 9 to 10 a.m. while all other UN members and observers (including the Palestinian Authority) meet in private strategic and information-sharing sessions in each of the five UN regional groups. That country is Israel. This is apartheid United Nations–style. . . . As for the substantive assault on Israel, which this year began Thursday, the Commission record over 30 years speaks for itself:

- Israel has been the only state subject to an entire agenda item every year.
- The Commission on Human Rights has spent more time on Israel than any other country.
- While 11 percent of its total substantive meeting has been on Israel alone, 24 percent of its time has been spent on all other UN states combined.
- 27 percent of its country-specific resolutions critical of a state have been on Israel alone.

"The real double standards? No resolution in the history of the commission has ever been passed on states such as Syria, China, Saudi Arabia or Zimbabwe.

"The fault is not that of the victims, who over the years have complained to the UN by the thousands about gross and systematic human rights abuses in countries such as Bahrain, Chad, Liberia, Malawi, Mali, Pakistan, Saudi Arabia, Syria, United Arab Emirates, Yemen and Zimbabwe. But every year, the commission holds closed-door meetings—the first one held Friday—in which it buries these complaints and refuses to subject such states to the public condemnation of resolutions.

"Commission debates on the Israel agenda item explain a lot. On Thursday, the Palestinian representative, Nabil Ramlawi (whom the Libyan chair calls 'His Excellency, the distinguished Ambassador of Palestine'), said:

'The world condemned the old Nazism in the past . . . during the Second World War. . . . The world also condemned Zionist Israel for the same criminal crimes it has been perpetrating against the Palestinian people . . . for over 50 years now, starting . . . in 1948. . . . [T]he world . . . has not yet eliminated the New Zionist Nazism and "Israel was created through crimes against humanity it perpetrated and which continue today." ' " (Anne Bayefsky, describing the accusations[3])

THE REALITY

Israel is the only nation in the Mideast that operates under the rule of law. Its record on human rights compares favorably to that of any country in the world that has faced comparable dangers. Its Supreme Court is among the best in the world, and it has repeatedly overruled the army and the government and made them operate under the rule of law. Israel has among the best records in the world with regard to the rights of women, gays, the physically and mentally challenged, and so on. It also has freedom of speech, press, dissent, association, and religion.

The Palestinian Authority, on the other hand, shows no respect for human rights. It tortures and kills alleged collaborators without even a semblance of due process. It tolerates little dissent and it is intolerant of alternative lifestyles. Palestinian propagandists invoke "human rights" merely as a tactic against Israel.

THE PROOF

Faced with comparable dangers both internal and external, no nation in history has ever tried so hard to require its military to operate within the rule of law. The Israeli Supreme Court, by all accounts one of the finest in the world, has played a far greater role in controlling the Israeli military than any court in history has ever played in the conduct of military affairs, including in the United States. Although obviously sensitive to the need for security, the Israeli Supreme Court has repeatedly enjoined the Israeli government and its military from undertaking actions in violation of the highest standards of the rule of law.

In virtually every other democracy, including the United States, the courts are extremely limited in their ability to prevent the military from taking whatever action it deems necessary to preserve national security. As the *New York Times* reported: "One of the most unusual aspects of Israeli law is the rapid access that petitioners, including Palestinians, can gain to Israel's highest court. In April 2002, during the fiercest fighting of the current conflict, in the Jenin refugee camp in the West Bank, the high court was receiving and ruling on petitions almost daily."[4]

Professor Yitzhak Zamir, a former Justice of the Israeli Supreme Court with "a reputation as a strong advocate of civil rights," said that he did not know of "any other country where civilian courts had such broad jurisdiction to review military actions."[5] Even Raji Sourani, the director of the Palestinian Center for Human Rights in Gaza and a strident critic of Israel, says that he remains "constantly amazed by the high standards of the legal systems."[6]

The modern Israeli Supreme Court, under the leadership of its president, Professor Aharon Barak, has taken an activist role in striking the appropriate balance between security and liberty. It has protected the rights of Palestinians, noncombatants, prisoners of war, and others, often at considerable risk to Israeli civilians and soldiers.

The Israeli Supreme Court has been the only high court to directly take on the issue of applying physical pressure (nonlethal torture) to captured terrorists in an effort to secure information necessary to prevent ongoing terrorist attacks. Notwithstanding its recognition that such extreme measures may at such times save lives, it has prohibited their use, thereby acknowledging that Israel must fight the war against terrorism "with one hand tied behind its back," because that is what the rule of law requires. It has prohibited the Israeli military from attacking ambulances, despite its recognition that ambulances are often used to transport explosives and suicide bombers.[7]

> We see fit to emphasize that our combat forces are obliged to abide by the humanitarian rules regarding care for the wounded, the ill, and the bodies of the deceased. The abuse committed by [Palestinian] medical personnel in hospitals and in ambulances obliges the I.D.F. to act in order to avoid such activities, but does not, in and of itself, make sweeping breach of humanitarian rules permissible. And indeed, this is the declared position of the State. This position is appropriate not only as far as international law, on which the Petitioners based their argument, is concerned, but also in light of the values of the State of Israel as a Jewish and democratic state.
>
> The I.D.F. shall once again remind the combat forces, down to the level of the single soldier in the field, of this commitment of our forces, based on law and morality—and according to the State, even on utility—through concrete instructions which will prevent, to the extent possible, and even in severe situations, activities which are not in line with the rules of humanitarian aid.[8]

Following that decision, Palestinian terrorists continued to use ambulances. The *New York Times,* on May 21, 2003, reported a case in which "a would-be bomber hid three times in an ambulance in a bid to get past Israeli troops. . . . He then joined forces with a 40-year-old woman, a mother of three, who strapped a bomb to her chest and accompanied him on a taxi ride."

The Israeli Supreme Court has prohibited Israel from holding prisoners as "bargaining chips" for the exchange of prisoners illegally being held by its enemies.[9]

On September 3, 2002, the court decided a case in which the Israeli military ordered the expulsion of the sister and brother of a terrorist who had organized several suicide bombings. They were expelled from the West Bank for a period of two years and moved to the Gaza Strip on the basis of a finding that the sister had sewn explosive belts and the brother served as a "look out when his brother and members of his group moved two explosive charges from one place to another."[10] The court ruled that the expulsion order, which constituted a temporary "assignment of residence" within the occupied territories rather than a transfer out of the territories, was valid only if "the person himself [who is being expelled] presents a real danger":

> One cannot assign the residence of an innocent relative who does not present a danger, even if it is proved that assigning his residence may deter others from carrying out terrorists acts. One cannot assign the residence of someone who no longer presents a danger. Assigning someone's place of residence may be done only on the basis of clear and convincing administrative evidence. It must be proportionate.[11]

In a companion case, the court reversed the expulsion order:

> It was however decided that with regard to the petitioner Abed Alnasser Mustafa Ahmed Asida—the brother of the terrorist Nasser A-Din Asida—the measure of assigned residence could not be adopted. The reason for this was that even though it was proved that this petitioner knew of the deeds of his terrorist brother, his involvement amounted merely to lending his brother a car and giving him clean clothes and food at his home, and no connection had been established between the petitioner's acts and the terrorist activity of the brother. It was therefore held that there was an inadequate basis for determining the petitioner to be sufficiently dangerous for his residence to be assigned.[12]

In its conclusion, the court made the following observation:

> The State of Israel is undergoing a difficult period. Terror is hurting its residents. Human life is trampled upon. Hundreds have been killed. Thousands have been injured. The Arab population in Judaea and Samaria and the Gaza Strip is also suffering unbearably. All of this is because of acts of murder, killing and destruction perpetrated by terrorists. . . . The State is doing all that it can in order to protect its citizens

and ensure the security of the region. These measures are limited. The restrictions are, first and foremost, military-operational ones. It is difficult to fight against persons who are prepared to turn themselves into living bombs. These restrictions are also normative. The State of Israel is a freedom-seeking democracy. It is a defensive democracy acting within the framework of its right to self-defence—a right recognized by the charter of the United Nations. . . . [N]ot every effective measure is also a lawful measure. . . . Indeed, the position of the State of Israel is a difficult one. Also our role as judges is not easy. We are doing all we can to balance properly between human rights and the security of the area. In this balance, human rights cannot receive complete protection, as if there were no terror, and State security cannot receive complete protection, as if there were no human rights. A delicate and sensitive balance is required. This is the price of democracy. It is expensive, but worthwhile. It strengthens the State. It provides a reason for its struggle.[13]

The entire text of this decision, which is available on the Web,[14] should be required reading for those who claim that Israel does not comply with the rule of law.

It is fair to say that although Israeli actions in combating terrorism have been far from perfect, Israel has been in greater compliance with the rule of law than any other country facing comparable dangers. In contrast to Israel, the Egyptians, the Jordanians, and the Palestinians routinely torture suspects and do not limit their torture to nonlethal applications. In 2002, the Palestinian Authority acknowledged that it tortured a suspected collaborator in order to get him to incriminate his aunt, who was then shot without any semblance of a trial.[15] Jordan has not only tortured suspected terrorists but also their relatives in an effort to loosen the tongues of uncooperative terrorists.

It is interesting to recall that when the Chinese government killed demonstrators at Tiananmen Square in 1989, the first person to congratulate Jiang Zemin for putting down the demonstration was Yasser Arafat, speaking on behalf of the Palestinian people. This is what he wrote:

> On behalf of the Arab Palestinian people, their leadership and myself, I . . . take this opportunity to express extreme gratification that you were able to restore normal order after the recent incidents in People's China. I wish you, close friends, more progress in your endeavour to achieve the hopes, goals, aspirations, stability and security of our friends, the Chinese people.[16]

The same Palestinian propagandists who so loudly and hypocritically complain whenever Israel deviates even one iota from human rights perfection are quick to praise and support every tyrannical destroyer of human rights, ranging from Saddam Hussein to Muammar Khadafi to Fidel Castro.

Like every other nation, Israel has made mistakes in overreacting to terrorism and other threats to its civilian population. It is far from perfect, but a comparative and contextual assessment of its actions demonstrates that it deserves to be singled out for praise, not criticism, for its efforts to combat terrorism within the rule of law and with sensitivity to the rights of innocent noncombatants.

In a 1987 speech, Justice William Brennan, perhaps the most civil libertarian justice in U.S. Supreme Court history, made the following observation of Israel's efforts to balance security and civil liberties:

> It may well be Israel, not the United States, that provides the best hope for building a jurisprudence that can protect civil liberties against the demands of national security. For it is Israel that has been facing real and serious threats to its security for the last forty years and seems destined to continue facing such threats in the foreseeable future. The struggle to establish civil liberties against the backdrop of these security threats, while difficult, promises to build bulwarks of liberty that can endure the fears and frenzy of sudden danger—bulwarks to help guarantee that a nation fighting for its survival does not sacrifice those national values that make the fight worthwhile. . . . The nations of the world, faced with sudden threats to their own security, will look to Israel's experience in handling its continuing security crisis, and may well find in that experience that expertise to reject security claims that Israel has exposed as baseless and the courage to preserve the civil liberties that Israel has preserved without detriment to its security. . . .
>
> I [would not] be surprised if in the future the protections generally afforded civil liberties during times of world danger owed much to the lessons Israel learns in its struggle to preserve simultaneously the liberties of its citizens and the security of its nation. For in this crucible of danger lies the opportunity to forge a worldwide jurisprudence of civil liberties that can withstand the turbulences of war and crisis. In this way, adversity may yet be the handmaiden of liberty.[17]

When a student leader like the one quoted at the beginning of this chapter declares Israel to be the prime human rights violator in the world, he or she is guilty either of abysmal ignorance or malignant bigotry. In either case, he is in very large, although not very good, company. Most reasonable people would rather be lectured about civil liberties and human rights by Justice William Brennan than by Eric Reichenberger, Yasser Arafat, or the U.N. Commission on Human Rights.

If there is any remaining doubt about the superiority of Israeli democracy and commitment to the rule of law in comparison to Arab and Muslim nations, and even most Western nations, let it be resolved by the Palestinians themselves, who are familiar with Israel's political and judicial institutions. Khalil Shikaki, a Palestinian political scientist who has been polling Palestinians since 1996 about "what governments they admire," found the following:

> Every year Israel has been the top performer, at times receiving more than 80 percent approval. The American system has been the next best, followed by the French and then, distantly trailing, the Jordanian and Egyptian.
>
> In its early days, the Palestinian Authority held fourth place, with about 50 percent approval. Now, it is dead last, under 20 percent. Corruption, mismanagement and the stagnation of the Palestinian predicament have turned the culture of criticism against the Palestinian rulers.[18]

The Palestinians who were polled would also like to see a constitution that would "substantially strengthen and protect the judiciary [which] is now the weakest element of Palestinian governance." This too is modeled on the Israeli judiciary. Not surprisingly, Arafat "prefers a weak judiciary." Most dictators do.

29 Is There Moral Equivalence between Palestinian Terrorists and Israeli Responses?

THE ACCUSATION

There is a moral equivalence between those who *deliberately* target innocent children, women, the elderly, and other civilians and those who *inadvertently* kill civilians in the process of trying to prevent further terrorist attacks.

THE ACCUSERS

"Suicide bombers are terrorists, and so are the far worse Israeli crimes that we [the United States] carry out." (Noam Chomsky[1])

"*Killing the Future: Children in the Line of Fire,* a new report issued today by Amnesty International, details the way in which Palestinian and Israeli children have been targeted in an unprecedented manner since the beginning of the current *intifada.*

"'Children are increasingly bearing the brunt of this conflict. Both the Israeli Defense Force (IDF) and Palestinian armed groups show an utter disregard for the lives of children and other civilians,' Amnesty International said today.

'Respect for human life must be restored. Only a new mindset among Israelis and Palestinians can prevent the killing of more children.'

"The impunity enjoyed by members of the IDF and of Palestinian groups responsible for killing children has no doubt helped create a situation where the right to life of children and civilians on the other side has little or no value.

"'Enough of unacceptable reasons and excuses. Both the Israeli government and the Palestinian Authority must act swiftly and firmly to investigate the killing of each and every child and ensure that all those responsible for such crimes are brought to justice,' the organization stated." (Amnesty International Press Release[2])

"[Pope John Paul II has issued an] unequivocal condemnation of Terrorism, from whatever side it may come."[3]

"We condemn equally . . . both the suicide bombings . . . and the violence of the Israeli occupation." (National Council of Churches delegation to the Middle East[4])

"Palestinians will argue that the violence of the Israeli Occupation is far greater, and that the daily combination of torture, house demolitions, humiliating searches, targeted assassinations, and the siege of towns and villages is far worse than anything experienced by the Israeli population. They may be right." (Rabbi Michael Lerner[5])

THE REALITY

Every reasonable school of philosophy, theology, jurisprudence, and common sense distinguishes between deliberately targeting civilians and inadvertently killing civilians while targeting terrorists who hide among them.

THE PROOF

Terrorist attacks against Israelis and Jews have included the following targets:

- A nursery school in which eighteen children and teachers were machine gunned to death
- An elementary school in which twenty-seven children and teachers were killed
- A Jewish community center in which eighty-six civilians were killed
- A Turkish synagogue in which twenty-seven Jews at prayer were killed
- A Swiss airliner headed to Israel in which all forty-seven civilian passengers were killed
- A passenger terminal at Lod Airport in which twenty-seven civilians, mostly Christian pilgrims, were killed

- A Passover seder in which twenty-nine Jews were killed
- A discotheque for teenagers in which twenty-one mostly Russian Jews were killed
- A Hebrew University cafeteria in which nine people were killed
- An airplane filled with Israeli tourists returning from a Chanukah vacation in Kenya

Only the last of these attacks failed. This targeted murder of children, the elderly, and other vulnerable citizens is utterly without any moral justification. Amnesty International has declared such terrorist acts to be "crimes against humanity." Many terrorist acts are not even directed against Israeli civilians—unjustified as that is—but are directed against Jews who live outside of Israel, regardless of their views about Israel. This is anti-Semitic hate violence, pure and simple.

When the Klu Klux Klan perpetrated similar outrageous attacks, although on a far smaller scale, there was universal condemnation. No one condemned equally the deliberate bombings by the Klan and the occasional overreactions by the FBI. Yet there are those who seek to justify the current anti-Jewish outrages as the work of freedom fighters. The reality is that right-wing extremists and Islamic militants are working together in Germany and other European countries to spread "violent anti-Semitism on university campuses."[6] Neo-Nazis have also cooperated with Islamic terrorists in Argentina to perpetrate anti-Jewish violence.

The victims of the Holocaust and other genocides did not take revenge by killing innocent children, even the children of actual perpetrators of the genocides. Yet Israel's enemies—from the Palestinians to the Iranians to the neo-Nazi groups that have worked in collaboration with them—have not hesitated to target children or anyone else, Jew or non-Jew. And many in the international community insist on describing Israel's attempts to prevent these outrages as morally equivalent to the outrages themselves. Among the worst offenders are certain religious leaders who should know better and whose own theologies make a crucial distinction between deliberately intended consequences, such as targeting children, and unintended consequences, even when they cause the accidental death of a child in the process of targeting a dangerous terrorist. The *New Catholic Encyclopedia* defines the principle of "double effect" as "a rule of conduct frequently used in moral theology to determine when a person may lawfully perform an action from which two effects will follow, one bad, and the other good." It then gives the following example, which perfectly describes Israel's policy of fighting terrorism:

In modern warfare the principle of the double effect is frequently applicable. Thus, *in waging a just war a nation may launch an air attack on an important military objective of the enemy even though a comparatively small number of noncombatants are killed. This evil effect can be compensated for by the great benefit gained through the destruction of the target.* This would not be true if the number of noncombatants slain in the attack were out of proportion to the benefits gained. . . . Furthermore, if the direct purpose of the attack were to kill a large number of noncombatants so that the morale of the enemy would be broken down and they would sue for peace, the attack would be sinful. . . . It would be a case of the use of a bad means to obtain a good end.

As the philosopher Jean Bethke Elshtain has pointedly observed in reaction to the claim of moral equivalence by some clergymen and theologians:

If we could not distinguish between an accidental death resulting from a car accident and an intentional murder, our criminal justice system would fall apart. And if we cannot distinguish the killing of combatants from the intended targeting of peaceable civilians, we live in a world of moral nihilism. In such a world, everything reduces to the same shade of gray and we cannot make distinctions that help us take our political and moral bearings.[7]

This failure to understand—or worse, to understand but not to acknowledge—the fundamental difference between deliberately targeting civilians and accidentally killing civilians in the course of self-defense reflects moral obtuseness at best and outright bigotry at worst. It also encourages those who deliberately employ the murder of civilians as a means toward achieving "moral equality" with their more humane enemies in the court of public opinion. The cruel irony is that for some bigots Israel is not *even* regarded as the moral equivalent of its terrorist enemies. Noam Chomsky, for example, regards Israeli and American counterterrorism actions as far worse than the terrorism itself.

The argument I am making is not that two wrongs make a right. It is always possible to find wrongs on all sides. The argument—and it is an argument central to civilization and justice—is that the concept of wrongs is not always a matter of degree; there are qualitative differences between *unintended* wrongs and *purposeful* wrongs. Two dead civilians are not morally equivalent if one was targeted for murder, and the death of the other was the unfortunate consequence of best efforts, including risks to one's own soldiers, to prevent the murder of civilians. Both are wrongs, just as the death of two hospital patients from overdoses of a cancer-treating drug are wrongs. But anyone who cannot, or will not, distinguish between a case where a black patient was deliberately overdosed by a racist nurse and another case where the patient died after consenting to aggressive cancer therapy that he knew carried a high risk of death is either morally blind or willfully bigoted. *Everybody* understands this difference, and everyone believes in it *in other contexts.* But when it comes to Israel, simple intelligence and basic morality are suspended by some who insist on applying a double standard to the Jewish state.

Even if Israel is properly criticized for overreacting in particular cases by placing civilians at risk, there is still no moral equivalence between exploding an antipersonnel bomb made of nails soaked in rat poison whose sole purpose is to maximize civilian deaths and injuries, on the one hand, and targeting terrorists under circumstances in which it is likely that some innocent civilians may die, on the other hand. Both are wrong, but the former is far, far more morally culpable than the latter, because of the differing purposes. No civilized society regards premeditated first-degree murder as morally equivalent to negligent homicide. This is true of the Bible, the Koran, and international law—except apparently when it comes to Israel, where longstanding distinctions and universally accepted rules of morality seem to be forgotten.

It is important for some people to believe that all morality is relative, and there is no absolute evil in the world. This is especially true of people who came of age after the Hitler–Stalin era. Even following the death of those two perfectly evil monsters, there were others who were pure evil, such as Pol Pot and Idi Amin. But they lived in distant lands and were not part of the daily consciousness of most Americans as Hitler and Stalin were. The Vietnam War was seen by many as a clash between morally equivalent aggressors. Fidel Castro was viewed by many on the left as having done some good and some bad.

Yet there is true evil in the world, and the deliberate targeting of children, women, and old people based on their ethnicity or national origin is pure evil, with absolutely no justification. To fail to acknowledge such terrorism as pure evil invites relativism about everything. If it is permissible to target babies and schoolchildren just because they are Jewish, is there anything that is beyond the pale of acceptability? In *The Brothers Karamazov,* Fyodor Dostoyevsky posed this question in the famous dialogue about relativism between Ivan and Alyosha:

> Ivan: "Imagine that you are creating a fabric of human destiny with the object of making men happy in the end, giving them peace at least, but that it was essential and inevitable to torture to death only one tiny creature—that baby beating its breast with its fist, for instance—and to found that edifice on its unavenged tears, would you consent to be the architect of those conditions? Tell me, and tell the truth." Alyosha replied without hesitation: "No, I wouldn't consent."

Remember that Hitler and Stalin both claimed justifications for their policies of mass murder and had large followings that included intellectuals, professionals, and artists. Yet we now understand that nothing could possibly justify the annihilation of tens of millions of innocent civilians, although some Palestinian and Arab leaders still bemoan the fact that Hitler did not complete the job.

Why then are decent people today afraid to call evil by its name? Why do so many insist on finding moral equivalence? And why do so many people describe the worst of evils—the deliberate targeting of children—with positive-sounding terms like "freedom fighting," while describing reasonable efforts to prevent these Nazi-like evils as Nazism itself? Noam Chomsky likes to remind his audiences that Hitler and Stalin both claimed that their genocide was really antiterrorism, as if to suggest that everything labeled antiterrorism—from the building of death camps in which a million children were gassed to the targeted assassination of a single terrorist commander—is morally equivalent.

The day after President Bush brought Israeli prime minister Sharon and Palestinian prime minister Abbas together at Aqaba, Hamas leader Ismail Abu Shanab vowed to continue the suicide bombings, after complaining bitterly that Abbas had acknowledged that Jews had suffered throughout history: "He spoke about Israeli suffering as if Palestinians committed the Holocaust against the Jews, while in truth it is the Palestinians who are being subject to an Israeli holocaust."[8] This historical ignorance or self-deception about the actual role of Palestinian leaders in the Holocaust, coupled with immoral comparisons between Nazi death camps and Israeli self-defense against terrorism, has itself become a barrier to peace.

The political analogue to moral equivalence is even-handedness. It might follow from the false premise that the Palestinians and Israelis are equally at fault for the breakdown of the peace process and the escalating violence, that the international community should be even-handed in dealing with both sides. But it also follows from the undisputed fact that Palestinian leaders are blameworthy for their repeated rejection of the two-state solution and for the resulting escalation of violence, that the two sides should not be treated in an even-handed manner. To reward rejection and violence with even-handedness is to encourage such conduct. There must be a high price paid by those who reject peace in favor of violence, as the Palestinians have since the 1920s. There must be a benefit for those who were willing to accept a peaceful two-state solution in 1937, 1947, and 2000–2001, as Israel was.

Moreover, there must be a price paid by those who start aggressive wars of annihilation and extermination, as the Arab states and Palestinian fighters have repeatedly done. And there should be a benefit for those who successfully defend their civilian population against such aggressive wars. Any other approach will encourage the waging of aggressive wars.

There must also be a price paid by those who have repeatedly allied themselves with, and actively supported, the worst sorts of evil, ranging from Nazism to Saddamism. Similarly, those who support the winning sides of just wars have traditionally been rewarded with favorable treatment.

The concept of even-handedness seems benign, almost moral. As a people committed to equality, Americans generally support even-handedness. We would certainly expect it from an umpire or a referee at a sporting event. We demand it of our government in the treatment of people of different races, religions, genders, and sexual orientations. But even-handedness is not automatically a desirable criterion for dealing with nations and groups that have behaved quite differently—some far better than others—as judged by universally accepted moral criteria. No one expected even-handedness for the Germans and the Japanese following the Second World War, and no one expected even-handedness when the Justice Department confronted the Ku Klux Klan. Most relevantly, no one expects even-handedness between Osama bin Laden's al-Qaeda and those who are seeking to destroy his capacity to inflict further harm on innocent people. We should favor those who seek peace over those who have shown a preference for war. We should favor those who are not seeking to destroy a U.N. member state over those who are.

Shifting from the theoretical to the practical, even-handedness is rarely even. Those who advocate even-handedness between Israel and its enemies generally favor a strong tilt against Israel in favor of the Palestinians. Certainly that has long been true of the United Nations, which talks the talk of even-handedness but votes the vote of a strong bias against Israel and a preference for the Palestinians, not only over Israel but also over all other occupied and stateless people. The same has been true of most European and Asian countries.

Even Amnesty International has failed the test of even-handedness by falsely claiming that no Palestinian minor has ever been involved in a suicide bombing and that the Israeli Army "targets" innocent Palestinian children. The United States, which has generally been even-handed in fact, as between Israel and the Palestinians, is widely perceived as being unfairly favorable to Israel, whereas those who are in fact unfairly favorable to the Palestinians are widely perceived as even-handed. The United States has voted against Israel at the Security Council on many occasions, sometimes most regrettably, as when it condemned Israel for destroying Iraq's nuclear reactor—an action for which the United States is now quite grateful. Many nations that claim to be even-handed have almost never voted to condemn Palestinian actions.

Even the false argument over why the United States "tilts" toward

Israel while the rest of the world is even-handed is often tinged with a not-so-subtle anti-Semitism. "The Jews control America," it is claimed, and that is why the United States is so pro-Israel. One rarely hears comparable complaints about Muslim or oil influences on French policy. Americans, whether Jewish or non-Jewish, who support Israel because they believe that is the best policy for the United States have a perfect right to try, by democratic means, to influence U.S. policy, especially when so much of the rest of the world is so one-sidedly anti-Israel, as reflected by the one-sided voting results at the U.N. and other international bodies.

If even-handedness is ever to be achieved within the entire international community, it will only happen if the United States does not seek to emulate European conceptions of even-handedness. If the United States were ever to become as even-handed as the international community has been, it would surely encourage continuing aggression against the Jewish state. It would also be morally wrong. Even-handedness toward those whose actions are not morally equivalent is an immoral and dangerous form of artificial symmetry.

30 Should Universities Divest from Israel and Boycott Israeli Scholars?

THE ACCUSATION

Israel's actions, more than those of any other nation, warrant divestment and boycott.

THE ACCUSERS

"We the undersigned . . . call on MIT and Harvard to divest from Israel." (Noam Chomsky, signing a petition for divestment)

"Divestment is wrong in principle. . . .

"Divestment is 'unprincipled' and 'it would be loved by Alan Dershowitz, Lawrence Summers and Marty Peretz who are delighted to have more atrocities and violence against Palestinians.' These men are 'extremists who want to maximize U.S.–Israeli atrocities and crimes.'" (Noam Chomsky[1])

THE REALITY

These campaigns to single out Israel for demonization are immoral, bigoted, and based on misinformation.

The campaign currently being waged against Israel on college and university campuses throughout the world is fueled by ignorance, bigotry, and cynicism. Led by efforts at Harvard University, the Massachusetts Institute of Technology, and other schools to end university investment in Israel and to boycott Israeli speakers and academics, this campaign seeks to delegitimize and isolate Israel as a pariah state. The campaign also seeks to convey to college students the false notion that Israel is among the worst human rights violators in the world and is guilty of genocide, torture, racism, ethnic cleansing, and Nazi tactics, whereas the Palestinians and their Arab supporters are victims of Israeli aggression.

Although it is unlikely that divestiture will be implemented on these campuses, the goal of the campaign is similar to, and grows out of, previous attempts to single out Israel by equating Zionism with racism and by complying with the now discredited and illegal Arab boycott of Israeli and Jewish goods.

THE PROOF

The intellectual godfather of this campaign is none other than Noam Chomsky, who has called for the abolition of the state of Israel and the substitution of a "secular binational state" based on the models of Lebanon and Yugoslavia. Chomsky has also defended the findings of the notorious anti-Semite and Holocaust denier Robert Faurisson, who claims that the Jews were responsible for World War II and that no Jews were gassed at death camps. Chomsky has said that he saw "no hint of anti-Semitic implications in Faurisson's work," including his denial of the Holocaust, which Chomsky claims is based on "extensive historical research."

Chomsky went so far as to write an introduction to one of Faurisson's anti-Semitic books. Although he sees no hint of anti-Semitism in blaming World War II on the Jews and in denying that Jews were gassed in death camps, Chomsky is quick to accuse of racism those who defend Israel's right to defend itself from terrorism. Chomsky is joined in his ignoble petition by some who would take the money now invested in the Mideast's only democracy and have it sent to Libya, Syria, Cuba, the Palestinian Authority, and others who support and finance terrorism. They are a motley assortment of knee-jerk anti-Zionists, rabid anti-Americans, radical leftists such as the Spartacus League (which also defends the "right" of North Korea to develop and sell nuclear weapons), and even some of Chomsky's former students who now teach in Israel.

It should not be surprising that the petition has garnered so little support among more respectable and experienced human rights advocates, since there is no intellectually or morally defensible case for singling out Israel for divestiture. Universities invest in a wide array of companies that have operations in countries all over the world, including many that systematically violate the human rights of millions of people. And these other countries are not defending themselves against those who would destroy them and target their civilians. Yet this petition focuses only on the Jewish state, to the exclusion of all others, including those which by any reasonable standard are actually among the worst violators of human rights.

As an advocate, teacher, and student of human rights for almost forty years, I feel confident in asserting that Israel's record on human rights is among the best in the world, especially among nations that have confronted comparable threats. Israel has the only independent judiciary in the entire Middle East and one of the most highly regarded supreme courts in the world. It is the only court in the Middle East from which an Arab or a Muslim can expect justice, as many have in winning dozens of victories against the Israeli government, the Israeli military, and Israeli citizens. There is no more important component in the protection of human rights and civil liberties than an independent judiciary willing to stand up to its own government. I challenge the proponents of divestiture to name a court in any other Arab or Muslim country that is comparable to the Israeli Supreme Court.

Israel is the only true democracy in the Middle East and the only country that has virtually unlimited freedom of speech. Its media are generally very critical of the government. Any person in Israel—whether Jewish, Muslim, or Christian—can criticize the Israeli government and its leaders. No citizen of any other Mideastern or Muslim state can do that without fear of imprisonment or death. Nor can Palestinians openly criticize their leaders without fear of reprisal. As Arafat famously threatened the mayor of Bethlehem, after the mayor had proposed a truce that would have halted Palestinian terrorism: "Whoever thinks of stopping the Intifada before it achieves its goal, I will give him 10 bullets in the chest."[2] Arafat first denied ever making such a statement, and then when our State Department produced a tape recording, Arafat denied it was a threat. Finally, when Arab translators said it could have no other meaning, Arafat denied that it was directed at the mayor but rather at himself! "I said that if I tried to stop the intifada, the small boy who is standing beside me would shoot *me*."[3] The mayor of Bethlehem had no difficulty understanding exactly what Arafat was saying: he immediately withdrew his proposal for a truce.[4] One wag recently put it this way: citizens of Israel and the Palestinian Authority have exactly the same right of free speech—they may both criticize Ariel Sharon and praise Yasser Arafat.

As previously documented, Israel is the only country in the world that has openly confronted the difficult issue of the civil liberties of the ticking-bomb terrorist, ruling that despite the potential benefits of employing physical pressure, such pressure is now illegal. Brutal torture, including lethal torture, is commonplace in every other Mideastern and Muslim country. Indeed, the United States sometimes sends suspects to Egypt, Jordan, and the Philippines precisely because it knows that they will be tortured in those countries.

There is more gender, religious, sexual orientation, and ethnic equality in Israel then in any other Mideastern or Muslim country. The rights of women, gays, and others are far more fully recognized and implemented in Israel than anywhere in the Arab world. The Israeli army does not discriminate against gays, as even the U.S. Army does, and the Israeli Knesset now includes an openly gay member. (Yet signs have been seen at anti-Israel demonstrations reading "Queers for Palestine," despite the reality that if anyone were to display such a sign in the Palestinian Authority, he would risk being killed! Indeed, gay Palestinians who were tortured because of their sexual orientation have sought asylum in Israel.) Israeli Arabs sit in the Knesset, serve on the Israeli Supreme Court, and have their own newspapers. The list could go on and on, and by every single standard Israel would surpass other countries against which no divestiture petition has been directed. To be sure, Israel is far from perfect. I have been critical of some of its policies, but there are mechanisms within Israel for improving its civil liberties and human rights record. These mechanisms do not exist in other Mideastern and Muslim nations.

Even when judged against European nations, Israel's human rights record does very well. It is far better than that of France on virtually any criterion, even if one forgets about the Algerian War, in which the French tortured and murdered thousands of people. It is at least as good as the British record in dealing with terrorism in Northern Ireland and the U.S. record of dealing with al-Qaeda terrorism. The Israeli legal system is far superior to those of Italy, Spain, and many other European countries, and at least as good as the system in the United States.

There are, of course, difficult issues to be resolved between Israel and the Palestinians. These include the settlements, the establishment of Palestinian self-governance, and the prevention of terrorism. These issues will require compromise on all sides. Any American should certainly feel free to criticize Israel, as well as any other country in the world whose record on human rights is not perfect. But to single out the Jewish state of Israel as if it were the worst human rights offender is bigotry pure and simple, and those who sign the Chomsky-inspired petition should be ashamed of themselves and shamed by others.

I have offered an alternative to singling out Israel for divestiture. Let universities invest their funds *in the order* of the human rights records of the various countries. If that were to be done, investment in Israel would increase dramatically, while investments in Saudi Arabia, Egypt, Jordan, the Philippines, Indonesia, the Palestinian Authority, and most other countries of the world would decrease dramatically. An alternative would be to invest in the order of the permitted degree of *internal* criticism of the nation's human rights record. The theory behind this variation is that divestiture, which is an *external* pressure, is most needed for countries that tolerate no *internal* pressures for change. Under this approach, investment in Israel would also skyrocket.

In a talk at the campus Memorial Church in 2002, Harvard's president, Lawrence Summers, condemned the divestiture campaign and other efforts at singling out Israel for consideration. He began his talk by reminding his audience of "some of the global events of the last year":

- There have been synagogue burnings, physical assaults on Jews, or the painting of swastikas on Jewish memorials in every country in Europe. Observers in many countries have pointed to the worst outbreak of attacks against the Jews since the Second World War.

- Candidates who denied the significance of the Holocaust reached the runoff stage of elections for the nation's highest office in France and Denmark. State-sponsored television stations in many nations of the world spew anti-Zionist propaganda.

- The United Nations'–sponsored World Conference on Racism—while failing to mention human rights abuses in China, Rwanda, or anyplace in the Arab world—spoke of Israel's policies prior to recent struggles under the Barak government as constituting ethnic cleansing and crimes against humanity. The NGO declaration at the same conference was even more virulent.

Summers then discussed issues closer to home:

Of course academic communities should be and always will be places that allow any viewpoint to be expressed. And certainly there is much to be debated about the Middle East and much in Israel's foreign and defense policy that can be and should be vigorously challenged.

But where anti-Semitism and views that are profoundly anti-Israeli have traditionally been the primary preserve of poorly educated right-wing populists, profoundly anti-Israel views are increasingly finding support in progressive intellectual communities. Serious and thoughtful people are advocating and taking actions that are anti-Semitic in their effect if not their intent.

Summers gave the following examples:

- Hundreds of European academics have called for an end to support for Israeli researchers, though not for an end to support for researchers from any other nation.

- Israeli scholars this past spring were forced off the board of an international literature journal.

- At the same rallies where protesters, many of them university students, condemn the IMF and global capitalism and raise questions about globalization, it is becoming increasingly common to also lash out at Israel. Indeed, at the anti-IMF rallies last spring, chants were heard equating Hitler and Sharon.

- Events to raise funds for organizations of questionable political provenance that in some cases were later found to support terrorism have been held by student organizations on this and other campuses with at least modest success and very little criticism.

- And some here at Harvard and some at universities across the country have called for the University to single out Israel among all nations as the lone country where it is inappropriate for any part of the university's endowment to be invested. I hasten to say the University has categorically rejected this suggestion.

Finally, Summers defended the right of anyone to criticize Israel and any other nation or institution:

> We should always respect the academic freedom of everyone to take any position. We should also recall that academic freedom does not include freedom from criticism. The only antidote to dangerous ideas is strong alternatives vigorously advocated. I have always throughout my life been put off by those who heard the sound of breaking glass in every insult or slight, and conjured up images of Hitler's Kristallnacht at any disagreement with Israel. Such views have always seemed to me alarmist if not slightly hysterical. But I have to say that while they still seem to me unwarranted, they seem rather less alarmist in the world of today than they did a year ago.

This balanced presentation led to Noam Chomsky including Summers in the category of "extremists who want to maximize U.S.-Israeli atrocities and crimes." It also led British journalist Robert Fisk to accuse Summers—who he described as "the Jewish president of Harvard"—of participating in a "vicious campaign of slander [against] anyone who dares to criticize Israeli policies."[5]

I wrote a column in support of President Summers, in which I challenged a housemaster at Harvard who had signed the petition to a debate:

> In my 38 years of teaching at HLS, I don't recall ever writing in praise of any action by a Harvard President, but this time I must congratulate President Lawrence Summers for his willingness to say out loud what

many of us in the Harvard community have long believed: namely, that singling out Israel, among all the countries in the world, for divestment, is an action which is anti-Semitic in effect, if not in intent.

Universities should encourage widespread debate and discussion about divisive and controversial issues. A housemaster who peremptorily signs a petition and then hides behind "other priorities" does not serve the interests of dialogue and education. I hope that [he] will accept my challenge, and that if [he does] not, I will be invited by [his] students to help fill the educational gap left by the cowardice of those who have signed this petition and refuse to defend their actions in public debate.

His students did invite me but he refused to participate in any debate or discussion, and I "debated" an empty chair with a copy of the petition in front of his students at Winthrop House.

President Lee Bollinger of Columbia University also denounced the divestment petition, responding to those who compared it to similar petitions against South African apartheid; he characterized the analogy to Israel as "both grotesque and offensive." Three hundred other college and university presidents expressed concern over intimidation and hatred directed against Jewish supporters of Israel on many campuses. I wrote the following in support of their statement:

There are some who argue that the Presidents' ad will chill campus debate. Quite the opposite is true. The ad, along with Harvard President Lawrence Summers' statement that the divestiture campaign is anti-Semitic in its effect, has stimulated healthy debate.

President Summers went out of his way to make it clear that criticism of Israel is not anti-Semitic, either in intent or effect. No one I know is seeking to stifle criticism of Israel or of the current government, or to chill support for Palestinian statehood and human rights.

What is the equivalent of anti-Semitism is the singling out of the Jewish nation for divestment, boycott, U.N. condemnation or other sanctions, in face of, and despite its far better record on human rights than any other nation in the Middle East and most other nations in the world.

It is certainly possible that some who have signed the divestiture or boycott petitions do not believe that their actions are anti-Semitic. They may be ignorant of the reality that they are being used by enemies of Israel who would delegitimate and isolate the world's only Jewish nation. The recent campaigns for divestiture and boycott grow out of two earlier campaigns that were undoubtedly motivated by a desire to destroy the Jewish state. The first was the Arab boycott, which lasted for many years and was finally defeated. The second was the now discredited United Nations resolution equating Zionism with racism. The current efforts to equate Israel with the apartheid regime of South Africa will also fail, because the analogy is demonstrably false. The goal of this campaign is not actually to achieve divestiture, but rather to miseducate young and impressionable college students into believing that Israel is among the worst human rights violators in the world, despite its generally superb record on human rights and its great concern for minimizing civilian casualties by exposing its own soldiers to the risks of door to door "retail" fighting, rather than "wholesale" bombing of the kind done by many other countries, including our own. The fact that Israel is the only country in the Middle East with freedom of expression, an independent judiciary, a commitment to the equality of women and gays are all ignored in this effort to isolate Israel. Ignorance may be a defense to bigotry, but it has no place on a university campus.

The immoral campaign on campuses against Jews who support Israel must be combated in the marketplace of ideas. The Presidents' letter is an important component of this struggle against bigotry. Too many good people are remaining silent in the face of anti-Semitism. It is time to stand up and be counted.

It was clear from the widespread condemnation of the anti-Israel divestment petition that no major American university would seriously consider divesting from Israel. Those who initiated the divestment campaign were, of course, aware of this reality. Actual divestment was not the goal of the campaign. Its goal was to miseducate and misinform students around the world about Israel's human rights record. *After* most of the signatures had already been secured, Noam Chomsky virtually admitted this when he told a Harvard audience that although he had signed— indeed spearheaded—the anti-Israel divestment petition, he was actually *opposed* to divestment from Israel! Chomsky said, "I am opposed and have been opposed for many years, in fact, I've probably been the leading opponent for years of the campaign for divestment from Israel and of the campaign about academic boycotts."[6] He also declared it to be "wrong in principle" and "unprincipled."[7]

When asked why he signed the divestment petition in view of his principled opposition to divestment, the renowned linguist explained, "No one who signs a petition is expected to approve of every word, even of large parts, if the main thrust is appropriate and sufficiently important."[8] But, of course, divestment is the main thrust of the petition—at least to many who agreed to sign it. But not to Chomsky, whose secret agenda— the delegitimation of Israel through the spread of disinformation—he did not share with the signatories. He kept his opposition secret from most of the signatories until after their signatures had been obtained.

Although Chomsky eventually characterized the call for divestment as "a big mistake," he would not—as some professors have now done—remove his influential name from it, since he believes that its substantive demands are valid. But are they? A close look at the demands themselves demonstrates that they are bogus on their face—even without any comparison with other countries.

The petition demands that Israel comply with U.N. Resolution 242, the *U.N. Committee Against Torture 2001 Report,* the Fourth Geneva Convention, and U.N. Resolution 194 with respect to the rights of refugees. Apparently, most of the signatories of this petition, which included 130 Harvard and MIT faculty members at last count, are unaware of the fact that Israel has *already* complied with or has offered to comply with each of these conditions.

United Nations Resolution 242, one of whose draftsmen was the very liberal Justice Arthur Goldberg (for whom I had served as a law clerk), does not call on Israel to give back *all* of the territories captured during the defensive war of 1967. The compromise agreed to by the Security Council was that Israel would give back "territories"—meaning most but not all—in exchange for complete termination of all claims or states of belligerency by Arab countries. A resolution put forward by the Soviet Union and its client states calling for Israel to withdraw from all the territories was not adopted.

Both Justice Goldberg and Lord Carrington of Britain, the primary drafters of the resolution that was accepted, have stated unambiguously that it did not contemplate withdrawal from "all the territories," recognizing, as Lord Carrington put it, "it would have been wrong to demand that Israel return to its positions of June 4, 1967, because these positions were undesirable and artificial."[9] The only two countries that have met the condition for a return of captured territories—namely a complete termination of belligerency against Israel—are Egypt and Jordan.

As previously documented, Israel returned every inch of land sought by Egypt when Egypt renounced belligerency, and Jordan has abandoned almost all of the claims to land now occupied by Israel. The small area that was claimed by Jordan was returned as soon as it made peace with Israel, and a tiny area in dispute between Egypt and Israel was submitted to arbitration and Israel turned it over to Egypt when the arbitrator ruled in favor of Egypt.

Moreover, in the year 2000, at Camp David and Taba, Israel offered to give up between 94 percent and 96 percent of the disputed land on the West Bank and all of the Gaza Strip and to accept a Palestinian state. That offer, together with the return of the territories to Egypt and Jordan, would have left Israel in possession of a tiny percentage of the land referred to by Resolution 242 (other than the Golan Heights, which Israel has offered to return in exchange for peace with Syria). It surely constituted full compliance with the language of Resolution 242 on the part of Israel. But there has been no compliance with Resolution 242 by the rejectionist Arab states and organizations, which continue to hold states of belligerency against Israel. Yet the divestiture petition imposes no conditions on these states, many of which also receive U.S. foreign aid and investments from Harvard and other universities.

The second demand is that Israel end the use of "legal torture," as outlined in the *U.N. Committee Against Torture 2001 Report.* The writers of this condition are either ignorant or mendacious. As previously documented, two years before the petition was circulated the Israeli Supreme Court outlawed the use of all physical pressure in eliciting information from potential terrorists. Israel is the only country in the Middle East to have abolished any kind of torture, in fact as well as in law. Jordan and Egypt, both of which receive substantial U.S. aid and investment, openly practice torture of the most violent and lethal nature. Yet the divestiture petition demands that only Israel stop doing something that it has already stopped doing without making any demands on countries that continue to engage in torture. There are scores of countries with worse records. Why single out Israel? The answer is obvious to any who are not afraid to ask questions with unpleasant answers.

Another condition laid out in the divestiture petition is that Israel acknowledge in principle that refugees be allowed to return to their former lands, or else be compensated for their losses, to comply with U.N. Resolution 194. At both Camp David and Taba, Israel offered the option for Palestinians to be compensated for their losses, and the Palestinians rejected it. Moreover, no Arab state has yet offered compensation to the hundreds of thousands of Jewish refugees who were forced to flee countries they and their families had lived in for hundreds of years after Arab countries declared war on Israel in 1948. Yet the petition demands nothing of these Arab countries.

The final condition, the cessation of building new settlements and the dismantling of existing settlements, is an issue that deeply divides Israelis. A majority of Israelis agree that no new settlements should be built and that most of the existing settlements should be vacated as part of an overall peace in the area. Even a significant number of the settlers have now expressed a willingness to leave their homes in exchange for peace. But the Palestinians have refused to accept peace offers made by the Israeli government. Many moderate Palestinians agree that Arafat's rejection of the peace offer made at Camp David and at Taba was a tactical mistake and that the resumption of terrorism against Israel is morally indefensible.

Even Prince Bandar of Saudi Arabia, a strong supporter of Palestinian rights who was directly involved in the failed negotiations, has acknowledged that Arafat's refusal to accept Barak's generous offer was "a crime against the Palestinians"—in fact, "against the entire region." Prince Bandar, who has said that Arafat "lied to him" and that it is "an open secret within the Arab world that Arafat was not truthful," has placed responsibility squarely on Arafat for the death of the "1,600 Palestinians . . . and 700 Israelis." As he put it in an interview with *The New Yorker,* "In my judgment not one life of these Israelis and Palestinians dead is justified."

Prince Bandar saw Arafat's rejection as part of a half-century-long pattern: "Since 1948, every time we've had something on the table, we say no. Then we say yes. When we say yes, it's not on the table any more. Then we have to deal with something less. Isn't it about time we said yes?"[10] Abba Eban made a similar point when he said, "The Palestinians have never missed an opportunity to miss an opportunity," and "they can't seem to take yes for an answer." Yet despite the acknowledgment by many people on all sides of the conflict that the blame for rejecting Barak's peace offer lies entirely at the feet of Arafat, the one-sided divestiture petition faults only Israel.

When I spoke to the students at Harvard's Winthrop House—the house whose master had signed the Harvard/MIT divestiture petition—many of the students seemed unaware of these facts about Israel's compliance. I suspect that many of the signatories of the petition are also ignorant of the complex realities underlying the continuing hostilities in the Middle East. But its drafters are not. They set out quite deliberately to misinform, miseducate, and misdirect their own students—a particularly nasty form of educational malpractice.

Any moral person who is aware of the true facts would not sign a petition singling out Israel for divestiture. Those who signed it are either misinformed or malignant. There is no third alternative.

31 Are Critics of Israel Anti-Semitic?

THE ACCUSATION

Anyone who criticizes Israel is automatically accused of anti-Semitism, thereby stifling legitimate criticism of that country's government and policies.

THE ACCUSERS

"It's the classic Zionist ploy to defame people by identifying criticism of Israel with anti-Semitism." (Edward Said[1])

"[T]he government of Israel is placed on a pedestal, and to criticize it is to be immediately dubbed anti-Semitic." (Archbishop Desmond Tutu[2])

THE REALITY

I have never heard a mere critic of Israel called anti-Semitic.

THE PROOF

Tyrants understood that if you repeat a big lie often enough people would begin to believe it. The big lie that is being repeated all around the United States, especially on college and university campuses, is that anyone who is critical of Israeli policies or the Sharon government will automatically be labeled an anti-Semite. It would be terrible if this were true, since criticism of Israel is important, as is criticism of any imperfect democracy. But the reality is that in the many years that I have been speaking about the Arab–Israeli conflict, I have never heard anyone actually label a mere critic of Israel or Sharon as anti-Semitic. Nor have I ever heard mere criticism of Israel described as anti-Semitism.

Yet the big lie persists. Susannah Heshel, a professor of Jewish studies at Dartmouth, has made the following charge: "We often hear that criticism of Israel is equivalent to anti-Semitism." Michael Lerner, the editor of *Tikkun,* has made a similar charge. So has Noam Chomsky. Most recently, a leading professor at Harvard, Paul Hanson of the Divinity School, has made this charge. I hereby challenge anyone who claims that mere criticism of Israel is often labeled anti-Semitism to document that serious charge by providing actual quotations, in context, with the source of the statements identified. I am not talking about the occasional kook who writes an anonymous postcard or e-mail. I am talking about mainstream supporters of Israel who, it is claimed, have often equated mere criticism of Israel with anti-Semitism.

Surely that is not what Harvard University president Lawrence Summers did when he said that "there is much to be debated about the Middle East and much in Israel's foreign and defense policy that can be and should be vigorously challenged."[3] Nor is it what Thomas Friedman of the *New York Times* did when he wrote the following: "Criticizing Israel is not anti-Semitic, and saying so is vile. But singling out Israel for opprobrium and international sanction—out of all proportion to any other party in the Middle East—is anti-Semitic, and not saying so is dishonest."[4]

Surely it is not what I have done when I have welcomed criticism of Israel, while accusing of bigotry those who would single out Israel for economic capital punishment, despite the reality that Israel's human rights record is far better than that of any other country in the region and at least as good as that of any other country that has faced comparable dangers. I have often myself been critical of particular Israeli policies, especially with regard to settlements. Yet I have never been accused of anti-Semitism, nor have Israel's many critics within the Israeli media.

Indeed, the Israeli government's harshest substantive critics are Israelis, both inside and outside the government—and sometimes even in the cabinet itself! No one has ever called them anti-Semitic. The one prominent person I am aware of who equated anti-Zionism with anti-Semitism was Martin Luther King Jr., who responded to a question posed by a student who attacked Zionism by telling the student that attacks on Zionists were often a euphemism for attacking Jews: "You're talking anti-Semitism."[5] But King's statement was made not in the context of criticizing Israeli policies but rather from a general attack on Zionism and the right of the

Jewish state to exist. King believed strongly that all good people must "protect its right to exist," as Congressman John Lewis, one of King's key assistants, recently recalled:

> On March 25, 1968, less than two weeks before his tragic death, he spoke out with clarity and directness stating, "peace for Israel means security, and we must stand with all our might to protect its right to exist, its territorial integrity. I see Israel as one of the great outposts of democracy in the world, and a marvelous example of what can be done, how desert land can be transformed into an oasis of brotherhood and democracy. Peace for Israel means security and that security must be a reality."
>
> During the recent U.N. Conference on Racism held in Durban, South Africa, we were all shocked by the attacks on Jews, Israel and Zionism. The United States of America stood up against these vicious attacks.
>
> Once again, the words of King ran through my memory, "I solemnly pledge to do my utmost to uphold the fair name of the Jews—because bigotry in any form is an affront to us all."[6]

It is important to understand that although criticism of Israel is not by itself anti-Semitism, there are certain kinds of criticism of Israel that are clearly anti-Semitic, even if the word *Jew* is never mentioned. An obvious instance is Amiri Baraka claiming in his poem that Israel and Sharon knew about the attack on the World Trade Center before it happened and warned 4,000 Israelis to stay away. Can anyone doubt that this variation on the blood libel is anti-Semitic to the core? Can anyone dispute that those who target Jews for physical attack—whether in France, Germany, or Russia—are engaging in anti-Semitic actions?

Professor Irwin Cotler, a leading scholar of human rights, has identified the following nine sets of what he calls "new anti-Semitism":[7]

- *Genocidal anti-Semitism.* The public calls for the destruction of Israel and the Jewish People. Examples are:

  The Covenants of terrorist groups like Hamas that commit themselves to the destruction of Israel and the Jewish People

  Religious legal rulings (fatwas) that call for the destruction of Israel and the Jewish people

  State-incited calls for genocide (e.g., the Iranian threat to annihilate Israel)

- *Political anti-Semitism*

  The denial of the Jewish people's right to self-determination

  The de-legitimization of Israel as a state

  The attribution to Israel of all the world's evils—Israel as the "poisoner of international wells"

- *Ideological anti-Semitism* (which surpasses the Zionism = Racism rhetoric) to "Nazify" Israel
- *Theological anti-Semitism.* The convergence of Islamic anti-Semitism and Christian "replacement" theology, drawing on classical hatred of Jews
- *Cultural anti-Semitism.* The mélange of attitudes, sentiments, and discourse of "fashionable" salon intellectuals
- *Economic anti-Semitism,* which goes beyond the Arab boycott of Israel to include extra-territorial application of restrictive covenants against countries trading with Israel
- *Holocaust denial*
- *Racist terrorism against Jews*
- *Denial to Israel of equality before the law in the international arena.* The singling out of Israel for differential and discriminatory treatment in the international arena

Whether or not one accepts each of these sets, there can be little doubt that some of these must be included in any comprehensive catalog of bigotry.

Certainly, denying the Holocaust, or blaming it on "the Jews," which has been a staple of Palestinian extremist rhetoric, constitutes bigotry. Even the "progressive" prime minister of the Palestinian Authority wrote a book denying the Holocaust, which he now apparently regrets. And the themes of outright Holocaust denial and blaming the Holocaust on the Jews are pervasive in the Friday sermons that are telecast by the Palestinian Authority.[8] It is not surprising that two of the issues that unite the extremists on the far right and the far left are Holocaust denial and unwavering support for Palestinian terrorism. It might be difficult to imagine two more different people with more different worldviews than Patrick Buchanan, the paleoconservative, and Noam Chomsky, the radical left anarchist. Yet they both strongly support the Palestinians and hate Israel. They also have both flirted with Holocaust denial, as have many Palestinian and Arab leaders.

Pat Buchanan has expressed doubts about whether Jews were gassed at Treblinka. His "evidence" was the following vignette: "In 1988, 97 kids, trapped 200 feet underground in a Washington, D.C. tunnel while two locomotives spewed diesel exhaust into the car, emerged unharmed after 45 minutes."[9] An article in the *New Republic* pointed out that "much of the material on which Buchanan bases his columns [about the Holocaust] is sent to him by pro-Nazi, and anti-Semitic cranks." Asked where he got the information about Treblinka, he replied, "Somebody sent it to me." The article concludes that Holocaust deniers know "they can expect a hearing from Buchanan."[10]

Buchanan's support for Nazi war criminals, such as Klaus Barbie and Karl Linnas, and for the abolition of the government office that investigates them, led former Justice Department official Alan Ryan to comment that "great numbers of people are asking themselves: Why is Pat Buchanan so in love with Nazi war criminals?"[11]

Noam Chomsky's flirtation with Holocaust denial is even stranger. Buchanan is simply a classic anti-Semite, as many of his fellow conservatives now acknowledge. But Chomsky is a Jew whose parents were Hebrew teachers. He went to the same Hebrew-speaking camp that I did and was actually a member of a left-wing pro-Israel group during his youth. But the published record speaks for itself.

The story begins with a strange Frenchman named Robert Faurisson. Faurisson, who was an obscure lecturer on French literature at the University of Lyon, wrote a book and gave talks in which he mocked Holocaust victims and survivors as perpetrators of a hoax. The Holocaust, according to Faurisson, never took place. The Hitler gas chambers never existed. The Jews bear responsibility for World War II. Hitler acted reasonably and in self-defense when he rounded up the Jews and put them in labor camps, not death camps. The "massive lie" about genocide was a deliberate concoction begun by American Zionists—in context he obviously means Jews. The principal beneficiary of this hoax is Israel, which has encouraged this "enormous political and financial fraud." The principal victims of this fraud have been the German people and the Palestinian people. Faurisson also called the diary of Anne Frank a forgery.[12]

Not surprisingly, as soon as Faurisson's crackpot tome was published, it was seized upon by Jew-haters throughout the world. In the United States, the notorious Liberty Lobby, which distributes *The Protocols of the Elders of Zion* and other anti-Semitic best-sellers, translated the most hateful portions of the work and distributed them widely within its network, touting the fact that Faurisson was a professor! His videotaped speeches were distributed for use at neo-Nazi gatherings. I sent for one such video and watched Faurisson smile when describing the "alleged victims" of the "nonexistent" gas chambers. His neo-Nazi audience laughed as he mocked the testimony of survivor eyewitnesses.

Following the publication of Faurisson's book, the University of Lyon suspended him for a semester, claiming that it could not guarantee his safety. This decision, understandable as it may have been considering the fact that Lyon suffered greatly during the Nazi occupation, was improper and foolish. A teacher has the right to be protected even for espousing idiotic views.

Chomsky was asked to join in protesting Faurisson's suspension. I am sure that he welcomed the opportunity, because Faurisson's writings and speeches are stridently anti-Zionist as well as anti-Semitic. Indeed, Professor

Chomsky has himself made statements about Zionist exploitation of the tragedy of World War II that are not, in my view, so different from some of those of Faurisson. He has also compared Israel with Nazi Germany.

Chomsky defended Faurisson not only on the issue of free speech but also on the *merits* of his scholarship and character. He signed a petition that characterized Faurisson's falsifications of history as "findings" and said that they were based on "extensive historical research."[13] Had Chomsky bothered to check on Faurisson's historical research, he would have found it to be faked.[14]

There was no extensive historical research. Instead, there was the fraudulent manufacturing of false antihistory. It was the kind of deception for which professors are rightly fired—not because their views are controversial but because they are violating the most basic canons of historical scholarship. Yet Chomsky was prepared to lend his academic legitimacy to Faurisson's "extensive historical research." Now, not only was the Holocaust "disproved" by a professor but the professor's research and findings were certified by another professor—this one from MIT!

Chomsky went even further. After signing the petition, he wrote an essay that he allowed to be used as a foreword to Faurisson's next book about his career as a Holocaust denier! In this book, Faurisson again calls the gas chambers a lie and repeats his claims about the hoax of the Holocaust. Chomsky, in his foreword, feigns ignorance of Faurisson's work—"I do not know his work very well"—but concludes that Faurisson's arguments are not anti-Semitic and that Faurisson himself is neither an anti-Semite nor a Nazi but rather "a sort of relatively apolitical liberal."[15]

A few years later, after it became unmistakably clear that Faurisson was consciously lending his name to all sorts of anti-Semitic and neo-Nazi groups, Chomsky repeated his character reference: "I see no anti-Semitic implications in denial of the existence of gas chambers, or even denial of the Holocaust. Nor would there be anti-Semitic implications, per se in the claim that the Holocaust (whether one believes it took place or not) is being exploited, viciously so, by apologists for Israeli repression and violence. I see no hint of anti-Semitic implications in Faurisson's work."[16]

I simply cannot understand how a Jew who was himself alive during the Holocaust and who calls virtually anything with which he disagrees "racism" can fail to see even a hint of anti-Semitism in the work of a man who describes the Holocaust as a "hoax" and "fraud" perpetrated by Jews. Nor can I understand how a Jew could say with reference to the Holocaust, "whether one believes it took place or not"—thus suggesting that reasonable people could believe either that it did or did not take place.

I came across this statement in a *Boston Globe* article that characterized Chomsky as a defender of underdogs and wrote the following letter to the editor:

While some may regard Chomsky as an eminent linguist, he does not understand the most obvious meaning of words in context. To fail to see any "hint of anti-Semitic implications" in Faurisson's collective condemnation of the Jewish people as liars is to be either a fool or a knave. Failure to recognize the anti-Semitic implications of Holocaust denial is like saying there would be no racist implications in a claim that Blacks enjoyed slavery, or no sexist implications in a statement that women want to be raped. The Holocaust is the central historical event of modern Jewish history. Efforts to deny or minimize it are the current tools of the anti-Semite and neo-Nazi. Not surprising, both Faurisson and Chomsky are frequently quoted with approval by those hate-mongers.

Chomsky's actions in defending the substance of Faurisson's bigoted remarks against valid charges of anti-Semitism—as distinguished from defending Faurisson's *right* to publish such pernicious drivel—disqualify Chomsky from being considered an honorable defender of the "underdog." The victims of the Holocaust, not its defenders or deniers, are the underdogs.[17]

Chomsky responded by arguing that Faurisson was an anti-Zionist rather than an anti-Semite because he denounced "Zionist lies." He charged that "Dershowitz's easy translation of 'Zionist' to 'Jewish' is illegitimate," and that, "in fact, it is a standard gambit of anti-Semites."[18]

Following this exchange, I challenged Chomsky to a public debate on the issue of whether it is anti-Semitic or anti-Jewish to deny the Holocaust. This was his answer: "It is so obvious that there is no point in debating it because *nobody* believes there is an anti-Semitic connotation to the denial of the Holocaust" (emphasis added).[19] That answer, which suggests the perverse world Chomsky lives in, speaks for itself.

One is left to speculate about Chomsky's political and psychological motives for becoming so embroiled in the substantive defense of a neo-Nazi Holocaust denier. The civil liberties–free speech rationale does not work for Chomsky: civil libertarians who defend the free speech of neo-Nazis do not get into bed with them by legitimating their findings as having been based on "extensive historical research" and by defending them against well-documented charges of anti-Semitism. Moreover, providing a foreword for a book is *joining* with the author and publisher in an effort to sell the book. It is intended not merely to leave the marketplace of ideas open. It is intended to influence that marketplace substantively in favor of the author's ideas.

Paul L. Berman, writing for the *Village Voice*, got it exactly right: "Chomsky's view of anti-Semitism is positively wild. His definition is so narrow, neither the *Protocols of the Elders of Zion* nor the no-Holocaust delusion fit into it. . . . I am afraid that his present remarks on anti-Semitism and Zionist lies disqualify him from ever being taken seriously on matters pertaining to Jews."[20]

Yet Chomsky, despite his long track record of mendacity about Israel and his perverse views of anti-Semitism, continues to be taken quite seriously on matters pertaining to Jews by legions of students and professors around the world. He has even taught a course that includes this subject at Harvard's Kennedy School of Government despite the fact that he is a linguist with no professional credentials in this area, other than his one-sided opinions.

The Chomsky–Faurisson episode illustrates some important issues discussed in this book. Chomsky's bizarre definition of anti-Semitism—a definition that excludes denial of the Holocaust and the claim that it is a Zionist hoax—reminds us how anti-Zionism often provides a cover for anti-Semitism. When Faurisson says that the Holocaust is a hoax perpetrated by Zionists, he means Jews. Many non-Zionist Jews in the United States and elsewhere have been involved in Holocaust education and memorialization. Faurisson and Chomsky defend any accusation leveled against the Jewish people as long as the accuser uses the right code word: *Zionists.* But these accusations easily translate from "Zionist" to "Jew." "Revisionist" historians like Faurisson are regularly cited by radical imams who preach hatred of Jews in the weekly sermons. For example, Sheikh Ibrahim Madhi—who, when he is not calling the Jews "donkeys" and demanding the destruction of Israel, is a lecturer on ecology at Al-Aqsa University in Gaza—delivered the following "historical" analysis in September 2001: "One of the Jews' evil deeds is what has come to be called 'The Holocaust' that is the slaughter of the Jews by Nazism. However, Revisionist [historians] have proven that this crime, carried out against some of the Jews, was planned by the Jews' leaders, and was part of their policy."[21]

This sermon—which Chomsky would not regard as anti-Semitic—was telecast on Palestinian Authority Television, as was the following sermon, delivered by Dr. Ahmad Abu Halabiya, who was an official member of the Fatwa Council, appointed by the Palestinian Authority:

Have no mercy on the Jews, no matter where they are, in any country. Fight them, wherever you are. Wherever you meet them, kill them. Wherever you are, kill those Jews and those Americans who are like them—and those who stand by them—they are all in one trench, against the Arabs and the Muslims—because they established Israel here, in the beating heart of the Arab world, in Palestine. They created it to be the outpost of their civilization—and the vanguard of their army, and to be the sword of the West and the crusaders, hanging over the necks of the monotheists, the Muslims in these lands. They wanted the Jews to be their spearhead."[22]

Even those who believe that singling out Zionists or the Zionist state for criticism is not anti-Semitic must surely acknowledge that there is a difference between mere *criticism* of Israel and *singling it out* for unique sanctions such as divestiture or boycott. It is true that those who advocate the latter have been accused of anti-Semitism, but it is false that those who fit into the former category have been so labeled. Yet the recent big lie lumps these distinct categories together. The time has come for those who are spreading this big lie either to put up by documenting their charge or to stop misleading the public.

32 Why Do So Many Jews and Even Israelis Side with the Palestinians?

THE ACCUSATION

The fact that so many Israelis and Jews support the Palestinian side and so few Palestinians, Arabs, and Muslims support the Israeli side is evidence that the Palestinian side is right.

THE ACCUSERS

"[F]ollowing in the line of Judah Magnus, the great critical efforts of non- or anti-Zionist Jews like Elmer Berger, Israel Shahak, Noam Chomsky, Maxine Rodinson, Livia Rokach, I.F. Stone, many of them sponsored or directly encouraged by Arab efforts in the West, [produced material] forever dismissing the myth of Zionist innocence." (Edward Said and Christopher Hitchens[1])

"Some of the young Israeli revisionist historians . . . [Tom Segev, Benny Morris, and so on] are Zionists, but their work is done with a genuine will to understand the past; what they say about the horrors of 1948, they say openly without a desire to lie or conceal the past. Their counterparts in the establishment still operate with the old scruples." (Edward Said and Christopher Hitchens[2])

"Zionism is anti-Semitic because it essentializes Jews. Many Jews do not support Israeli oppression of the Palestinian people." (Amer Zahr,

217

University of Michigan law student, at a panel discussion sponsored by Michigan's pro-Palestinian student group[3])

"The true Jews remain faithful to Jewish belief and are not contaminated with Zionism. The true Jews are against dispossessing the Arabs of their land and homes. According to the Torah, the land should be returned to them." (Website of Neturei Karta USA, the ultra-orthodox anti-Zionist sect[4])

THE REALITY

The reality is that complete freedom of information and freedom of speech among Israelis and Jews allows for the widest array of views to be presented, whereas virtually total control over information to most residents of Arab and Muslim states, coupled with extreme sanctions for expressing dissenting views, makes any realistic comparison impossible.

THE PROOF

Israelis and Jews have no limitations on receiving views regarding the Israeli–Palestinian dispute. They can watch Arab and Islamic television programs, read the most virulent anti-Zionist material, and express any views they wish on the conflict. Moreover, Jews and Israelis have traditionally held the widest array of views ranging from political and religious anti-Zionism to messianic concepts of the Jewish state.

The media tends to emphasize dissenting rather than mainstream views. For example, the 500 to 600 Israeli reservists who refused to serve in the territories constituted less than 1 percent of those who did serve and a far smaller number than those who were above the age of service and insisted on volunteering to defend Israel. Yet the media, for understandable reasons, paid far more attention to the dissidents than to those in the mainstream.

Moreover, many Jewish organizations in the United States, anxious to hear the widest range of views, welcomed the dissenters and gave them a full hearing. The American and European media generally tend to present the views of articulate Israelis, such as Amos Oz and Yossi Beilin as well as leaders of peace now and B'Tselem, who tend to be quite critical of current Israeli policies. Although most of these Israeli critics themselves remain Zionists and support Israel's right to exist as a Jewish state and to defend itself against terrorists by proportional means, their criticisms—well understood *within* Israel—are misused outside of Israel by those who would delegitimize and destroy the Jewish state.

This contrasts sharply with the Palestinian, Arab, and Muslim approach to dissent. Even the most minimal of dissenting voices are imprisoned and often executed. (Recall the fatwa against Salman Rushdie.) Moreover, many Palestinians, Arabs, and Muslims throughout the world are denied access to information that could influence their perspectives in favor of Israel. For example, they are shown repeated images of Palestinian civilians being killed without being shown the mangled bodies of Jewish babies, women, and the elderly. They are shown pictures of houses being destroyed without being told that they were emptied of residents prior to the bulldozers arriving. There is absolutely no comparison between the free flow of information among Jews and Israelis on the one hand, and among Palestinians, Muslims, and Arabs on the other hand.

Moreover, Jews and Israelis have traditionally included some extremists on virtually every issue. There is an old joke about two Israelis being found on a desert island after having been stranded for five years. The first thing they reported to their rescuers was that they had formed seven political parties between them. The Israeli population today includes messianic anti-Zionists, Stalinists, Maoists, Trotskyites, one-worlders, flat-Earth believers, Holocaust-deniers, and other conceivable—and some inconceivable—views.

I recall a conversation with a prominent Israeli lawyer who has devoted her life not only to defending Palestinian terrorists in court but to supporting their cause in the political arena and befriending them personally. She is a virulent anti-Zionist and an active member of the Stalinist wing of the Communist party. When I asked her how she could be a Stalinist, her answer was simple and moving, if ultimately unconvincing: "Stalin saved me and my family from Hitler; I could never forget that." (I regret not having thought to ask her how she could support and befriend people who deny or minimize the Holocaust in which so many of her own family were murdered.) In addition to these dissident Jewish views, more than a million Muslims and Arabs are citizens of Israel and have complete freedom of information and expression.

Prior to the collapse of the Camp David and Taba peace talks, there was far more disagreement among Israeli doves about whether Arafat was a real peace partner and whether Palestinian peace efforts were serious. Now, although there is still an active peace camp, there are very few Israelis who place any faith in Arafat's willingness or ability to make peace. As Yoram Kinuik, one of the founders of the Israeli peace movement, put it, "Since the failure of the Camp David talks, when the truth came out, I've had to face the fact that the Arabs simply don't accept Israel being here. [Our peace] partner is the suicide bomber."[5] The fact that so many are now optimistic about the appointment of a new prime minister, despite the fact that Abu Mazen wrote a book denying the Holocaust, is a testament to the perseverance of the peace camp, as well as to the paucity of Palestinian leaders with acceptable views.

Many Israelis are so anxious to make peace that some are willing to distort the history and deny clear facts when the history and the facts seem to make it more difficult to make peace. For example, when Yasser Arafat was caught giving a secret briefing to Arab leaders in which he revealed his true plan to destroy the Jewish state, many Israelis refused to believe the story. Many Israeli peace advocates are also willing to accept revisionist, and often false, historical accounts that produce a more "even-handed" narrative of the past, because they believe that such a narrative, as contrasted with the actual history, is more conducive to peace.

Finally, there is a somewhat irrational but historically accurate factor that contributes to the disparity between Jewish and Israeli dissent, on the one hand, and the lack thereof on the other side. There has always been a small element within the Jewish community that for largely inexplicable reasons has been hypercritical of everything associated with Judaism, Jews, or the Jewish states. Karl Marx, Noam Chomsky, and Norman Finkelstein come easily to mind. The reasons for this lie more in the realm of Sigmund Freud and Jean Paul Sartre than in the realm of political or media discourse. But it has been a sad reality over time.

I do not mean to suggest by this observation that all anti-Zionists and Israel-bashers are self-hating Jews. People can be wrong on the merits without requiring any psychological explanation. But the reality is that there are some Jews who despise anything Jewish, ranging from their religion, to the Jewish state, to individuals who are "too Jewish." To recognize the accuracy of this empirical observation is not necessarily to undercut the importance of dealing with anti-Zionist and anti-Israel arguments on their merits and demerits. It is to offer a partial explanation for what seems so incongruous to some—namely, the ferocious, sometimes even joyous, and, as the feminist writer Phyllis Chesler has put it, "erotic," nature of knee-jerk Israel-bashing on behalf of some Jews.

There are also some Jews for whom Israel's growing unpopularity among the radical left is something of an embarrassment. These Jews want to be liked by those whose politics they support on other issues. Accordingly they tend to distance themselves from Israel and often support the Palestinian side without much thought about the merits of the case. Opposing Israel and supporting the Palestinians is, for some Jews, a way of establishing their left-wing credentials and proving that their political correctness trumps any ethnic solidarity. This phenomenon creates a multiplier effect that results in some Jews who previously supported Israel now abandoning that support as more and more radical leftists take up the Palestinian cause as part of their agenda.

A related phenomenon has seen some Jews, especially in Europe, abandoning their support of Israel because of fear. In 1967, following its spectacular victory in the Six-Day War, Israel was seen as a source of protection for Jews around the world. American and European Jews, basking vicariously in Israel's victory, experienced a new pride in being Jews. Today Israel is seen by many European Jews as a source of danger, because anti-Zionism has become the current justification or excuse for violence against Jews. This has resulted in some fair-weather supporters of Israel abandoning their support during difficult times.

It is a fundamental fallacy to conclude that one side of a dispute must be right if some people who are ethnically identified with *that* side support the *other side*. For example, the fact that there is a handful of Jewish Holocaust deniers—as well as some prominent Jews, like Noam Chomsky, who are prepared to endorse the "extensive research" done by a Holocaust denier—does not mean that the Holocaust did not occur. Nor does the fact that some Italian Jews supported Mussolini in the early 1930s prove that fascism was right. Yet a staple of pro-Palestinian propaganda is the argument that is structured as follows: "See, even a Jew like [fill in the name] believes that Israel is wrong and the Palestinians are right about [fill in the issue]." This "argument by ethnic admission" is both logically and empirically fallacious.

Conclusion
Israel — the Jew among Nations

In order to assess the status of Israel in the international community, it may be useful to look at the Middle East's only democracy as "the Jew" among nations. Privately admired for its pioneering spirit, intelligence, aggressiveness, and tenacity, the State of Israel has been publicly condemned as racist, militant, xenophobic, uncompromising, authoritarian, and stiff-necked. During its century and a quarter–long struggle for nationhood and survival following millennia of forced dispersion and exile, the modern prestate and State of Israel has been far from perfect in its adherence to its own professed elevated values and those of international law, human rights, and civil liberties (described collectively as "the rule of law").

But, as stated at the outset, it is the thesis of this book that no nation in the history of the world that has faced comparable threats to its survival—both external and internal—has ever made greater efforts at, and has ever come closer to, achieving the high norms of the rule of law. Yet no civilized nation in the history of the world, including totalitarian and authoritarian regimes, has ever been as repeatedly, unfairly, and hypocritically condemned and criticized by the international community as Israel has been over the years. The net result is that the *gulf* between Israel's *actual* record of compliance with the rule of law and its *perceived* record of compliance with the rule of law is greater than for any other nation in history.

I challenge anyone to dispute this conclusion by naming another country in which the gulf is equal or greater. None even comes close, although for some America-bashers the United States may be a distant second to

Israel. The underlying reason for this misleading gulf is that Israel's imperfections—and there are many—have been greatly exaggerated by large segments of the international community, the media, the academy, and public opinion, while the comparative imperfections of other countries have been minimized.

In the interests of fairness and peace, the world must come to see Israel in a realistic way. It must stop looking only for imperfections, and then magnifying them all out of proportion both to Israel's own positive accomplishments and to the imperfections of other nations.

Israel is a tiny nation, with few natural resources and little natural wealth, that has had to devote an enormous percentage of its gross national product to defending itself against external and internal enemies. Yet it has not only created a good life for its Jewish citizens, it has helped its Arab citizens live better lives—as measured by income, health, longevity, and other accepted criteria—than the Arabs of any neighboring countries. It should not be surprising that a poll of the Arab-Israeli residents of Umm el-Fahm conducted by the Arab-Israeli weekly paper *Kul Al-Arab* in 2000 showed a striking 83 percent opposed to including their city in a Palestinian state. The reason given by a majority of those opposed was that they wanted to remain under democratic rule and they enjoyed a good quality of life.[1] Although there is much to be criticized, and progress to be made, in the economic inequality between Jews and Arabs living in Israel, the world should acknowledge the benefits that the democratic state of Israel brings to the Arabs living and working within its borders.

Opponents of Israel tend to emphasize the disparity between Israeli Arabs and Jews, while hardly mentioning how much better Israeli Arabs fare than their counterparts in the Arab states. In the United States and Europe newspapers routinely cite the fact that Israeli Arabs have the lowest average family income of any ethnic group in Israel, as well as the highest infant mortality rate (as do minority groups in most countries, including our own).[2] Few point out, however, that Arab families tend to be much larger *despite* the infant mortality rate, or that women are discouraged from working in the Arab community—facts that explain some of the discrepancies. Even the very critical group Sikkuy, which monitors civic equality among Jews and Palestinians, acknowledges that there have been good-faith efforts on the part of the Israeli government to improve Arab infrastructure and educational institutions.[3]

Israel's health care system also dwarfs that of its neighbors, to the benefit of all its citizens. Israel has national health insurance, which guarantees health care to all of its citizens, regardless of race or religion. Access to such care has helped to raise the life expectancy of Israeli Arabs to well above that of Arab neighbors, and to drive their infant mortality rates to well below. Although life expectancy is somewhat lower for Israeli Palestinians than for Israeli Jews—seventy-seven years for women and seventy-four for men rather than eighty and seventy-six respectively[4]—it is still well above that of Syria, which is only in the upper sixties for both.[5]

Syria is a resource-rich country, but like Iraq, its wealth has been used to line its leaders' pockets rather than on national health. Arafat is now one of the richest men in the world, but little of his extorted bounty is spent on hospitals or health care. It is unfair to criticize Israel for its lack of perfect parity while not criticizing these other leaders for their complete lack of effort. In truth, Israeli health care has likely saved more Palestinian lives than the care available in many of the neighboring countries combined.

The Israeli economy also creates health benefits beyond its borders. Israel has become a world leader in biotechnology, with Israeli companies leading the way in elements of cancer and autoimmune disease research. There are now over 160 biotech companies in Israel, with hundreds of millions of private dollars invested, providing thousands of jobs and hundreds of health-improving products—80 percent of which are for export.[6] With close ties to Israel's flourishing research universities and educational system, as well as support from the government, Israeli biotech has become industry leading, providing advances in research on Parkinson's and Alzheimer's, multiple sclerosis, and other diseases that are the cause of great suffering. Now, tragically, it has become the world's leader in the medical treatment of injuries caused by terrorism. Israeli companies and Israeli government research dollars are saving lives both in Israel and abroad, and the same simply cannot be said of any other country in the region despite their much greater share of natural resources. That Israel should be so villainized for its inequalities—inequalities that plague every country—despite its disproportionately large contributions in health care, simply shows that an unfair view is taken of the real benefits that the Israeli economy and health care system provide, both in Israel and around the world.

Even aside from medicine, Israeli research on many subjects, ranging from computer technology to archeology, is among the most respected in the world.

The point that is often ignored is that Israel has become—through hard work, ingenuity, and most of all, dedication to freedom and the rule of law—a flourishing and diverse democracy with a bustling economy, a vibrant and critical media, a creative artistic culture, and a commitment to equality based on gender, sexual orientation, and race. Other countries in the region, which have more natural resources and comparable amounts of foreign aid, have failed to translate these assets into benefits to their people. Moreover, the relatively strong Israeli economy materially contributes to the well-being of *all* Israelis, regardless of their religion, ethnicity, or race, and the gap between Jewish and non-Jewish Israelis will surely close even further if peace is achieved.

Professor Amnon Rubenstein—a strong supporter of a peaceful two-state-solution and a frequent critic of Israeli government policies—well summarized Israel's achievements on its fifty-fifth birthday:

> Israel can look backwards with tremendous pride. Minute in size, not much bigger than a sliver of Mediterranean coastline, it has withstood continuing Arab onslaughts, wars, boycott and terrorism; it has turned itself from a poor, rural country to an industrial and post industrial powerhouse; despite the long road ahead, and the need for further integration, it has reduced social, educational and health gaps between its various components, including gaps between Arabs and Jews. Some of its achievements are unprecedented: Israeli Arabs have a higher life-expectancy than most European whites; its democracy functions, inside Israel proper, in times of great national emergency; it boasts of the most activists and interventionist courts in the world, who do not fear to tread where other courts shun intervention; it has maintained freedom of the press in time of war; it stands out as a singular democratic, first-world island in a sea of Arab and Moslem poverty and backwardness.

Yet, these realities are often ignored or distorted in a deliberate effort to demonize Israel.

I can easily understand why the oil interests of the world might seek to distort the facts in order to favor the Arabs, who control much of the world's oil and gas reserves, over the Israelis, who gave back the only oil fields they had in order to make peace with Egypt. I can understand why Islamic fundamentalists favor the Palestinians, who have promised to establish an Islamic state, over the Israelis, who have a largely secular Jewish democracy. I can even understand why anti-Semites, like Pat Buchanan and David Duke, favor the radical, anti-Christian, and anti-American Palestinians, whom they would ordinarily despise if they were fighting anyone else but the Jews. I can understand why sexists, homophobes, and racists would favor those who discriminate against women, gays, and non-Muslims, over the Israelis, who are committed to equality.

I can understand why those who do not value human life favor groups who promote suicide bombing and the murder of civilians, over Israel, which values every human life. I can understand why those who do not care about children favor terrorists, who abuse their own children by turning them into suicide bombers and placing their bomb factories next to kindergartens, and who abuse the children of others by targeting them for terrorism, over Israelis, who try to keep children away from combat.

I can understand why the extreme radical left, which favors instability over stability, would favor the radical destabilizing impact of Palestinian terrorism over the stability of Israel. I can understand why some who hate the United States, freedom, and democracy favor those who have sided with America's enemies—the Kaiser, Hitler, Stalin, Saddam Hussein, and Osama bin Laden—over one of America's most loyal and valuable democratic allies.

I can understand why the neo-fascist right, which bemoans Hitler's failure to complete his genocide, would favor the destruction of Israel. I can understand why those who believe that conflict should be resolved by violence rather than by negotiations would favor the Palestinian leader, who walked away from Camp David and Taba without offering any peace proposal and renewed the violence, over Israel, which has always been willing to negotiate and accept compromise. I can understand why all of these would favor the Palestinian cause over the Israeli cause.

But I cannot for the life of me understand why peace-loving people committed to equality and self-determination should favor the side that rejects all the values they hold dear and oppose the side that promotes these values. What then explains the widespread support for the Palestinians and the widespread opposition to Israel? I am not, by asking this question, including constructive criticism of Israel or support for the legitimate aspirations of the Palestinian people, who have suffered greatly, although mostly at the hands of their own destructive leadership and their exploitation by other Arab nations.

Nor am I referring to reasonable opposition to any particular prime minister, government, party, or policy of Israel. Many supporters of Israel oppose—even strongly oppose—particular aspects of Israel at a given time, as I do. I am asking about something qualitatively different: a visceral dislike—sometimes hatred—of Israel, coupled with uncritical support of the Palestinian cause, even by those (such as some Quakers) who would normally be appalled by terrorism, those (such as some pro-American patriots) who would normally be outraged at the widespread Palestinian support for America's enemies, those (like some feminists) who would usually rail against the sexist practices of many Palestinians, those (like some civil libertarians) who would never tolerate the lawlessness of the Palestinian authority, those (like some leftists) who would normally be opposed to the financial corruption of the Palestinian leaders and their exploitation of Palestinian workers, and those (like some internationalists) who would never justify the claim of many Palestinians to destroy a member nation of the United Nations and to target noncombatants for terrorism.

When it comes to opposition to Israel and support for the Palestinian cause, consistency seems to be forgotten. The Jewish state is sui generis. It is impossible to explain the attitudes of many otherwise rational people and institutions by reference to principles of rationality, morality, or consistency. All of these seem to fly out the window when the Jewish state is being discussed.

Various explanations have been offered for this anomaly. First, good people favor the underdog, and the stateless Palestinians are the underdogs in their struggle against the occupation by the powerful Israeli state. Second, the Palestinians are people of color, while the Israelis are white Europeans. Third, Israel is a tool of the imperialist United States, while the Palestinians are a third world people. Fourth, good people have come to expect more of the Jews than they do of the Arabs. Fifth, decent people know that they cannot influence Arab behavior, but they can influence the behavior of Israel. Each of these arguments—really rationalization—is demonstrably false and some smack of blatant racism.

Viewed from the global perspective, Israel, as the world's only Jewish nation, is clearly the underdog. The Palestinians have the widespread support of a billion Muslims. Add to that the United Nations, the European community, the third world, the Vatican, many influential academics, the international left, the far right, and many Protestant churches. The Palestinians have far more support than the Tibetans, the Kurds, the Armenians, the Chechens, and other real underdogs. Moreover, the nations that are oppressing these other underdog groups—China, Turkey, and Russia—are far more powerful than tiny Israel with the population of approximately 5.37 million Jews and 1.26 million Arabs. Yet these other "underdogs" receive little support from those who champion the Palestinians.

Israel is the underdog in yet another, even more dangerous, way. It cannot afford to lose even a single war without exposing its population to genocide and its nationhood to politicide. Wars waged against Israel are wars of extermination that target its cities and population centers. Its enemies are seeking its total destruction.

Israel, in contrast, avoids targeting cities and civilians and does not seek the destruction of any neighboring state. The stakes are far greater for Israel than for any of its enemies, and despite its current military strength—which is absolutely necessary as a deterrent against enemy aggressions—Israel is clearly the underdog over the long term of history. The underdog rationale for supporting the Palestinians is short-sighted and inconsistent with the lack of support for real underdogs.

With regard to support for people of color, Israel is truly a nation of color. It has one of the most diverse populations in the world, including black Africans from Ethiopia; brown Africans and Asians from North Africa, Yemen, Egypt, Iraq, and Morocco; Jews from Central Asia, Russia, and the Caucasus; and families from Romania, Latin America, and the former Yugoslavia. Nelson Mandela was simply wrong when he described Israel as a "white" nation as contrasted with Iraq, which he called a "black" nation.

As far as Israel being a tool of the United States, that is simply false. It is an ally. Both countries are democracies fighting against terrorism. Israel is also an independent nation pursuing its own self-interest. It was established with the support of the Soviet Union, which originally recognized it because of its socialist roots. It allied itself with England and France when Egypt nationalized the Suez Canal. It has assisted black African nations with its technical expertise and other forms of aid.

The United States has often opposed Israel's policies, as in the Suez matter and when it could have destroyed the encircled Egyptian army in 1973. The United States supported Israel's efforts to make peace with the Palestinians in 2000–2001, and President Bill Clinton laid the entire blame for the collapse of the Camp David and Taba negotiations at the feet of the Palestinians, where it belongs. The close but independent relationship between the United States and Israel—based on mutual principles of democracy, equality, and the rule of law—is an argument for supporting Israel, not for applying a double standard of condemnation against it, except for those who hate everything the United States stands for, like Noam Chomsky, who believes that the United States is the leader of the real "Axis of Evil." Not surprisingly, Chomsky's "Axis of Evil" also includes Israel and Turkey,[7] and excludes Libya, Iran, Cuba, North Korea, and even Saddam Hussein's Iraq.

The argument that more should be expected of the Jews and less of the Arabs, and that the "rational" Israelis are more subject to pressure than the "irrational" Palestinians, is primitive racism. It also creates self-fulfilling prophecies by expecting the Arabs to act irrationally. An Israeli may be entitled to expect more of Israel, just as an American may be entitled to expect more of his own country and a Palestinian to expect more of his own people. But no outsider is entitled to expect more of one people than another. Even a Jew who has chosen not to become an Israeli citizen and to suffer its burdens and risks is not entitled, in my view, to apply a double standard to the Jewish state and not to other states.

Certainly, no one should expect less of well-educated, wealthy, and advantaged Palestinians (like Arafat) or Arabs (like bin Laden) than of their Jewish counterparts. Nor is it true that Americans should be able to demand more from Israel than from its Arab neighbors because Israel is the recipient of a large amount of financial aid from the United States. Such an approach *would* turn Israel into an American puppet, which it is not.

Israel, more than any Arab nation, *earns* its financial assistance by providing the United States with invaluable intelligence information, technological advice, and a democratic presence in the Mideast. Egypt, Jordan, Turkey, and the Palestinian Authority, which together receive aid comparable to that received by Israel, provide the United States little in return. They receive foreign aid in large part to bolster regimes that are in danger of internal insurrections. Israel, as a democracy, has no such need. The benign double standard argument is an extremely dangerous one bordering on racism and encouraging further violence.

If the previous rationalizations are rejected, what else remains to explain the irrational hatred so often directed against Israel and the obvious disparity between reality and perception that exists with regard to Israel? One obvious and disturbing explanation is the lingering anti-Semitism in many parts of the international community, which carries over from "the Jew" to the Jewish nation. A second is that the Palestinian movement has made a concerted and somewhat successful effort to demonize Israel by exaggerating its imperfections in human rights. A third is that Israeli opponents of the government in power—past and present— have internationalized domestic opposition by highlighting the imperfections of human rights and broadcasting them abroad, thus confirming in the minds of many the exaggerations made by Israel's enemies.

A fourth explanation is that even friends of Israel—domestic and external—seem to expect more of Israel in terms of human rights because it is the Jewish state. A fifth is that even some people of goodwill enjoy sticking it to the Jews, who they believe have always claimed some moral superiority, when the Jewish state behaves like other states. Thomas Friedman said, "The anti-Semitism coming out of Europe today suggests that deep down Europeans want Mr. Sharon to commit a massacre against Palestinians, or they want to describe what he did in Jenin as a massacre, so that the Europeans can finally get the guilt of the Holocaust off their backs and are able to shout: 'Look at these Jews, they're worse than we were!'"[8]

A sixth explanation is that some non-Jews who have become accustomed to seeing and sympathizing with Jews as helpless victims have difficulty accepting the image of the strong Jewish state with the military capacity to fight back. But whatever the explanations—and none of them alone or in combination begin to justify the double standard—it is essential to the rule of law that this gulf be reassessed.

During the first 2000 years of the Common Era, the soul of any given city, nation, culture, or religion could be fairly assessed by the way it regarded and treated its Jewish neighbors. Today, the soul of the international community can be fairly assessed by the way in which it treats the Jew among nations. Judged by this standard, the United Nations fails miserably, as do many of the great nations of Europe, Asia, Africa, and South America. Indeed, if the United Nations were ultimately to fail, as the League of Nations did, it may well be as the result of losing its moral authority over Israel.

When the General Assembly voted to declare Zionism a form of racism, it became complicit in anti-Semitism and suffered an enormous loss of prestige and support in the United States and some other parts of the world (although not in others). When the U.N. Conference on Women in Mexico City in 1975, and in Copenhagen in 1980, devoted more time and energy to condemning Zionism than sexism, it became a cruel joke. When the U.N. Conference on Racism in Durban became, in the words of Canadian Parliament member and human rights scholar Irwin Cotler, "a racist conference against Jews,[9] it became a megaphone for bigotry.

More than the credibility of the General Assembly or the entire United Nations is put at risk by the unfair treatment accorded the Jewish state. The International Criminal Court will fail if it cannot be trusted to be evenhanded toward Israelis, even if it is fair with regard to others. Southern courts during Jim Crow and South African courts during apartheid were often fair in cases between white litigants, but they could not be trusted to do justice between black and white litigants. The same has generally been the case with regard to international organizations when Israel is involved. Even Amnesty International—an otherwise wonderful organization, which I support—has contributed to the false comparisons between Israel and outlaw nations that do not respect the rule of law. The World Health Organization, without hearing any evidence, once condemned Israel for providing poor health care in the West Bank, despite the dramatic increase in life expectancy and decrease in infant mortality. A medical team was then sent to investigate. The team, composed of doctors from Romania, Indonesia, and Senegal, concluded that "the medical care in the Arab territories occupied by Israel has shown slow but steady improvement in the nine years since the 1967 war." When this favorable expert report was received, the World Health Organization voted 65 to 18, with 14 abstentions, not to accept it, since it did not conform to its political agenda.[10]

> In December 2001, the contracting parties of the Geneva Convention convened for the first time—and they did it to criticize Israel. This was the only time in 52 years that any nation was condemned. Similarly the UN Commission on Human Rights has repeatedly singled out Israel for discriminatory treatment while ignoring the real human rights violators.[11]

Routine public condemnation of Israel for actions that rarely incur condemnation when undertaken by other nations is only one manifestation of this pervasive double standard. A simple test of this proposition would be to imagine an extraterrestrial messenger sent to Earth to assess the relative compliance of this planet's nations to the rule of law. If the messenger were to limit his review to U.N. resolutions and the record of international condemnations over the past third of a century, he would report back to his supervisors that Israel is the outlaw nation of the earth with the worst record of compliance with the rule of law.

The extraterrestrial messenger would report that this pariah among nations has been condemned for waging aggressive war, for capturing and keeping territory of other nations, for dispossessing citizens of their homes, for destroying the homes of innocent civilians, for torturing prisoners, for conducting secret trials, for imprisoning people without trial, for bombing civilian targets, for enforcing religious and gender discrimination, and for a host of other violations of the rule of law. Being a sophisticated messenger, our extraterrestrial would look not only at the history of condemnation of Israel but also at the *comparative* history of condemnations directed against *other* nations. Such comparative assessment would only confirm his conclusion that Israel was the planet's worst offender in terms of the seriousness of the offenses, their persuasiveness, and their recidivism. He would learn little from studying U.N. resolutions about the human rights violations of China, Cuba, Egypt, Jordan, Algeria, Belarus, the Philippines, and other nations that have a much poorer record of compliance with the rule of law than Israel.

The extraterrestrial messenger is but a figment of a law professor's imagination. But this same law professor has traveled the real world lecturing and speaking about the rule of law to university and other audiences of young earthlings from New Zealand to South Africa, from China to Russia, from Australia to Germany, from Canada to Poland, from Italy to Norway, and every major city in North America. My report of the *perceptions* of many young, highly educated men and women throughout the world would not be very different from the conclusions reached by the extraterrestrial messenger.

Although most young earthlings realize that human rights violations are not unique to Israel—they have heard about Iran, Iraq, Libya, Algeria, China, North Korea, and other flagrant and persistent violators—many believe that Israel is *among* the worst offenders. This perception, as I have demonstrated, is not only unfair and dangerous to Israel but is destructive of the rule of law itself, which cannot survive in the absence of a single standard fairly applied to all nations. When "human rights" becomes a tactic, selectively and successfully invoked by the worst violators against those who make serious efforts to comply with the rule of law, human rights lose all objective meaning and their continued utility in the ongoing struggle for international justice becomes diluted.

Even some experienced diplomats eventually fall for the big lie when it is repeated often enough. United Nations Secretary General Kofi Annan has "remarked that it cannot be that the entire world is against Israel, yet Israel is right."[12] But anyone who remembers the "blood libel" (the claim that Jews ritually murder Christian children and use their blood to make matzah) or the *Protocols of the Elders of Zion* (the Czarist forgery) will understand that millions of people can believe a totally false accusation.

The great moral issue facing the world at the dawn of this millennium is whether Israel's attempt to protect itself against terrorism will result in a massive increase in worldwide anti-Semitism—anti-Semitism directed against the Jewish state itself, its supporters, and Jews throughout the world. Two indisputable propositions are (1) that Israel's current efforts to protect its innocent civilians against those who would murder children, women, the elderly, and others is no worse—and in many respects is considerably better—than protective efforts taken by other democracies that have faced far less virulent threats, and (2) that no other country—whether Catholic, Protestant, Muslim, or without religion—has faced the kind of condemnation that Israel and its supporters have encountered, particularly since Yasser Arafat walked away from Israel's peace offers at Camp David and Taba and dramatically increased the campaign of terrorism against Israeli civilians.

As many objective commentators have observed, not since the horrible days of the late 1930s and early 1940s has the world experienced so perverse and sustained an outpouring of primitive anti-Semitism. Andrew Sullivan, who wrote extensively for the *New York Times Magazine*, put it this way just before the war against Iraq:

> America's anti-war movement, still puny and struggling, is showing signs of being hijacked by one of the oldest and darkest prejudices there is. Perhaps it was inevitable. The conflict against Islamo-fascism obviously circles back to the question of Israel. Fanatical anti-Semitism, as bad or even worse than Hitler's, is now a cultural norm across much of the Middle East. It's the acrid glue that unites Saddam, Arafat, Al-Qaeda, Hezbollah, Iran and the Saudis.[13]

The writer Oriana Fallaci has stated it even more dramatically: "I find it shameful and see in all this the rise of a new fascism, a new Nazism. A fascism, a Nazism, that is much more grim and revolting because it is conducted and nourished by those who hypocritically pose as do-gooders [and] progressives."[14]

As with most previous outbreaks of anti-Semitism, some have sought to blame it on the victims. "It's the Jews' fault," wrote Dostoyevsky in his notorious article on the Jewish question in 1879. The great Russian writer argued that the hatred of Jews "must have stemmed from something." And instead of looking for the sources within the haters, he looked to the actions of the hated and declared that "the Jew himself is guilty." He continued: "The Jew, wherever he has settled, has . . . humiliated and debauched the people." According to Dostoyevsky, it was the Jews who "ruined" the Lithuanians "with vodka," and it is the Jews who will re-enslave the "millions of liberated Negroes" in the American South: "The negroes have now been liberated from their slave owners, but . . . that will not last because the Jews, of whom there are so many in the world, will jump at this new little victim."[15]

Dostoyevsky's views of the worldwide Jewish conspiracy are not much different from the views expressed by Hitler in *Mein Kampf* or in the Czarist forgery *The Protocols of the Elders of Zion*. In Dostoyevsky's bizarre world "the Jews are reigning everywhere over stock exchanges," "they control capital," "they are the masters of credit," "they are also the masters of international politics," and "what is going to happen in the future is known to the Jews themselves." He predicted that "their reign, their complete reign is approaching!"[16] He believed that "Judaism and the *Jewish idea*" is "clasping the whole world instead of Christianity."[17] His conspiracy theory was based on the following logic. He found it "impossible to conceive of a Jew without God," refusing to believe "in the existence of atheists even among the educated Jews." He believed that the Jews "all of them—both the lowest Yiddisher and the highest and most learned one—the philosopher and the cabalist-rabbi—all believe that the messiah will again unite them in Jerusalem and will bring by his sword all nations to their feet." He also believed that "this is the reason that the overwhelming majority of the Jews have a predilection but for one profession—the trade in gold." When the messiah comes, according to Dostoyevsky, "it will be easier [for the Jews] to carry [the gold] away."[18] Dostoyevsky could not explain why the Jews would want to carry the gold away when they already are "reigning in Europe, are directing there at least the stock exchanges and therefore politics, domestic affairs, and the morality of the states."[19]

Nor was Dostoyevsky's bigotry directed only at Judaism in the abstract. He deemed it "difficult to find anything more irritable . . . than the educated Jew."[20]

It is quite remarkable that a man of Dostoevsky's brilliance and insight in so many areas could have harbored such primitive fantasies about the Jews. It must be recalled, however, that Dostoyevsky's fame is based on his fiction writings and not on his nonfiction rantings. Like many anti-Semites throughout history, and even today, Dostoyevsky disclaimed any a priori anti-Jewish feelings, saying it is "the Jew himself who is responsible" for all the hatred directed against him. These views were echoed by Hitler, Stalin, Cardinal Glemp, and other notorious anti-Semites throughout the ages.

Now the claim is, "It's the Israelis' fault," or "It's Sharon's fault." But the facts no more support this accusation than Dostoyevsky's reasoning.

An interesting point of comparison might be the best, certainly the Western world's favorite, Arab–Muslim nation: Jordan. A creation of British imperialism, Jordan occupied the West Bank for twenty years. It annexed it, imposed emergency martial laws on its residents, and excluded all Jews from it. In September 1970, King Hussein of Jordan killed and injured more Palestinians in one month than Israel has during three years of responding to the suicide bombing intifada.[21] Torture, especially of Palestinians, is rampant in Jordan and has been developed into a fine art. Not only are suspected terrorists tortured but so are their relatives. They have so perfected the technique that our CIA has come to rely on them, along with Egypt and the Philippines. Everything bad that Israel has done to Palestinians, Jordan has done far worse. And yet there are no divestment or boycott campaigns directed at that kingdom, only against the democracy to its west.

As a civil libertarian and human rights advocate, I personally disapprove of many of Israel's compromises with perfection in the rule of law, as I do with my own country's imperfections. Were I an Israeli citizen, I would be campaigning for changes and improvements in Israel. But the international community—unlike Israeli citizens—has no right to single out Israel for criticism as the worst offender when that beleaguered nation is among the most committed to the rule of law. For the international community to accuse Israel of being the worst or among the worst violators of the rule of law is the international equivalent of the old anti-Semitic blood libel. To demonstrate how the international community's unfair treatment of Israel is itself a barrier to peace, let me pose an important *what if* question.

What if Israel were to accede to every demand being made by the Palestinian Authority, the United Nations, and the European Community? What if, after taking all of the steps demanded of it, terrorism against its civilians continued, even escalated? What would the international community then expect Israel to do? What would the international community do? What could Israel count on it to do?

These are the questions being asked by moderate Israelis and their American supporters who crave peace. They are particularly troubling questions in light of how the international community responded after Ehud Barak offered the Palestinians nearly all of their wish list and the Palestinian leadership responded by escalating the terrorism.

The standard answer being offered today is that any peace would, of course, be conditional on good-faith efforts by the newly created Palestinian state to end the terrorism. But recent public opinion polls taken by Palestinians themselves show that a significant majority of Palestinians favor a continuation of terrorism until all of Palestine, which includes Israel, is liberated. To be sure, it is possible that these figures are inflated by the current violence and would diminish if real peace were achieved.

But it is possible that the opposite may be true: if a Palestinian state is achieved by terrorism—or if that perception exists among most Palestinians—then many will urge an escalation of terrorism to achieve the ultimate goal of many of the Palestinian groups, including Hamas, Hezbullah, Islamic Jihad, and even elements within the Fatah movement.

There is precedent for this latter scenario: when Israel left southern Lebanon as a result of increasing Hezbollah terrorism, several Palestinian groups called for an increase in terrorism. Thomas Friedman summarized this perspective as follows: "Ever since the unilateral Israeli withdrawal from Lebanon, Palestinians have watched too much Hezbullah TV from Lebanon, which had peddled the notion that Israel had become just a big, soft Silicon Valley, and that therefore, with enough suicide bombs, the Jews could be forced from Palestine, just as they had been from South Lebanon."[22]

Given the expressed goal of these increasingly popular radical groups, those who urge the eventual creation of a Palestinian state, as I do, cannot ignore the realistic possibility that such a state might well continue to support, encourage, or at the very least tolerate continuing terrorism against Israeli civilians in an effort, futile as it might be, to make the Israelis give up and abandon their hard-earned state. When Israel declared statehood in 1948, one of the first actions taken by its new prime minister, David Ben-Gurion, was to attack and sink a ship loaded with weapons destined for Menachem Begin's paramilitary group, the Irgun. "A state must have a total monopoly on its use of force," he declared, and all paramilitary groups were forcibly disbanded. Does anyone really believe that Yasser Arafat, or any popularly elected Palestinian leader, would show such courage against his own constituents? Arafat's personal involvement in (and denial of) the shipment of terrorist weapons from Iran in 2002 certainly raises some questions about his reliability in ending terrorism.

Any objective observer of the Mideast situation must acknowledge the significant probability that a Palestinian state could serve as a launching pad for renewed terrorism—and worse. Until and unless that frightening scenario is addressed, with concrete guarantees from the United States and the international community, it will be more difficult for a political consensus to be reached in Israel in favor of such a state.

It is not enough to say that Israel retains the right to defend itself and to retaliate against terrorism, because when Israel has done so in the past, it has been condemned by the international community and the United Nations. Such condemnation would only grow stronger if Israel were to attack a newly formed Palestinian state that was giving lip service to stopping terrorism but was secretly supporting it, or even just closing its eyes to it. The United Nations could not be counted on, as evidenced by UNRWA's refusal to do anything about terrorism that is openly planned and organized in its refugee camps. Only the United States, with the cooperation of other nations, could provide the needed guarantees. But little thought is currently being given to eliminating this pressing *what if* barrier to peace because so much attention is being focused on blaming Israel for the current impasse.

If the only consequence of condemning Israel disproportionately to its faults were to be unfairness toward the Jewish state, that would be bad enough considering the history of discrimination toward Jews and Jewish institutions over the millennia, but the consequences are far more severe. The double standard applied to Israel endangers the rule of law and the credibility of international institutions. The disproportionate, sometimes even exclusive, focus on Israel's imperfections gives the international community a ready excuse to ignore far more serious and sustained violations of human rights. It also encourages those who deliberately engage in violence in order to provoke an Israeli reaction that they know will result in disproportionate and excessive criticism of Israel.

Finally, and perhaps most subtly, the cacophony of unreasonable, double-standard, extremist condemnation of Israel drowns out the reasonable, comparative, and contextual criticism of particular Israeli policies, governments, and actions. When the Jewish nation is so unfairly criticized, some of its supporters—even those who would normally be critical of particular actions—tend to become defensive because they realize that adding to the criticism only lends support to improper efforts to demonize the Jewish state. The end result is that those who attack Israel unfairly make it more difficult to criticize Israeli policies fairly, and they sometimes discourage Israel from accepting reasonable criticism and acting on it. They also contribute indirectly but palpably to the violence that plagues efforts to bring about a just and lasting peace.

As a strong supporter of freedom of speech and a lifelong practitioner of freedom to criticize, I would certainly never try to prevent the expression of any views regarding Israel, but I am also a strong believer in the reality that words matter and that unreasoned condemnation can sometimes come with a heavy price. The selective and unjust criticism of Israel carries with it an especially heavy price measured in lives and limbs. For some enemies of Israel, this risk is worthwhile—indeed, it is specifically calculated to produce violent results. But for many people of goodwill there is an unawareness that the very unfairness of the condemnation directed singularly toward Israel contributes to results of which they would surely disapprove.

In sum, therefore, the case for Israel is strong indeed, especially when viewed comparatively and contextually, but even when judged against any reasonable objective standards. Israel is a small democracy surrounded by hostile enemies and battling for its very survival. It is fighting a many-pronged war against enemies both within its borders and outside them, as well as against hostile nations and groups seeking to delegitimate it within the international community. Its actions in defense of its citizens and its nationhood have been far from perfect over the years. It has made mistakes, it has overacted, and it has sometimes lacked generosity toward its enemies. But the same, and worse, can be said of most other democracies.

What cannot be said of other democracies is that any have behaved better—more lawfully, more generously—when faced with equivalent threats to its citizens and to its survival. Whenever Israel or any nation deviates from perfection, it should be criticized by its own citizens and by outsiders. But no nation—and certainly no nation whose people have historically been subject to so much prejudice, persecution, and discrimination—should be subjected to the kind of double-standard, unique condemnation to which the Jewish nation is now being unfairly subjected.

Before I turn to proposals for a future peace, let me directly address the growing number of students and young people who are joining the legion of bigots who can see no right on the side of Israel and no wrong on the side of those who seek to destroy the Jewish state and transfer its Jewish population. You are on the wrong side of history. You are on the wrong side of morality and justice. You have, perhaps inadvertently, joined hands with forces of evil that have for millennia imposed a double standard against everything Jewish.

You are on the side of those who supported Hitler's Holocaust and now deny that it occurred. You are assisting those who are once again targeting babies, children, women, and the elderly just because they are Jewish. You are in very bad company. Nor can you continue to hide behind claims of ignorance, because the facts are so easily available to anyone who wants to think for himself or herself.

If tragedy were once again to befall the Jewish people, or the Jewish nation in which more than 5 million of them make their home, history will judge you harshly, as it has your ideological predecessors. Think for yourself. Learn the facts. Listen to all sides. And if you are a person of goodwill, I am confident that you will no longer see this complex issue as one-sidedly anti-Israel. You owe it to yourself and to history not to remain complicit with a new variant on the world's oldest prejudice.

THE CASE FOR PEACE: NECESSARY FIRST STEPS

Israel's best chance for peace is to remain strong militarily while also helping to strengthen the hands of those Palestinians who truly believe in a two-state solution—those who would be satisfied with a Palestinian state living side by side with a Jewish state not merely as a temporary tactic but as an enduring solution to this century-long problem. Although current polls suggest that most Palestinians and many Arabs around the world see a Palestinian state as a tactical first step toward the eventual destruction of Israel, the best hope for peace is that time and progress will change these numbers.

There will always be some who oppose Israel's very existence and who are prepared to blow themselves up, along with Israeli civilians, to achieve that unrealistic goal. All terrorism will not come to an end—now or ever—even if Israel were to do everything in its power to help establish a strong Palestinian state. Israel, like the United States, will probably have to live with a certain amount of terrorism over its lifetime, just as African Americans had to endure Ku Klux Klan violence for many years. But the Klan is finally dead (or at least on life support) and perhaps someday Palestinian terrorism will also die a belated death. Yet it will be a slow death because it enjoys more support among Palestinians and Islamic extremists than Klan violence ever enjoyed among American racists.

The complete termination of all Palestinian terrorism should not be a prerequisite to the creation of a Palestinian state alongside a secure Israel. To impose such a condition would be to give terrorist groups a veto over progress toward peace—a veto they would exercise with violence, as they have in the past when progress was being made. But a total and honest effort by the Palestinian Authority, and those groups and individuals over which it exercises de facto control, to stop all terrorism must be an unconditional prerequisite to statehood. A Palestinian state must seek to maintain an absolute monopoly over military, paramilitary, guerrilla, and terrorist violence, as the Jewish state did in 1948 when it forcibly and permanently disarmed Etzel and Lechi. Even before it becomes a state, the Palestinian Authority must show that it is willing and able to disarm all terrorist groups, and especially those—such as the Tanzim and Al-Aqsa Martyrs Brigade—that regard themselves as part of the Fatah movement. Surely, there can be no serious consideration of statehood if the Palestinian Authority continues to import illegal weapons for terrorist groups as it did in January 2002, when the *Karine A* was caught and its captain admitted that he was bringing in weapons by order of Yasser Arafat.

Creating a strong Palestinian state next to a strong Israel will require Palestinians to give up their unrealistic dream and Israel's dreaded nightmare of several million people returning to Israel who claim to be refugees from Israel. This so-called Palestinian right of return, more than any Israeli action, including the misguided continued occupation and the wrong-headed expansion of settlements, is *the major* barrier to a permanent peace between Israelis and Palestinians.

Few Palestinians actually want to return to Israel to become part of an Arab minority living in a Jewish state (unless they are fearful of a Muslim–Palestinian tyranny).[23] Most would surely prefer to live as part of a Muslim majority in an economically viable and politically democratic Palestinian state. As argued earlier, a claimed right to return has always been a tactic designed to swamp Israel with millions of Palestinians so as to turn the Jewish nation into a third Palestinian state and yet another of the numerous Islamic states.

As a resolution passed by the refugee conference at Homs, Syria, made clear in 1952, "Any discussion aimed at a solution of the Palestinian problem which will not be based on ensuring the refugees' right to annihilate Israel will be regarded as a desecration of the Arab people and an act of treason."[24] Israel's right to exist as a Jewish state must be deemed by the international community and must be conceded by the Palestinian leadership to trump any claimed right of return.

Nor would the Palestinians be giving up a real right. No other refugee group in history—certainly none created by the kind of complex forces that led an equivalent number of Arabs to leave Israel and Jews to leave Arab countries—has ever been given an actual right to return that had the effect, if not the intent, of changing the character and nature of the country that they left.

Moreover, the vast majority of Palestinians who now claim the right to return to Israel have never literally set foot in Israel. They, their children, and often their grandchildren were born in refugee camps deliberately established by Israel's enemies to perpetuate and expand a refugee problem designed to destroy Israel. Among the few who actually left more than half a century ago and who are still alive, many lived in Israel for only a few years. Recall that the definition of a Palestinian refugee, unlike that of any other refugee in the history of the world, is someone who lived in Israel for *only two years* and left for any reason whatsoever, including economic convenience, family reunification, hatred of Jewish neighbors, or tactical decisions made by Arab leaders. This is one of the weakest refugee claims in history, yet it is the one that has gotten the strongest support from the international community. Again, the gulf between reality and perception is unprecedented, perhaps because the nation accused of creating this exaggerated refugee problem is the Jewish nation.

The time has come—indeed the time is long overdue—to put an end to this right of return charade by so-called Arab refugees. Even Noam Chomsky has urged Palestinian leaders to stop pandering to their followers by promising them a right to return that they have no possibility of securing.[25] Until the world acknowledges that the Arab refusal to accept the existence of Israel following the U.N. partition created an exchange of population that must now be deemed to be permanent, there will be no prospect of peace between the Arabs and Israel. But as soon as the world recognizes Israel's right to continue to exist and thrive as a Jewish state, without the threat of millions of hostile refugees returning to destroy it, the prospects for peace will increase dramatically.

Professor Michael Waltzer of Princeton's Institute for Advanced Studies has argued that the Palestinians will never achieve statehood unless they give up the right to return and to demographically destroy Israel as a Jewish state. He has also correctly observed that few, if any, Palestinian leaders have been ready to argue that giving up the right of return is the necessary price of statehood. That seems to me the right position, since the claim to return effectively reopens the 1947–1948 conflict, which is not a helpful thing to do more than half a century later. All the other refugees from the years immediately after World War Two, from Central Europe to Southeast Asia, have been successfully resettled. Palestinians are still in camps because a decision was made, by their own leaders and by the adjacent Arab states, to keep them there: this was a way of insisting that Israel's independence war was not yet over. Today, however, if the Palestinians are to win their own independence war, they must acknowledge that Israel's is already won. Perhaps some number of refugees will return to Israel, some greater number to Palestine (how many will depend on the pace of investment and economic development). The rest must finally be resettled. It is time to address their actual misery rather than their symbolic claims. There will continue to be a Palestinian diaspora, just as there continues to be a Jewish diaspora. A clear statement by Arafat acknowledging this simple truth would represent a big step toward undeclaring the first war.[26]

Not only has Yasser Arafat refused to take this step, the Palestinian Authority recently took a giant step backward by including the right of return in their new constitution and insisting that it remain on the table as part of the "road map." Moreover, although the new Palestinian prime minister has recognized Israel's "right to exist," he has thus far refused an American request, made as recently as June 1, 2003, that the Palestinian Authority recognize Israel's right to exist "specifically as a Jewish State."[27] This refusal preserves the Palestinian claim that Israel should allow millions of Arab refugees to "return" and to turn Israel into another state with a Palestinian majority. It is the hope of most Israelis that the Palestinians will eventually drop this unrealistic demand, since it was Arafat's refusal to do so that doomed the earlier peace negotiations in 2000–2001.

President Hosni Mubarak took a positive first step in this direction by declaring that "the Palestinian demand for the 'right of return' is totally unrealistic and would have to be solved by means of financial compensation and resettlement in Arab countries."[28] This, of course, is precisely what was offered at Camp David and Taba—a $30 billion compensation package plus an acknowledgment of "wrongs" done to the refugees, and the right of some refugees to return to Israel. But Arafat walked away, claiming that Barak's offer would not resolve the refugee problem. Any hope of achieving a real peace will be dashed unless the Palestinian leadership gives up this pretextual "right of return," which is nothing less than a veiled "right" to destroy Israel by demographic, rather than by terroristic, means.

The Muslim world must also give up its chauvinistic and racist claim that the existence of a Jewish state, no matter how small, on "sacred Muslim land" is a violation of Islamic law. This absurd and self-serving claim, first made by the anti-Semitic grand mufti in the 1920s and continuously repeated since then in Palestinian charters, constitutions, and sermons, must be categorically and publicly rejected by the Palestinian leadership once and for all not as a tactic but as a recognition that a Jewish state has as much right to exist in the area as does a Palestinian state.

Ethan Bronner, who covered the Middle East from 1991 to 1997 and is now an editorial page editor for the *New York Times,* recently told of an interview with the late King Hussein of Jordan that shows how deeply the opposition to Israel's legitimacy is ingrained even among the most moderate of Arab leaders:

> I once asked King Hussein . . . whether he considered Zionism legitimate. Did he accept that there was any historical basis to the Jews' claim to a portion of Palestine as their homeland? He looked at me as if I were from Mars and ducked the question. Perhaps by the time of his death in 1999 he had softened his view. But his reaction still exemplifies that of the vast majority of Arabs today."[29]

Bronner also reports that Saeb Erekat, a "moderate" Palestinian leader, announced during the Camp David negotiations in 2002 that it is the Muslim position that "there never was a Jewish Temple" in Jerusalem, despite near unanimity among historians and archeologists that the holiest site in Jerusalem was on the Temple Mount. This falsification of history is part of a Palestinian effort to dispute any historical claims by Jews not only to Jerusalem but to any part of Israel.

The Arab and Muslim nations of the world must also come to accept not only Israel's continued existence as a fact but also its *right* to exist as a Jewish state in safety and security. The threats of genocide and politicide that are continually made in many quarters must end once and for all. Arab and Muslim leaders must tell their people that Israel will not be attacked because it has the right to exist permanently, not because it is tactically inadvisable to do so "at this time"—and these statements must be made and repeated in Arabic to their people, not only in English and French to diplomats.

Israel's permanent security must be assured against enemies both external and internal. Until and unless that occurs, Israel must continue to maintain a qualitative military superiority over the combined armed forces of its potential enemies as the best assurance of peace in the region, since Israel can count on no one else to assure its survival.

Israel, in turn, must give up any claim, as it offered to do at Camp David and Taba in 2000, over the West Bank and the Gaza Strip, subject only to the kind of small territorial adjustments contemplated by U.N. Resolution 242 to assure its security. It must also end the Jewish settlements in the Gaza Strip and throughout the heart of the West Bank, although, over time, Jews should be free to live safely anywhere in Palestine as Palestinians can, and do, live in Israel. On May 25, 2003, Israeli prime minister Ariel Sharon announced that "[t]he moment has arrived to divide this tract of land between us and the Palestinians."[30] His government voted to accept the road map, including the creation of a Palestinian state. Now the Palestinian Authority must demonstrate its determination to dismantle the Palestinian terrorist organizations, and to make best efforts to prevent further acts of terrorism. It remains to be seen whether its current leaders have the courage and power to implement their obligations under the road map.

In an important article in *Dissent,* in the fall of 2002, Professor Walzer pointed out that four wars are being fought simultaneously:

The first is a Palestinian war to destroy the state of Israel.

The second is a Palestinian war to create an independent state alongside Israel, ending the occupation of the West Bank and Gaza.

The third is an Israeli war for the security of Israel within the 1967 borders.

The fourth is an Israeli war for Greater Israel, for the settlements and the occupied territories.[31]

Walzer then argued that for most Palestinians the war for Israel's destruction seems to have priority over the war for Palestinian statehood alongside Israel. His proof is that at Camp David and Taba "statehood could have been achieved without any war at all." Yet it was turned down because it left Israel intact as a Jewish state. For most Israelis, on the other hand, the "defensive war for Israel's security" takes priority over any war for "greater Israel." The proof is that an Israeli government, almost certainly supported by a majority of its population, was prepared to end the occupation and dismantle the settlements in exchange for real peace and security. Yet Arafat walked away from Barak's proposal without offering a counterproposal.

For peace to become a reality, the Palestinians who support the goal of the first war—the destruction of Israel—must become convinced that it is not only impossible to achieve, it is also wrong. And the Israelis who support the fourth war—for a permanent occupation and an extensive network of settlements—must become convinced of the same thing. The problem is that there are many more Palestinians who believe in the first war than there are Israelis who believe in the fourth war, and these Palestinians are far more willing to use terrorist violence in a futile but deadly effort to achieve their ignoble goal of destroying the Jewish state.

The most important and enduring steps toward peace are thus attitudinal: Palestinian leaders must stop teaching their children to hate Jews and Israelis, must stop publishing maps that eliminate Israel, and must stop misleading the "refugees" into believing that they will someday return to their homes in a Muslim Israel. Israeli leaders must stop encouraging settlements and must discourage those who harbor the illusion of a greater Israel that includes large portions of Judea and Samaria. Jewish biblical claims must be abandoned in the name of pragmatic compromise, just as Islamic Koranic claims must be surrendered. Most important, the international community, the academic left, religious leaders, and people of goodwill throughout the world must stop trying to demonize and delegitimate the Jewish nation for its reasonable efforts to protect its population while seeking partners for peace. This unthinking and one-sided condemnation of Israel has itself become a significant barrier to peace.

A two-state solution of the kind proposed by former U.S. president Bill Clinton and former Israeli prime minister Ehud Barak, and now apparently accepted by Prime Ministers Ariel Sharon and Mahmed Abbas (Abu Mazen), holds enormous promise for both the Palestinians and the Israelis of a democratic, economically viable Palestine that poses no danger to Israel's security. Democracies do not generally go to war against each other, and economically viable democracies have real incentives to settle their differences peacefully and to prevent terrorist groups from operating within their borders. By abandoning unrealistic claims and recognizing each other's right to live in peace, Israel and Palestine can become beacons of enlightenment, progress, and hope in an increasingly dangerous world.

I write these closing paragraphs in a spirit of cautious optimism, having just watched Israel's prime minister Ariel Sharon, the Palestinian Authority's prime minister Mahmoud Abbas, Jordan's King Abdullah and our own President George W. Bush shake hands and speak words of peace and reconciliation at Aqaba. But handshakes alone will not bring peace, nor words reconciliation after so many decades of bloodshed. Difficult and long-term actions on the ground will be needed to build mutual confidence.

On the very day of the Aqaba summit, Palestinian extremists vowed to continue the violence, as Yasser Arafat complained that Israel had offered "nothing tangible." Even Mahmoud Abbas seemed to be preserving the option of destroying Israel demographically by refusing to acknowledge its right to exist as a Jewish state.

On the same day, some Jewish settlers from the West Bank rallied in opposition to the peace efforts, carrying signs claiming that "Mr. Bush's road map is on a collision course with the creator's road map." The good news is that an overwhelming majority of Israelis, including a considerable number of settlers, seem prepared to implement the road map, so long as the road leads to an enduring peace and a genuine two-state solution— one with a Jewish majority, the other with an Arab majority. A considerable number of Palestinians also seem ready to compromise in the interests of peace.

If a peaceful two-state solution were finally to become reality, it would be a blessing for all. But it would also have tragic overtones, since this eminently reasonable and fair solution could have been achieved long ago if the Arab leadership had not rejected the *Peel Report,* the U.N. partition, and the Camp David-Taba proposals. So many lives were wasted by so repeated an unwillingness on the part of so many Arab leaders to recognize the right of the Jewish people peacefully to establish a small Jewish state in those parts of the ancient Jewish homeland that they had cultivated and on which they constituted a clear majority. To avoid the bloody past becoming prologue yet again, we must learn from the tragic mistakes that needlessly took all these lives.

I now rest the case for Israel that I make in this book. I realize, however, that the defense can never rest when it comes to the Jewish state. No matter what steps Israel takes toward peace and the two-state solution, there will always be some for whom nothing short of Israel's destruction will suffice. For that reason, Israel's best defense must remain its determination to survive and its ability to defend its citizens against those zealots—some armed with bombs, others with bigotry—who cannot abide the reality of a strong independent and democratic Jewish state.

NOTES

Introduction

1. Thomas Friedman, "Campus Hypocrisy," *New York Times,* October 16, 2002.
2. See chapter 28 in this book.
3. See chapter 28 in this book.
4. Chomsky's preference for a federal model "along Yugoslav lines" is articulated in *Middle East Illusions* (Oxford: Rowman & Littlefield, 2003), pp. 105–106. His use of Lebanon as a model comes from a debate with me in 1970.
5. *Atlantic Unbound* (online publication of *Atlantic Monthly*). Interview of Said by Harry Bloom, September 22, 1999, www.theatlantic.com/unbound/interviews/ba990922.htm.
6. See Benny Morris, *Righteous Victims* (New York: Vintage Books, 2001), p. xiv.
7. See chapter 9 in this book.
8. *Atlantic Unbound,* September 22, 1999.
9. See chapter 17 in this book.
10. See chapter 17 in this book.
11. See chapters 16 and 17 in this book.
12. See chapter 17 in this book.
13. James Bennet, "Arafat's Edge: Violence and Time on His Side," *New York Times,* March 18, 2002.
14. Bruce Hoffman, "The Logic of Suicide Terrorism," *Atlantic Monthly,* June 2003, p. 45.
15. See chapter 18 in this book.

CHAPTER 1
Is Israel a Colonial, Imperialist State?

1. "What Went Wrong?" *Al Ahram Weekly* (Egypt), December 12–18, 2002. All cites to *Al-Ahram Weekly* available at http://weekly.ahram.org.eg.
2. Radio 786, May 23, 2002.
3. Buber to Gandhi, quoted in Arthur Hertzberg, *The Zionist Idea* (Philadelphia: Jewish Publication Society, 1997), p. 464.
4. Paul Johnson, *Modern Times: The World from the Twenties to the Nineties* (New York: Harper & Row, 1983), p. 485.
5. The 10,000 Jews who sought refuge in Palestine constituted roughly 2 percent of the existing population. The million Jews who sought refuge in America constituted

approximately 2 percent of the existing population.
6. Martin Gilbert, *The Routledge Atlas of the Arab-Israeli Conflict,* 7th Edition (London: Routledge Taylor Francis Group, 2002), p. 1.
7. Clayton Miles Lehmann, "Palestine," http://www.usd.edu/erp/Palestine/history. htm.
8. Yitzchak Ben-Zvi, *The Exiled and the Redeemed* (Philadelphia: Jewish Publication Society, 1961), pp. 44–45.
9. Sheikh Abd Allah Al Meshad, "Jews' Attitudes toward Islam and Muslims in the First Islamic ERE," quoted in D. F. Green, ed., *Arab Theologians on Jews and Israel* (Geneva: Editions de l'Avenir, 1976).
10. *Palestine Royal Commission Report (Peel Report)* (London: His Majesty's Stationary Office, 1937), pp. 11–12.
11. James Finn to Earl of Clarendon, January 1, 1858.
12. James Finn to Viscount Palmerston, November 7, 1851.
13. Jacob de Haas, *History of Palestine* (New York: Macmillan, 1934), p. 393 quoting contemporaneous letter.
14. Wm. T. Young to Colonel Patrick Campbell, May 25, 1839.
15. Wm. T. Young to Viscount Palmerston, May 25, 1839.
16. Wm. T. Young to Viscount Canning, January 13, 1842.

CHAPTER 2
Did European Jews Displace Palestinians?

1. Kenneth R. Timmerman, "Top Egyptian Cleric Justifies Terrorism," *Insight on the News,* November 26, 2002.
2. "A Colonizing Project Built on Lies," *CounterPunch* (www.counterpunch.org), April 18, 2002.
3. Center for Policy Analysis on Palestine luncheon address, State Department briefing, Federal News Service, January 17, 1992.
4. Interview with David Barsamian of Alternative Radio, "Israel, the Holocaust, and Anti-Semites," October 24, 1986, in Noam Chomsky, *Chronicles of Dissent* (Monroe, Me.: Common Courage Press, 1992).

245

5. Mark Twain, *The Innocents Abroad* (New York: Oxford University Press, 1996), pp. 349, 366, 375, 441–442.
6. Efraim Karsh, *Fabricating Israeli History; the "New Historians"* (London: Frank Cass, 1997), pp. 4–6.
7. Ethan Bronner, Book Review, *New York Times,* November 14, 1999. Since Arafat walked away from the Barak-Clinton peace offers at Camp David and Taba in 2000–2001, Morris has written more critically of the Palestinians, while still criticizing many Israeli policies, actions, and decisions. See Benny Morris, "The Rejection," *New Republic,* April 21–28, 2003.
8. Morris, p. 123.
9. Quoted in Morris, p. 111.
10. Abraham Granott, *The Land System in Palestine: History and Structure* (London: Eyre & Spottiswoode, 1952), p. 278.
11. Edward Said and Christopher Hitchens, eds., *Blaming the Victims* (London: Verso, 2001).
12. Shabtai Teveth, *David Ben Gurion and the Palestinian Arabs* (New York: Oxford University Press, 1985), p. 32.
13. Jamal Husseini, February 9, 1939, quoted in Arieh Avneri, *The Claim of Dispossession* (New Brunswick: Transaction Books, 1984), p. 11.
14. M. Shahid Alam, "A Colonizing Built on Lies," *Counterpunch,* www.counterpunch.org, April 18, 2002.
15. James Parkes, *Whose Land? A History of the Peoples of Palestine* (New York: Taplinger, 1971), p. 212.
16. Avneri, p.11.
17. James Finn to the Earl of Clarendon, September 15, 1857.
18. Ibid.
19. J. B. Forsyth, *A Few Months in the East* (Quebec: J. Lovell, 1861), p. 188.
20. H. B. Tristram, *The Land of Israel: A Journal of Travels in Palestine* (London: Society for Promoting Christian Knowledge, 1865), p. 490.
21. Samuel Bartlett, *From Egypt to Palestine* (New York: Harper, 1879), p. 409. Cited in Fred Gottheil, "The Population of Palestine, Circa 1875," Middle Eastern Studies, vol. 15, no. 3, October 1979.
22. Edward Wilson, *In Scripture Lands* (New York: C. Scribner's, 1890), p. 316. Cited in Gottheil.
23. W. Allen, *The Dead Sea: A New Route to India* (London: 1855), p.113. Cited in Gottheil.
24. William Thomson, *The Land and the Book* (New York: Harper Bros., 1871), p. 466. Cited in Gottheil.

25. Reverend Samuel Manning, *Those Holy Fields* (London: The Religious Tract Society, 1874), pp. 14–17.
26. Roderic H. Davison, *Reform in the Ottoman Empire* (Princeton: Princeton University Press, 1963) p. 69, citing a Muslim writer in 1868.
27. Morris, p. 6.
28. Ibid.
29. John Lewis Burckhardt, *Travels in Syria and the Holy Land* (New York: AMS Press, 1983), p. 299.
30. See chapter 9 in this book.
31. The research of a French geographer, Vital Cuinct are relied on for this conclusion. See Joan Peters, *From Time Immemorial* (Chicago: JKAP Publications, 1984). Peters's conclusions and data have been challenged. See Said and Hitchens, p. 33. I do not in any way rely on them in this book.
32. A. Druyanow, *Ketavim Letoldot Hibbat Ziyyon Ve-Yishshuv Erez Yisra'el* (Writings on the history of Hibbat Ziyyon and the settlement of the land of Israel) (Odessa, Tel Aviv, 1919, 1925, 1932), vol. 3, pp. 66–67.
33. Ernst Frankenstein, *Justice for my People* (London: Nicholson & Watson, 1943), p. 127.
34. *Report by His Britannic Majesty's Government to the Council of the League of Nations on the Administration of Palestine and Trans-Jordan for the Year 1937,* Colonial No. 146, pp. 223–224.
35. Quoted in Peters, p. 11.
36. King Abdullah of Jordan, *My Memoirs Completed,* Harold W. Glidden, trans. (London: Longman, 1978), pp. 88–89.

CHAPTER 3
Was the Zionist Movement a Plot to Colonize All of Palestine?

1. *The Question of Palestine* (New York: Vintage Books, 1992 ed.), p. 84.
2. Lecture, Harvard University, November 25, 2002 (videotape).
3. Morris, p. 25.
4. Ibid.
5. Ibid., p. 57.
6. Ibid.
7. Ibid.
8. Ibid., pp. 57–59.

CHAPTER 4
Was the Balfour Declaration Binding International Law?

1. *The Question of Palestine* (New York: Vintage Books, 1992 ed.), pp. 15–16.

2. "Why We're on the Side of Justice," *Sunday Mail* (Australia), April 7, 2002.
3. Morris, p. 71.
4. Ibid., p. 72.
5. Ibid.
6. Ibid., p. 75.
7. Ibid., p. 74.
8. *Peel Report,* p. 24.
9. Ibid., p. 25.
10. Ibid., p. 33.
11. Ibid., p. 41.
12. Quoted in Morris, p. 82.
13. Jordanian nationality law, Article 3(3) of Law No. 6; and *Official Gazette,* no. 1171, February 16, 1954.
14. *Peel Report,* p. 308.
15. Quoted in Morris, p. 91.
16. Walter Laqueur and Barry Rubin, *The Israel-Arab Reader:* 6th Edition (New York: Penguin, 2001), p. 19.
17. Ibid.

CHAPTER 5
Were the Jews Unwilling to Share Palestine?

1. *The Question of Palestine,* pp. 12–13.
2. Ibid., p. 101.
3. Morris, p. 95.
4. Ibid., p. 96.
5. Quoted in Morris, p. 96.
6. Morris, p. 100 .
7. I use anti-Semitism in its original meaning as hatred of Jews in particular, not Semites in general.
8. Quoted in Peters, p. 37.
9. Letter from Husseini to the Minister for Foreign Affairs of Hungary, June 28, 1943.
10. Morris, p. 76.
11. Ibid., p. 76.
12. See testimony quoted in *Peel Report,* p. 141.
13. Ibid.
14. Morris, p. 112.
15. Ibid., p. 113.
16. Ibid., p. 114.
17. *Peel Report,* p. 68.
18. Morris, p. 116. As if to suggest some moral equivalence, Morris reports that 116 Arabs were killed. But most were armed perpetrators killed by the police, not unarmed, innocent civilians; see *Peel Report,* p. 68.
19. Morris, quoting Sir John Chancellor, p. 116.
20. *Peel Report,* p. 68.
21. Whatever the high commissioner, who was an overt anti-Zionist, may have thought of the Balfour Declaration, it was at this time binding international law, which could not unilaterally be abrogated by the British, even though they had initiated it.

CHAPTER 6
Have the Jews Always Rejected the Two-State Solution?

1. "Can Zionism Be Reconciled with Justice for the Palestinians?" *Tikkun,* July–August 2000.
2. "Middle East Diplomacy: Continuities and Change," *Z* magazine, December 1991, available at www.zmag.org/chomsky (last visited March 17, 2003).
3. Lecture, Harvard University, November 25, 2002.
4. *Peel Report,* p. 2.
5. Ibid., pp. 106–107.
6. Ibid., p. 59.
7. Ibid., p. 61.
8. Ibid., pp. 116–117.
9. Ibid., p. 370.
10. Ibid., p. 371.
11. Ibid., p. 141.
12. Ibid., pp. 375–376.
13. Ibid., p. 389.
14. Ibid., pp. 394–395.
15. Ibid., p. 395.
16. Ibid., p. 141, question to the grand mufti and his answer.
17. Ian Bickerton and Carla Klausner, *A Concise History of the Arab-Israeli Conflict* (Upper Saddle River, N.J.: Prentice Hall, 2002), p. 56.
18. Ibid.
19. *Peel Report,* p. 147.
20. Michael Oren, *Six Days of War* (Oxford: Oxford University Press, 2002), p. 93.

CHAPTER 7
Have the Jews Exploited the Holocaust?

1. Norman G. Finkelstein, *The Holocaust Industry: Reflections of the Exploitation of Jewish Suffering* (London: Verso, 2001).
2. Quoted in Morris, p. 125.
3. Morris, p. 124.
4. Ibid., p. 137.
5. Quoted in Morris, p. 137.
6. Morris, pp. 130, 134.
7. Sarah Honig, "Fiendish Hypocrisy II: The Man from Klopstock St.," *Jerusalem Post,* April 6, 2001.
8. Germany, Auswärtiges Amt., *Documents on German Foreign Policy, 1918–1945, from the Archives of the German Foreign Ministry,* series D, vol. XIII, no. 515, (Washington, D.C.: U.S. Government Printing Office, 1949), pp. 881–885. Cited at www.psych.upenn.edu/~fjgil/muftihitler.htm.
9. See Zvi Elpeleg, *The Grand Mufti* (London: Frank Cass, 1993), p. 100.

10. Itamar Marcus, "Nazi Alley, Hajj Amen Al Husseini Is Arafat's 'Hero,' " *Palestinian Media Watch,* www.pmw.org.il/new/bulletins-050802.html.
11. Said and Hitchens, p. 248.
12. Ibid.
13. Morris, p. 166.
14. Ibid., p. 165.
15. PA newspaper, *Al-Hayat Al-Jadeeda,* September 1, 1997.
16. Elpeleg, p. 164.
17. Martin Gilbert, *Winston S. Churchill,* vol. VII (London: Heinemann, 1966), pp. 90, 154
18. " 'Dialogue of Civilizations Seeks International Democracy,' States President Khatami, Tehran, February 27, 2001," from the website of the International Centre for Dialogue among Civilizations, www.dialoguecentre.org/news_detail 2.htm.
19. Morris, p. 11.
20. Ibid.
21. Elie Kedourie, quoted in Morris, p. 9.
22. Morris, p. 39.
23. Alan Dershowitz, *Shouting Fire: Civil Liberties in a Turbulent Age* (Boston: Little, Brown, 2002), pp. 33–48.
24. *London Times,* December 1, 1947.
25. *Peel Report,* p. 124.

CHAPTER 8
Was the U.N. Partition Plan Unfair to Palestinians?

1. In an interview in *Ha'aretz* with journalist Ari Shavit, "My Right of Return," August 18, 2000.
2. In an interview with Belgian journalist Baudoin Loos, "An Interview of Ilan Pappe," *Le Soir* (Belgium), November 29, 1999.
3. Faisal Bodi, "Israel Surely Has No Right to Exist," *The Guardian,* January 3, 2001. This view is also reflected in the Palestinian National Covenant of 1968.
4. See chapter 1 in this book.

CHAPTER 9
Were Jews a Minority in What Became Israel?

1. "A World-Wide Intifada? *Why?*" *Counter-Punch,* www.counterpunch.org/cook1207.html (last visited April 6, 2003).
2. "Israel: Five Decades of Pillage and Ethnic Cleansing," Marxism Alive Website, www.marxismalive.org/israelfive3.html (last visited April 6, 2003).
3. The same would be true of the Peel Commission proposal. Norman G. Finkelstein,

an anti-Zionist polemicist, argues that "the only germane demographic comparisons are between the Arab and Jewish populations in all of Palestine and, arguably, between the Arab and Jewish populations in the region of Palestine *that later became Israel."* (emphasis added) Said and Hitchens at p. 65. This is false. For purposes of assessing the fairness of the U.N. Partition in 1947, the relevant comparison is between Jewish and Arab populations *in the area allocated to the Jewish state* by that partition. The fact that Israel gained more territory *after being attacked* by Arab armies and Palestinian fighters is not relevant to the fairness of the original partition plan.

CHAPTER 10
Has Israel's Victimization of the Palestinians Been the Primary Cause of the Arab–Israeli Conflict?

1. Interview in *Ha'aretz* with Ari Shavit, "My Right to Return," August 18, 2000.
2. Elpeleg, pp. 45–46.
3. Sermon broadcast on Palestinian Authority Radio, April 30, 1999; released in a report from the Israeli Prime Minister's Office and cited in the *Boston Globe,* June 30, 2002.
4. Quoted in Nissim Ratzlav-Katz, "Joseph's Inheritance," *National Review,* August 8, 2002; and Charles A. Radin, "Sacred Sites Caught in Historic Conflict," *Boston Globe,* June 30, 2002.
5. See chapter 16 of this book.
6. "Fifty Years of Dispossession," *Al Ahram Weekly,* May 7–13, 1998.
7. *New York Times,* May 18, 2002.
8. As quoted by Yedidya Atlas, "Arafat's Secret Agenda is to Wear Israelis Out," *Insight on the News,* April 1, 1996, p. 16. The incident was originally reported by the Norwegian daily *Dagen* and widely quoted thereafter.
9. As quoted by Senator Warren Rudman, at a hearing of the Commerce, Justice, State, and Judiciary Subcommittee of the Senate Appropriations Committee, April 13, 1989.

CHAPTER 11
Was the Israeli War of Independence Expansionist Aggression?

1. "Zionist Theses and Anti-Theses," *The Palestine Chronicle,* November 27, 2002; www.palestinechronicle.com/article.php?story=2002112719193028 (last visited April 7, 2003).

2. Associated Press report published in *The Morning Call,* Allentown, Pa., May 17, 1948.
3. Morris, p. 201.
4. Ibid.
5. Ibid., p. 219.
6. Said and Hitchens, p. 266.
7. Morris., p. 233.
8. Ibid.
9. Ibid., p. 221.
10. Ibid., pp. 221–222.

CHAPTER 12

Did Israel Create the Arab Refugee Problem?

1. "Calling a Spade a Spade," *Al Ahram Weekly,* September 6–12, 2001.
2. In an interview in *Ha'aretz* with Ari Shavit, "My Right to Return," August 18, 2000.
3. Lecture, Harvard University, November 25, 2002.
4. Morris, p. 214.
5. Ibid., p. 204.
6. As we will see, the rare instances in which Arab civilians have been targeted were perpetrated not by the Israeli army but by irregulars and paramilitary groups that were put out of business once the Israeli army assumed control over the defense of Israel.
7. Morris, p. 255.
8. Ibid., p. 256.
9. Ibid.
10. Larry Collins and Dominique Lapierre, *O Jerusalem* (New York: Simon & Schuster, 1972), p. 400.
11. *Peel Report,* p. 141.
12. Morris, p. 219.
13. Ibid., p. 223.
14. Martin Gilbert, *Israel: A History* (New York: William Morrow and Co., 1998), p. 216.
15. Morris, p. 208.
16. Ibid., p. 209. Original reports placed the number of dead as high as 254, but this number was, it turned out, an exaggeration.
17. See Uri Milstein, *History of Israeli War of Independence,* vol. IV ed. by Alan Sacks (Lanham, Md.: University Press of America, 1996), p. 262.
18. Morris, p. 209.
19. BBC Report, *Israel and the Arabs: The 50 Year Conflict.*
20. Ibid.
21. Morris, p. 209.
22. There were other episodes involving individuals and paramilitary groups in which claims of massacre were made, but none of the scale and seriousness of Deir Yassin.
23. Morris, p. 211.
24. Ibid., p. 212.
25. Benny Morris, *The Birth of the Palestinian Refugee Problem (The Birth)* (Cambridge: Cambridge University Press, 1988), pp. 286–289.
26. Ibid., p. 289.
27. Ibid.
28. Ibid., p. 290.
29. Ibid., p. 296.
30. Lecture, Harvard University, November 25, 2002.
31. Quoted in Peters, p. 16.
32. "Abu Mazen Charges that the Arab States Are the Cause of the Palestinian Refugee Problem," *Wall Street Journal,* June 5, 2003.
33. Peter Dodd, *River Without Bridges* (Beirut: Institute for Palestine Studies, 1969), p. 43; as quoted in Peters, p. 445 n. 21.
34. Cited in Peters, p. 13.
35. General Assembly official records: 3rd session, supplement no. 11 (A/648), Paris, 1948, p. 47.
36. Morris, p. 253.
37. Quoted in Peters, p. 13.
38. Quoted in Peters, p. 22.
39. Morris, p. 253.
40. Ibid.
41. Ruth Lapidoth, "Legal Aspects of the Palestinian Refugee Question," Jerusalem Center for Public Affairs, no. 485, 24 Elul 5762, www.jcpa.org/jl/vp485.htm.
42. See www.unhcr.ch (Office of the High Commissioner for Human Rights) and www.un.org/unrwa/index.html (United Nations Relief and Works Agency).
43. Erik Schecter, "Divided Responsibilities: The U.N. and the Refugees," *The Jerusalem Report,* January 29, 2002; UNHCR, "Who Is a Refugee?" available at www.unhcr.org (last visited March 13, 2003), citing the 1951 Convention Relating to the Status of Refugees; UNRWA, "Who Is a Palestinian Refugee?" available at www.un.org./unrwa/refugees/pl.htm (last visited March 13, 2003).
44. Associated Press interview with King Hussein of Jordan, January 1960; quoted in Peters, p. 23.
45. David G. Littman, "The Forgotten Refugees," *National Review,* December 3, 2002.
46. Howard Sachar, *A History of Israel* (New York: Knopf, 1976), pp. 398–401.
47. Quoted in Peters, pp. 29–30.
48. Daniel Doron, "Palestinian Lies and Western Complicity," *National Review,* August 14, 2002.

49. Bernard Caplan, "Muslims Also Targeted Jerusalem's Christians," *Richmond Post-Dispatch*, June 29, 1997.

CHAPTER 13
Did Israel Start the Six-Day War?

1. "International Community Bargains with Rights of Palestinians," *Aftenposten* (Norwegian daily), posted on the web site of *Spectre* e-magazine, www.spectrezine.org /war/Palestine (last visited April 6, 2003).
2. Oren, p. 93.
3. Ibid., p. 84.
4. Morris, p. 306.
5. Ibid., p. 310.
6. Quoted in Oren, p. 253.
7. Morris, p. 310.
8. Ibid., p. 310.
9. Oren, p. 92.
10. Ibid., p. 63.
11. Ibid., p. 82.
12. Ibid., p. 99.
13. Ibid., pp. 186–187.
14. Ibid., p. 186.
15. Ibid., p. 306.
16. Ibid., pp. 306–307.

CHAPTER 14
Was the Israeli Occupation without Justification?

1. In a letter defending the anti-Israel documentary of British journalist John Pilger, "Letter: Faultless Film," *The Independent* (Britain), September 23, 2002.
2. "War on Terrorism or Illegal Occupation?" *War Times Newspaper*, www.war-times. org/pdf/palestine020405.pdf (last visited April 8, 2003).
3. U.N. Security Council, Resolution 242, November 22, 1967.
4. Morris, p. 330.
5. Ibid.
6. Ibid.
7. Ibid.
8. Abba Eban, *Abba Eban* (New York: Random House, 1977), p. 446.
9. Lecture, Harvard University, November 25, 2002.

CHAPTER 15
Was the Yom Kippur War Israel's Fault?

1. Laqueur and Rubin, p. 143.
2. "The Spirit of October," *Al-Ahram Weekly* (Egypt), October 8–14, 1998.
3. Morris, p. 390.
4. Ibid., p. 413.

5. Quoted in Morris, p. 406.
6. Morris, p. 419.
7. Ibid., p. 223.
8. Quoted in Laqueur and Rubin, p. 148.
9. Ibid., p. 143.
10. Morris, p. 387.
11. Tom Masland, "Nelson Mandela: The U.S.A. Is a Threat to World Peace," *Newsweek*, September 10, 2002.
12. Morris, p. 632.

CHAPTER 16
Has Israel Made Serious Efforts at Peace?

1. "Israel Sharpens Its Axe," *CounterPunch*, July 13, 2001, www.counterpunch.org /saidaxe.html, (last visited April 5, 2003).
2. Lecture, Harvard University, November 25, 2002.
3. Morris, p. 578.
4. Laqueur and Rubin, pp. 341–348.
5. Morris, pp. 578–579.
6. Report, *Jews, Israel and Peace in Palestinian School Textbooks*, www.edume.org/reports /7/1.htm.
7. See Itmar Marcus, "Palestine Media Watch Report #37," July 2, 2001, available at www.pmw.org.il/report-37.html.
8. Morris, p. 581.
9. Ibid., p. 596.
10. "In 1991 the Israelis killed fewer Palestinians—about 100—than the Palestinians did themselves—about 150." See Morris, p. 612.
11. Ephraim Yaar and Tamar Hemrann, "Peace Index: Most Israelis Support Attack on Iraq," *Ha'aretz*, March 6, 2003.
12. Thomas Friedman, *New York Times*, March, 18, 2002.
13. Serge Schmemann, "Mideast Turmoil: The Talks," *New York Times*, March 18, 2002.
14. Thomas Friedman, "The Hard Truth," *New York Times*, April 3, 2002.
15. "Clinton Minutes," *Ha'aretz*, December 31, 2000.
16. Ibid.
17. Benny Morris, "Camp David and After: An Exchange. (1) An Interview with Ehud Barak," *New York Review of Books*, June 13, 2002.
18. Laqueur and Rubin, pp. 565–567.
19. Alan Dershowitz, *Why Terrorism Works* (New Haven, Conn.: Yale University Press, 2002), p. 79. Khaled Abu Toameh, "How the War Began," *Jerusalem Post*, September 20, 2002.
20. *Guardian* (London), January 25, 2001.
21. Joel Brinkley, April 4, 2002.
22. Quoted in *Why Terrorism Works*, p. 82.

23. *New York Times,* quoted in *Why Terrorism Works,* pp. 79–80.
24. Scott Atran, "Who Wants to be a Martyr," *New York Times,* May 5, 2003, p. A27.
25. *Why Terrorism Works,* p. 80.
26. Ibid, p. 81.
27. Ibid.
28. Ibid.

CHAPTER 17
Was Arafat Right in Turning Down the Barak–Clinton Peace Proposal?

1. "The Infernal Scapegoat," September 25, 2001, www.mideastweb.org/infernalscapegoat.html.
2. Lecture, Harvard University, November 25, 2002.
3. M. Kondracke, "Powell Should Tell Arafat: 'It's Now or Never,'" *Roll Call,* April 11, 2002.
4. Elsa Walsh, "The Prince," *The New Yorker,* March 24, 2003, p. 61.
5. James Bennet, "Skipper Ties Cargo to Arafat's Group," *New York Times,* January 7, 2002.
6. The quote is Walsh's description of what Bandar was shown by the American negotiators.
7. *The New Yorker,* March 24, 2003, p. 55.
8. Ibid., pp. 49, 58.
9. Ibid., p. 49.
10. Ibid.
11. Ibid., p. 59.
12. Ibid., p. 57.
13. Benny Morris, "Rejection," *The New Republic,* April 21–28, 2003, p. 37.

CHAPTER 18
Why Have More Palestinians Than Israelis Been Killed?

1. On CNN's *Crossfire,* April 4, 2002, in response to comments made by Rev. Jerry Falwell.
2. "Mideast Peace Visions Shared," *The Journal News* (Westchester County, N.Y.), March 4, 2002, quoting Abbas Hamideh, cochairman of the New York–New Jersey branch of the Al-Awda Palestine Right to Return Coalition.
3. *Ajuri v. I.D.F. Commander, HCJ* (Israeli Supreme Court) 7015/02, September 3, 2002.
4. Bruce Hoffman, "The Logic of Suicide Terrorism," *Atlantic Monthly,* June 2003, p. 45.
5. "The Ambulance–Homicide Theory," *New York Times Magazine,* December 15, 2002, p. 66.
6. *Jerusalem Post,* April 18, 2002.
7. *Jerusalem Post,* May 22, 2001.
8. *Chicago Tribune,* April 5, 1994.
9. Ellis Shuman, German TV, "Mohamed A-Dura Likely Killed by Palestinian Gunfire." See also, James Fallows, "Who Shot Mohammed Al-Dura," *Atlantic Monthly,* June 2003, p. 49.
10. Quoted in Jean Elshtain, *Just War against Terror* (New York: Basic Books, 2003), p. 87.
11. Ibid.
12. David F. Green, "Fighting by the Book," *Boston Globe,* April 20, 2003.
13. Ibid. IDF Update, June 23, 2003.
14. Dan Radlauer, ICT Associate, "The 'Al-Aqsa Intifada': An Engineered Tragedy," June 20, 2002 (updated January 7, 2003), www.ict.org.il: "In absolute terms, even though more Palestinians than Israelis have been killed overall, Israeli female fatalities have far outnumbered Palestinian female fatalities. If we include all reliable reports of women and girls killed in the conflict, the ratio is 219 Israeli females compared to 92 Palestinian females—a ratio of almost 2.5 to 1. If we restrict the comparison to noncombatant Israeli females killed by Palestinians and noncombatant Palestinian females killed by Israel, the difference is even more dramatic: 69 Palestinians compared to 214 Israelis, a ratio of three to one."
15. Phyllis Chesler, *The New Anti-Semitism* (John Wiley & Sons, advance proof), p. 117.
16. Karen Birchard, "Hep B Case Makes Suicide Bombers an Infection Risk," *Medical Post,* MacLean Hunter Ltd., September 10, 2002.
17. Ibid.
18. Ibid.
19. Michael Ledeen, "Hebrew U Survivor: An Interview with Eliad Moreh," *National Review* online, August 6, 2002.
20. "Hepatitis Spread Via Suicide Bombers," *The Straits Times* (Singapore), July 26, 2002.
21. "Israeli soldier given 49 days in jail for killing Palestinian boy," *Deutshe Presse-Agentur,* February 25, 2001.
22. James Bennet, "Arafat's Edge: Violence, and Time, on His Side," *New York Times,* March 18, 2002.
23. Thomas Friedman, "Suicidal Lies," *New York Times,* March 31, 2002.
24. Said and Hitchens, p. 159.
25. "Hate Goes High Tech," *Frontline* magazine, Winter 2003, p. 5.

26. "Israel Kills a Top Hamas Leader," *New York Times,* March 8, 2003.
27. Anne Bayefsky, "Human Rights Groups Have Less Than Noble Agendas," *Chicago Sun Times,* April 6, 2003. This statement is quite remarkable considering the publicly available documentation—including specific names and dates—of the many terrorist acts committed by Palestinian adolescents and children. See Jeremy Cooke, "School Trains Suicide Bombers," *BBC News,* July 18, 2001; Justus Reed Weiner, "Palestinian Children and the Cult of Martyrdom," *Harvard Israel Review,* Summer 2003; "Participation of Children and Teenagers in Terrorist Activity during the 'Al-Aqsa' Intifada," www.mfa.gov.il.
28. Elshtain, p. 104, quoting Gerhardt Rempel, *Hitler's Children* (Chapel Hill: University of North Carolina Press, 1989), pp. 233k, 241.
29. Elshtain, p. 104.
30. Israeli Security Forces, "Blackmailing Young Women into Suicide Terrorism," Israeli Ministry of Foreign Affairs Report, February 12, 2002, www.mfa.gov.il/mfa/go.asp?MFAH0n2a0.
31. Itmar Marcus, Bulletin e-mail for *Palestinian Media Watch,* December 2, 2002.
32. James Bennet, "The Mideast Turmoil: Killer of 3; How 2 Took the Path of Suicide Bombers," *New York Times,* May 30, 2003.
33. Statements made by Slaim Haga, a senior Hamas operative, and Ahmed Moughrabi, a Tanzim operative, May, 27, 2002.
34. Thomas L. Friedman, "The Core of Muslim Rage," *New York Times,* March 6, 2002, quoted in *Why Terrorism Works,* pp. 89–90.
35. Atlanta Journal Constitution, www.ajc.com/news/content/news/0603/10iraqdead.html, last visited June 11, 2003.

CHAPTER 19
Does Israel Torture Palestinians?

1. "Uninteresting Terrorism and Insignificant Oppression," *All Things New,* www.scmcanada.org/atn/atn95/atn952_p19.html.
2. *Leon v. Wainwright,* 734 F.2d 770, 772–773 (11th Cir. 1984), quoted in *Why Terrorism Works,* p. 125. See also *Chavez v. Martinez* (slip opinion, U.S. Supreme Court, No. 01-1444). On May 27, 2003, the U.S. Supreme Court, in a sharply divided decision, ruled that the act of torturing a suspect in order to obtain a statement is not, in itself, a violation of the privilege against self-incrimination afforded by the 5th Amendment unless the state-

ment is then admitted against the suspect in a criminal case. The act of torturing may, however, constitute a violation of due process in extreme cases.
3. Richard Bernstein, "Kidnapping Has Germans Debating Police Torture," *New York Times,* April 10, 2003.
4. *Public Committee against Torture v. State of Israel,* HCJ (Israeli Supreme Court) 5100/94, July 15, 1999.
5. Ibid.
6. Adri Kemps (director, Dutch Section of Amnesty International) to Dr. Mario Soares, in protest of awarding the "Justicio en el Mundo" prize to Aharon Barak.
7. *Leon v. Wainwright,* 734 F.2d at 772–773.
8. Raymond Bonner, et al., "Questioning Terror Suspects in a Dark and Surreal World," *New York Times,* March 9, 2003.
9. One person died following shaking, but an independent investigation attributed his death to an unknown preexisting medical condition. See *Public Committee Against Torture,* HCJ (Israeli Supreme Court) 5100/9 4.
10. "Committee against Torture Concludes Eighteenth Session Geneva, 28 April–9 May," 1997 U.N. Press Release HR/4326.
11. Raymond Bonner, *New York Times,* March 9, 2003.
12. Ibid.
13. Jess Bravin and Gary Fields, "How Do Interrogators Make Terrorists Talk," Wall Street Journal, March 3, 2003.
14. *Al Odah v. United States,* 321 F.3d 1134 (2003).

CHAPTER 20
Has Israel Engaged in Genocide against Palestinian Civilians?

1. Posted by courtesy of Boyle at www.mediamonitors.net/francis1.html. Boyle goes on to set out a full-scale, step-by-step plan of action for the "state of Palestine" to bring the suit. To my knowledge, it was all talk and no lawsuit was ever brought.
2. Oren, p. 92.
3. Ibid., p. 93.
4. Ibid., p. 306.
5. Cleo Noel, the American diplomat murdered in March 1973, was the highest-ranking diplomat of color in the American Foreign Service. Some of the 273 marines killed by Palestinian terrorists in Beirut were black. Several of the airline passengers killed in the numerous attacks on airlines and terminals were black, as were several of the Jews murdered in Israel.

6. James Bennet, "A Nation at War: Parallels," *New York Times,* April 1, 2003.
7. Ibid.
8. Yigal Henkin, "The Best Way into Baghdad," *New York Times,* April 3, 2003.
9. David B. Green, "Fighting by the Book," *Boston Globe,* April 20, 2003.
10. Ibid.
11. Michael Walzer, "The Four Wars of Israel/Palestine," *Dissent,* Fall 2002.
12. Green, *Boston Globe,* April 20, 2003.
13. Jascha Hoffman, "The Good Soldier," *Boston Globe,* April 20, 2003.
14. Elshtain, pp. 21–22.
15. *New York Times,* April 30, 2003.
16. *Forward,* May 10, 2002.
17. Chris Hedges, "A Gaza Diary," *Harper's Monthly,* October 2001.
18. Dr. Umaya Ahmad al-Jalahma, *Al-Riydh,* quoted at Middle East Media Research Institute (MEMRI), Special Dispatch Series, March 13, 2002, no. 543. http://memri.org.

CHAPTER 21
Is Israel a Racist State?

1. Ahmed Bouzid, "The Right of Return—Israel and Palestine," *Media Monitors Network,* www.mediamonitors.net/bouzid3.html.
2. Na'eem Jeenah, "Zionism is a theory of ethnic cleansing and racism," *Islamic Association for Palestine,* www.iap.org/zionism3.htm.
3. Dr. Daud Abdullah, "The Right of Return in the Zionist Political Discourse," lecture for *Friends of Al-Aqsa.* Available at www.aqsa.org.uk/journals/vol4iss1/discourse.html.
4. James Bennet, "Letter from the Middle East: Arab Showpiece? Could It Be the West Bank?" *New York Times,* April 1, 2003.
5. Ruud Koopmans, "Germany and Its Immigrants: An Ambivalent Relationship," *Journal of Ethnic and Migration Studies,* October 1, 1999.
6. Agence France Presse, "Israel Airlifts Kosovo Refugees on Eve of Holocaust Memorial Day," April 12, 1999.
7. *Qadan v. Israel Lands Administration,* HCJ (Israeli Supreme Court) 6698/95, March 8, 2000.
8. The official website of The David Project shows examples of discrimination against "Dhimmi" of many different ethnic and religious persuasions in Arab countries, including Christians and Bahais. It also features a picture of a highway sign in Saudi Arabia with one lane for "Muslims Only." See www.davidproject.org/see/connectthedots.htm.

9. Article 3 (3) of Jordanian nationality law. Law number 6 (1954), official *Gazette,* No. 1171. February 16, 1954; reprinted in Uri Davis, *Citizenship and the State* (Reading, U.K.: Ithaca Press, 1997), p. 70.

CHAPTER 22
Is the Israeli Occupation the Cause of All the Problems?

1. Salmon Abu Sitta, "The Right of Return Is Alive and Well," *Popular Front for the Liberation of Palestine.* www.pflp-pal.org/right.html. Published in *The Jordan Times.*
2. "Baby Bomber Picture Generates Intense Fear," Media Review Network, www.mediareview.net/Baby%20Bomber%20picture%20generates%20intense%20fear.htm (last visited April 11, 2003).
3. John S. Hall, "Chinese Population Transfer in Tibet," 9 *Cardozo J. Int'l & Comp. L.* 173 (2001).
4. Ibid.
5. Regina M. Clark, "China's Unlawful Control over Tibet: The Tibetan People's Entitlement to Self-Determination," 12 *Ind. Int'l & Comp. L. Rev.* 293 (2002).
6. "Health Services Development in Judea–Samaria and Gaza, 1967–1994," Israeli Government website, www.mfa.gov.il/mfa/go.asp?MFAH0bzz0, 1999 (last visited April 11, 2003).
7. Thomas Friedman, *New York Times,* March 18, 2002.
8. Ibid.
9. *New York Times,* March 20, 2002, quoted in *Why Terrorism Works,* p. 180.

CHAPTER 23
Has Israel Denied the Palestinians Statehood?

1. Said and Hitchens, p. 291.
2. "Arab Word Looks the Other Way as Race-Based Hatreds Target It on Two Fronts," *Daily Star* (Lebanon), available at Lebanon Wire, www.lebanonwire.com/0206/02062612DS.asp (posted June 26, 2002).
3. Benny Morris, *New Republic,* April 21–28, 2002, p. 32.

CHAPTER 24
Is Israel's Policy of House Destruction Collective Punishment?

1. Statement of Syrian representative to the Security Council. This was the first statement

by the representative since Syria assumed one of the fifteen seats on the Security Council. Israel has been excluded from sitting on the Security Council.

2. Self-description by Danny Warren, who proudly boasted of coming from the "most racist town in the U.K." and wanting to "go back and tell my town what I discover." *Ha'aretz,* December 21, 2002.

3. Joel Leyden, "Initial IDF Report: Shot Palestinian Activist May Have Fired First," *Jerusalem Post,* April 12, 2003.

4. Warren Hoge, "Britain Holds 6th Person in Tel Aviv Blast," *New York Times,* May 4, 2003.

5. Ibrahim Barzak, "Protesters in Gaza Town Blame Palestinian Militants for Incursion," *Associated Press,* May 21, 2003.

6. Greg Myre, "Israel Stems Suicide Bombings, but at a Cost," *New York Times,* April 5, 2003.

7. Ibid.

CHAPTER 25
Is Targeted Assassination of Terrorist Leaders Unlawful?

1. Yael Stein, "Israel's Assassination Policy: Extra-Judicial Executions," *B'Tselem,* January 2001, available at www.btselem. org.

2. Ibrahim Barzak, *Associated Press,* May 31, 2003.

CHAPTER 26
Is Settlement in the West Bank and Gaza a Major Barrier to Peace?

1. Marwan Bishara, "West Bank Settlements Obstruct Peace: Israel's Empire State Building," *Le Monde Diplomatique,* June 2002, available at http://logosonline.home.igc. org/bishara.htm.

2. James Bennet, "Mideast Sides Maneuver, Expecting Peace Effort," *New York Times,* April 14, 2003.

3. *Forward,* May 2, 2003.

CHAPTER 27
Is Terrorism Merely Part of a Cycle of Violence?

1. Ash Pulcifer, "The Cycle of Violence Begins Again," *Yellowtimes.org,* www.yellowtimes. org/article.php?sid=1126.

2. "Mideast Hope Meets Its Enemy," *New York Times,* April 30, 2003.

CHAPTER 28
Is Israel the Prime Human Rights Violator in the World?

1. Eric Reichenberger, spokesman for Students Allied for Freedom and Equality, a pro-Palestinian group at the University of Michigan, at the anti-Israel divestment conference hosted by his organization in October 2002 (Daniel Treiman, "Students Rap Israel at Divestment Parley," *Forward,* October 18, 2002; also quoted by Nat Hentoff, Op.-Ed., "Israel at Stake on U.S. Campuses: Students and Faculty Call for Divestment," *Washington Times,* November 25, 2002).

2. Professor Irwin Cotler, "Beyond Durban: The Conference Against Racism That Became a Racist Conference Against Jews," Global Jewish Agenda, www.jafi.org.il/ agenda/2001/english/wk3-22/6.asp (last visited April 11, 2003).

3. Anne Bayefsky, "At U.N., Israel Bashing Is Always the First Priority," *Chicago Sun Times,* March 30, 2003.

4. Greg Myre, "Trial of Palestinian Leader Focuses Attention on Israeli Courts, *New York Times,* May 5, 2003.

5. Ibid.

6. Ibid.

7. Supreme Court Justice Dorit Beinisch, "The Role of the Supreme Court of Israel in Times of Emergency," *Globes,* November 21, 2002.

8. *Physicians for Human Rights v. Commander of I.D.F. Forces in the West Bank,* HCJ 2936/02, April 8, 2002.

9. Dan Izenberg, et al., "Supreme Court Orders Lebanese Freed: MIA's Slam 'Self-Destructive Judicial System,' " Jerusalem Post, April 12, 2000.

10. Ajuri, HCJ (Israeli Supreme Court) 7015/02.

11. "Israeli Supreme Court Decision on Deportation of Family Members of Terrorists," Jewish Virtual Library, American-Israel Cooperative Enterprise, www.us-israel.org /jsource/Terrorism/sctdec.html, September 3, 2002 (last visited April 8, 2003).

12. Ibid.

13. Ibid.

14. See www.court.gov.il.

15. Khaled Abu Toameh, "200 Suspected Collaborators Held in P.A. Jails," *Jerusalem Post,* August 15, 2002. See also, Serge Schemann, "For Arab Informers, Death; for the Executioners, Justice," *New York Times,* September 2, 2002, describing the execution of the

women of an entire family on suspicion of being collaborators with Israel.

16. "Parliamentary Debates 2001," Parliament of Ireland, www.irlgov.ie/debates-01/13dec/sect4.htm, December 13, 2001 (last visited April 8, 2003).

17. Justice William J. Brennan Jr., "The Quest to Develop a Jurisprudence of Civil Liberties in Times of Security Crisis," lecture, Hebrew University Law School, available at www.brennancenter.org/resources/downloads/nation_security_brennan.pdf.

18. James Bennet, "Letter From the Middle East," *New York Times*, April 2, 2003.

CHAPTER 29
Is There Moral Equivalence between Palestinian Terrorists and Israeli Responses?

1. Lecture, Harvard University, November 25, 2002.

2. "Israel/Occupied Territories/Palestinian Authority: Killing Children Under Scrutiny at UN," www.amnesty.org.au/children/killingfuture.html, September 30, 2003 (last visited April 11, 2003).

3. Statement of the Holy See, April 11, 2002, available at www.vatican.va.

4. "By My Spirit: What Will Make for Peace in the Middle East," statement of National Council of Churches delegation to the Middle East, available at www.ncccusa.org/nccmiddleeastdelegation/statement.html.

5. "State of the Spirit" address given at the founding conference of the Tikkun Community.

6. Peter Finn, "Germany Announces Ban on Islamic Extremist Group," *Washington Post*, January 16, 2003.

7. Elshtain, p. 20.

8. Boston Globe, June 7, 2003, p. A14.

CHAPTER 30
Should Universities Divest from Israel and Boycott Israeli Scholars?

1. Lecture, Harvard University, November 25, 2002.

2. Congressional Record, Senate, February 8, 1989, S1294.

3. Elaine Sciolino, "U.S. Says It Has Arafat Threat on Tape," *New York Times*, January 18, 1989.

4. Ibid.

5. Robert Fisk, "How to Shut Up Your Critics with a Single Word," *The Independent*, October 21, 2002.

6. David Weinfeld, "Chomsky's Gift," *Harvard Crimson*, December 12, 2002.

7. Chomsky, lecture, Harvard University, November 25, 2002.

8. Weinfeld, *Harvard Crimson*, December 12, 2002.

9. "Not Just Semantics," Editorial, *Orlando Sentinel*, August 7, 2000.

10. *The New Yorker*, March 24, 2003, pp. 48–63.

CHAPTER 31
Are Critics of Israel Anti-Semitic?

1. Thomas Bartlett, "A Surge of Anti-Semitism or McCarthyism?" *The Chronicle of Higher Education*, vol. 49, October 4, 2002.

2. "Apartheid in the Holy Land," *Guardian*, April 25, 2002.

3. Lawrence Summers, speech at Memorial Church, Cambridge, Massachusetts, September 17, 2002.

4. Thomas Friedman, "Campus Hypocrisy," *New York Times*, October 16, 2002.

5. Seymour Martin Lipset, "The Socialism of Fools—the Left, the Jews, and Israel," *Encounter*, December 1969, p. 41.

6. Representative John Lewis, " 'I Have a Dream' for Peace in the Middle East," San Francisco Chronicle, January 21, 2002.

7. Professor Irwin Cotler, "Beyond Durban," Global Jewish Agenda, www.jafi.org.il/agenda/2001/english/wk3-22/6.asp.

8. See, e.g., MEMRI, September 25, 2001, no. 276.

9. Patrick Buchanan, "Dividing Line," *New York Post*, March 17, 1990. Buchanan, as usual, had his facts wrong. The Jews of Treblinka were murdered by various methods of gassing, including the use of exhaust fuels and Zyklon B. Buchanan's "facts" about the Holocaust typically come from crackpot Holocaust deniers.

10. Jacob Weisberg, "The Heresies of Pat Buchanan," *New Republic*, October 22, 1990, p. 22.

11. Philip Shenon, "Washington Talk: The Buchanan Aggravation," *New York Times*, February 19, 1978.

12. Robert Faurisson, *Memoire en Defense* (Paris: La Vieille Taupe, 1980).

13. Paul L. Berman, "Gas Chamber Games: Crackpot History and the Right to Lie," *Village Voice*, June 10–16, 1981, p. 37.

14. For example, Faurisson relies on an entry dated October 18, 1942, from the diary of SS doctor Johann-Paul Kremer written during the three months he spent in Auschwitz in 1942. An eminent scholar checked Faurisson's use of the entry and demonstrated

that Faurisson's research was entirely phony. The diary entry read: "This Sunday morning in cold and humid weather I was present at the 11th special action (Dutch). Atrocious scenes with three women who begged us to let them live."

Faurisson concludes that this passage proves (1) that a "special action" was nothing more than the sorting out by doctors of the sick from the healthy during a typhus epidemic; (2) that the "atrocious scenes" were "executions of persons who had been *condemned to death*, executions for which the doctor was obliged to be present"; (3) that "among the condemned were three women who had come in a convoy from Holland [who] *were shot*"; (4) that there were no gas chambers since the women were shot and not gassed (emphasis added).

A French scholar named George Wellers analyzed this diary entry and the surrounding documentation for *Le Monde*. He did actual historical research, checking the Auschwitz archives for the date of the diary entry—a simple matter. He found that 1,710 Dutch Jews arrived at Auschwitz on October 18, 1942. Of these, 1,594 were immediately sent to the gas chambers. The remaining 116 people, all women, were brought into the camp; the three women who were the subject of the Kremer diary must have been among them. The three women were, in fact, shot, as Faurisson concludes. But the fact now appears here in Kremer's diary. How did Faurisson learn it? Professor Wellers was able to find the answer with some simple research. He checked Dr. Kremer's testimony at a Polish war crimes trial. This is what Kremer said at the trial: "Three Dutch women did not want to go *into the gas chamber* and begged to have their lives spared. They were young women, *in good health*, but in spite of that, their prayer was not granted and the SS who were participating in the action shot them on the spot" (emphasis added).

Faurisson, who said he had researched the trial, knew that his own source, Dr. Kremer, had testified that the gas chambers did exist. Yet he deliberately omitted that crucial item from his book while including the fact that the women were shot. Faurisson also knew that the three women were in good health. Yet he led his readers to believe that Dr. Kremer had said they were selected on medical grounds during an epidemic. Finally, Faurisson states that those who were shot had been "condemned to

death." Yet he knew they were shot by the SS for refusing to enter the gas chambers.

15. Brian Morton, "The Culture of Terrorism," *Nation*, vol. 246, no. 15, May 7, 1988, p. 651.
16. W. D. Rubinstein, "Chomsky and the Neo-Nazis," *Quadrant* (Australia), October 1981, p. 12.
17. Alan M. Dershowitz, "Chomsky Defends Vicious Lie as Free Speech," *Boston Globe*, June 13, 1989, p. 14.
18. Noam Chomsky, "Right to Speak Transcends Content of Speech," *Boston Globe*, July 4, 1989, p. 10.
19. Scot Lehigh, "Men of Letters," *Boston Phoenix*, June 16–22, 1989, p. 30.
20. Paul L. Berman, "Reply to Chomsky," *Village Voice*, July 1–7, 1981, p. 18.
21. MEMRI, September 25, 2001, no. 276.
22. Palestinian Authority Television, October 14, 2000.

CHAPTER 32
Why Do So Many Jews and Even Israelis Side with the Palestinians?

1. Said and Hitchens, p. 15.
2. Ibid., p. 9.
3. Reported by Chris Amos, "Activists Urge Reappraisal of Middle East Conflict," *Michigan Daily*, November 14, 2002.
4. www.nkusa.org/aboutus/index.cfm (last visited May 7, 2003).
5. *Forward*, November 29, 2002.

Conclusion: Israel—the Jew among Nations

1. Andrea Levin, "Israeli Arab Rights and Wrongs," *On CAMERA* column, February 14, 2003.
2. "The wage gaps between Jews and Arabs in Israel are very similar to those between whites and blacks in the U.S.," Amnon Rubenstein, "Jewish Professions, Arab Professions," Haaretzdaily.com, April 15, 2003. The article goes on to show that "ethnic-based income disparities exist even in classic welfare states" such as Holland.
3. See the *Sikkuy Report*, 2001–2002, p. 5, www.sikkuy.org.il/report/Sikkuy%20Report%202002.doc.
4. Israeli Central Bureau of Statistics, www.cbs.gov.il.
5. Steven Plaut, "The Collapsing Syrian Economy," *Middle East Quarterly*, vol. VI, no. 3, September, 1999.
6. Web site of the Israeli Foreign Ministry, www.isreal-mfa.gov.il.

7. Noam Chomsky, speech to Middle East Children's Alliance, San Francisco, March 21, 2002, www.zmag.org/content/Mideast/chomskymecatalk.cfm.

8. Thomas Friedman, "Nine Wars Too Many," *New York Times,* May 15, 2002.

9. Professor Irwin Cotler, "Beyond Durban," Global Jewish Agenda, www.jafi.org.il/agenda/2001/english/wk3-22/6.asp.

10. Juliana Pilon, "The United Nations' Campaign against Israel," *Heritage Foundation Report,* June 16, 1983.

11. Cotler, "Beyond Durban."

12. Ibid.

13. Posted on Andrew Sullivan's personal website at www.andrewsullivan.com/main_article.php?artnum=20021020.

14. Oriana Fallaci, "Oriana Fallaci on Anti-Semitism," *Panorama,* April 12, 2002.

15. F. M. Dostoyevsky, *The Diary of a Writer,* Boris Brasol trans. (Salt Lake City: Peregrine Smith Books, 1985), pp. 642–645.

16. Ibid., p. 650.

17. Ibid., p. 651.

18. Ibid., p. 647.

19. Ibid., p. 640.

20. Ibid., p. 638.

21. Estimates vary as to the number of Palestinians killed during "Black September," with some estimates as high as 4,000 (*One Day in September,* Sony Pictures, www.sonypictures.com/classics/oneday /html/blacksept, last visited April 10, 2003), while others cite the figure of 3,000 ("Some Key Dates in the Israeli-Palestinian Conflict," www.umich.edu/~iinet/cmenas/studyunits/israeli-palestinian_conflict/studentkeydates.html, last visited April 10, 2003).

22. Thomas L. Friedman, "Reeling but Ready," *New York Times,* April 28, 2002.

23. See poll conducted by the Palestinian Center for Policy and Research at Berzeit University, referred to in *Jewish Week,* April 18, 2003, p. 28.

24. Beirut al Nassa, July 15, 1957.

25. Chomsky, lecture, Harvard University, November 25, 2002.

26. Michael Walzer, "The Four Wars of Israel/Palestine," *Dissent,* Fall 2002.

27. James Bennet, "U.S. Statements Guide the Talks on the Mideast," *New York Times,* June 2, 2003.

28. *Jerusalem Post,* January 26, 1989.

29. Review of *Shattered Dreams* by Charles Enderlin, *New York Times Book Review,* May 4, 2003, p. 22.

30. James Bennet, "The Mideast Turmoil: Jerusalem; Israel Approves Bush's Roadmap to New Palestine," *New York Times,* May 26, 2003.

31. Walzer, "The Four Wars of Israel/Palestine."

INDEX

Feisal, Emir, 38
fellahin, 8, 25–26
"final solution, " 41, 52, 57
Finkelstein, Norman, 63
First Aliyah, 5–6, 8, 15, 20–21, 23–28
foreign aid, 228
Frankfurter, Felix, 38
freedom of speech, in Israel, 218, 219
Friedman, Thomas, 2, 114, 129, 162, 209
fundamentalists, 3, 106, 225

Garcia, Ernie, 123
Gaza Strip, 3, 16, 17, 111, 176–77, 241
gays, 200
genocide, 76, 81, 92, 140–53, 181
George, Lloyd, 37
Germans, collective punishment of, 167, 168
Ghoury, Emile, 85
Gilbert, Martin, 15
Golan Heights, 95, 101, 241
Goldberg, Arthur, 96
"Golden Medina," 20
Goldstein, Baruch, 143–44
grand mufti of Jerusalem. See Husseini
Gulf of Aqaba, 91, 92

Hadassah Hospital attack, 82
Haganah army, 75, 80, 82, 83
Haifa, 46, 83
Halbertal, Moshe, 145
Hamas
    charter, 106–107
    fundamentalist zeal of, 106
    and house demolitions by Israel, 171
    as rejectionists, 3, 71
    targeting of, 165
    and terrorism, 128–29, 131, 175
Haniya, Ismail, 128–29
Hanson, Peter, 144
Harvard/MIT divestiture petition, 197–207
Harvard University, 2
health care, 27, 28, 125–26, 161, 223–24
Hebrew kingdoms, independent, 15
Hebron, 5, 16, 17, 42, 69, 177
Hebron massacre, 42–44, 141
Herzl, Theodore, 15, 30
Heshel, Susannah, 209
Hezbullah, 65, 72
Hidden Question, The (Epstein), 30
Himmler, Heinrich, 54
history, disparate perceptions of, 4–6, 7
Hitchens, Christopher, 217
Hitler, Adolf, 2, 40–41, 44, 54, 194
Holocaust
    Arab and Muslim support of, 54–58, 59, 60
    and curtailment of Jewish immigration from
        Europe, 52
    denial of, 198, 211–15

Husseini and, 56–58
Jews accused of exploiting, 53–62
survivors, 59
holy cities, 6, 16, 17, 19
Holy Places, mandate to protect, 50
homeland solution. See two-state solution
house destruction, Israel's policy of, 166–67,
    170, 171–72
human rights, Israel's record on, 2, 181–88,
    199, 229, 231
Hussein, Saddam, 174, 175
Hussein (King of Jordan), 87–88, 103,
    232–34, 240–41
Husseini, Haj Amin al-
    Balfour Declaration and, 41
    hatred of Jews by, 41, 56
    Hebron massacre and, 42
    Hitler, Nazis, and, 40–41, 54, 56
    and Israeli War of Independence, 76
    self-determination and, 41, 42, 71
    terrorism incited by, 42–44
    and war of 1947–1948, 80–81

IDF. See Israeli Defense Force
Ihnat, John, 134
imperialism, accusations of, 13–21, 22, 29–31
international laws, 174–75
International Solidarity Movement, 170
interrogation techniques, 135–39
intifada, after Camp David-Taba negotiations,
    (Al-Aksa Intifada), 9–10, 112, 123–33
intifada, first, 106, 107
Iran, as rejectionist state, 3, 71
Iraq
    pro-Nazi coup in, 55
    and Six-Day War, 92, 93
    war against, 152
Irgun (Etzel), 81
Islam, as established religion, 155, 156
Islamic Jihad, 72
Israel
    achievements of, 223–25
    actual versus perceived record, 222–43
    art and culture in, 46–47, 224
    at Camp David-Taba negotiations, 8–11
    Code of Ethics for military, 145, 147, 150
    as democracy, 1, 222–27
    demonization of, 1, 2, 11–12, 197–98,
        223–34
    discrimination in, 157
    divestment from, call for, 197–
    double standard against, 7, 11, 12, 116,
        229, 236
    economic strength of, 224–25
    Jerusalem captured by, 93
    as "Jew" among nations, 11, 222
    occupation by, 95–99, 103, 158–62, 241
    Palestinian Arabs in, 28

terrorism *(continued)*
  by women, 131
  world, 143
Tiberias, Jewish presence in, 16, 17
Tibet, occupation of by China, 159–60, 163, 164–65
Toledo, Cecilia, 68
torture, 134–39, 152, 184, 199–200
Transjordan, 37, 65. *See also* Jordan
Turkish rule, 37
Twain, Mark, 23–24
two-state solution, 2–4, 177
  consensus for, 64, 65
  effects of, 69, 243
  Jews accused of rejecting, 45–52
  rejection of, 3, 7, 45–46, 65, 71–73, 97
  starting points, 4, 5
  and U.N. Partition Plan, 64–66, 69

United Nations
  Arab refugee problem and, 5, 86–87
  Commission on Human Rights, 182–83
  Committee Against Torture, 135, 137–38
  High Commission for Refugees, 86–87
  Relief and Works (Refugee) Agency, 86–87, 144, 235
  Security Council Resolution 242, 96–98, 205, 241
United Nations Partition Plan of 1947, 6, 7, 24, 27, 28, 61, 63–69
United States
  and Balfour Declaration, 35
  and civilian casualties, 148–49
  evenhandedness in Middle East, 195–96
  Israel's relationship with, 195–96, 228–29
  and targeted assassinations, 174, 175
  and torture, 134, 135, 137, 138–39, 152, 199–200
  and World War I, 33
universities, call to boycott Israeli scholars in, 197–207

vilayets (administrative units), 24–25
violence. *See also* civilians, targeting and killing

of; pogroms; terrorism
  after Balfour Declaration, 37, 40, 46
  after Camp David-Taba negotiations, 8, 9–11, 111–12
  cycle of, 178–80
  of intifada, 107
  after Peel Commission partition plan, 51
Voices of the Arabs, 92

Walsh, Elsa, 118–21
Walzer, Michael, 146, 239–40, 242
war, laws of, 174–75
War of Independence, Israeli, 74–77, 89
war of 1947 and 1948, 79–90
Weizmann, Chaim, 38
West Bank
  Alon Plan for, 98–99
  annexation of, 3, 87
  Barak's offer of, 110
  federation with Arab state, 3
  Israeli settlements on, 106, 110, 176–77
  Jordan's control of, 87
  and Palestinian Authority, 88, 98
West Jerusalem, 46, 69
Western Wall, 42, 112
Why Terrorism Works (Dershowitz), 105
Wilson, Woodrow, 33, 35, 65
Woodhead Commission, 49
World Conference Against Racism, 181–82
World War I, 31, 33
World War II, refugees of, 87

Ya'alon, Moshe, 146–47
Yom Kippur War, 100–103
Yugoslavia, 3

Zaaneen, Mohammed, 172
Zahr, Amer, 217
Zamir, Yitzhak, 183–84
Zatme, Mahroud, 174
Zion, longing for, 17–18, 21
Zionism, 21, 29–31
Zionist Congress, first, 15
Zionists, 38